Political Campaign Strategy

Be Just and Fear Not

S Stockwell

Associate Professor Stephen Stockwell is Head of the School of Arts at Griffith University's Gold Coast campus where he founded the journalism and public relations programs. Previously he was a journalist with community radio 4ZZZ, youth radio JJJ and the Australian Broadcasting Corporation's flagship TV current affairs program, *Four Corners*. He has also worked as a press secretary, media manager and campaign consultant. Outside politics his interests include surfing, bushwalking and independent rock music.

Political Campaign Strategy

Doing Democracy in the 21st Century

Stephen Stockwell

Australian Scholarly
Melbourne

First published 2005
Reprinted 2010
Australian Scholarly Publishing Pty Ltd
7 Lt Lothian St Nth, North Melbourne, Vic 3051
phone: 03 9329 6963   fax: 03 9329 5452
email: aspic@ozemail.com.au
web: www.scholarly.info

A Cataloguing-in-Publication entry for this title is
available from the National Library of Australia.

ISBN 1 74097 106 X

Page design and typesetting by Shawn Low
Printing and binding by On-Demand
Cover design by Jim Hsu

CONTENTS

Acknowledgements

While you always learn more from your enemies than your friends, I would like to take this opportunity to thank the many friends whose insights inform this book: Wayne Swan, Mike Kaiser, John Utting, Kerry Gardiner, Andy Nehl, Linden Woodward, Shaun Hoyt, Nicola Joseph, Tony Collins, Anne Jones, Damien Ledwich, Robbie White, David Barbagello, Alan Knight, Marian Wilkinson, Paul Williams, Paul Gillen, Helen Irving and Lee Cox. I would like to thank Griffith University for allowing me the time to write this book; my research assistants, Adele Somerville and Shona Upson, and my colleagues who have supported my work, Pat Wise, Nigel Krauth, Jane Johnston and Grahame Griffin. Finally I would like to thank my parents, Bill and Necia Stockwell; my wife, Ann Baillie, and our son, Matthew Baillie Stockwell, who have provided so much support and understanding over the years.

Introduction

Thirty years working in, reporting on and teaching about political campaigns have given me some of the most exciting, nerve-wracking, uplifting and soul-destroying moments of my life. This book arises from my dissatisfaction with the different academic accounts of political campaigns. Aside from the memoirs of a few campaign advisers, nothing comes close to capturing the roller-coaster ride which is how, for our sins, our actual democracy gets done in this day and age. Nothing comes close to capturing or explaining that moment where an astute reading of the popular consciousness and decisive use of the right turn of phrase can turn a disaster into success.

For all his personal faults, Bill Clinton will be remembered as a master of the campaign and nowhere were his skills more apparent than when his wife Hillary's campaign for New York senator was faltering in the aftermath of the Monica Lewinsky affair. Hillary's campaign people were in turmoil as women voters began to question Hillary's values. Bill dispassionately read the polling data and said to Hillary "Women want to know why you stayed with me." Hillary responded "Yes, I've been wondering that myself." Unembarrassed, Bill had the answer: "Because you're a sticker. That's what people need to know: you're a sticker. You stick at things you care about." (Gawenda 2005:21) Hillary's campaign rhetoric shifted subtly, women voters were reassured that she would stick by them and she was elected to the US senate. How do you explain these moments of alchemy and what do they mean for democracy? These are the interesting and important questions but very few academics confront them.

Political science treats campaigns as if they were the quantitative exercise of dry constitutional rights. Political marketing turns campaigns into empty rituals of consumption and commercial enterprise. Media studies give a pessimistic critique that portrays campaigns as tools to manipulate and control the public and undermine democracy. Those accounts all fail to capture the energy and excitement of the campaign. They have no conception of the campaign as life on the edge where real decisions have to be made quickly to persuade real people to take decisions that are going to have a real effect on their lives. And the most exciting thing is that this is democracy.

Many people have an idealised view of democracy because they treat democracy as an ideal. This is not a bad thing because part of democracy's work is to strive for high, even ideal standards. But more importantly democracy is a practical exercise that exists because it is carried out. Complain as people will about big government, global corporations and self-interested politicians losing touch, the only antidote to these problems is participation. Democracy gives us the power to persuade other people and it gives us the responsibility to do it as well but if citizens do not rise to this responsibility, in large numbers but in diverse ways, then democracy ceases to exist.

This book discusses political campaigns in a way that grapples with the complexity of the democracy that we actually have. It does this by exploring and clarifying the origins, techniques and different forms of the political campaign. The campaign paradigm has spread from elections and referenda to governmental media management and public education and the public affairs, lobbying and activism of interest groups. By coming to terms with the campaign paradigm, we can begin to appreciate how our democracy, as imperfect as it is, actually functions and its potential to be used and transformed by citizens. This book seeks to capture the rhetorical, ethical and strategic dimensions of the political campaign and explain its historical roots, methods and manifestations in terms of democratic theory. This is a vital first step in re-thinking democracy in a global context where the campaign has become the predominant form of politics.

Close study of the origins and operations of the political campaign provides the opportunity to make the argument, as democrats always have, for a fresh understanding of democracy that fits the times. This book moves beyond any particular disciplinary focus on political campaign strategy to draw together an eclectic mix of practical tools and theoretical insights from a range of disciplines including not only political science, marketing and media theory but also literature, classics, military history, statistics, psychology and game theory.

This book begins by looking at recent accounts of political campaigns and their place in democratic theory. The realisation emerges that representative democracy has a flaw: the mass media is not quite the perfect forum for the debate between citizens on which the legitimacy of democracy depends. If citizens cannot put their point of view in debate then how can they be morally obliged to accept the outcome of that debate? Popular culture's preoccupation with political campaigns (from *Pickwick Papers* to *The West Wing)* leads us to consider how a multiplicity of contending campaigns provides the deliberative forum for mass voices. The political campaign, for all its flaws, emerges as the only effective way to do democracy in a mass society and as a method ripe for citizen intervention and co-option.

Next, we look for the roots of the political campaign deep in human history. The political function of language was crucial to the evolution of human society and political campaigns have much to learn from the practical, linguistic magic of the shaman and the bard. As the early forms of democracy developed, the Greek Sophists applied rational analysis to that linguistic magic to understand how citizens could be persuaded, work that was systematised in the classical rhetoric of Aristotle. Further, the book examines the contribution of Machiavelli in the early modern period and his application of concepts from military strategy to politics. We also consider two forms of military strategy of particular relevance to political campaigns: guerrilla warfare for situations of offensive insurgence and siege warfare for defensive incumbency.

The book also summarises 20th century developments that led to the current form of the political campaign. To appreciate how campaigns work, we explore the theoretical bases and practical operation of political persuasion strategies in message development, qualitative and quantitative research, media management, advertising, direct contact and organisation. This work occupies the core of the book because it is crucial to understanding the possibilities campaigns offer.

The book then points to the political possibilities in the collision between campaign strategy and the information age. The permanent campaign has become the predominant form of governance evident not only in the electorally-connected work of government media minders but also in public education and information campaigns by which governments do their work. To counter the power of government and to lead it towards particular interests, corporate lobbying and citizen activism have emerged as the practices of public affairs. New technology provides the opportunity for new forms of political campaigning where networks of citizen-hackers create the connections between the local and emerging global forums. By refusing to be drawn into the utopian promises of on-line only cyber-citizenry, citizens can make use of cyber-strategy to build new spaces for democracy in the global environment.

1
MESSING WITH THE FABRIC OF REALITY – DEMOCRACY AND SPIN

Political Campaigns

Pity the poor spin doctors. Few occupations are more despised than theirs but then few occupations offer such power with so little responsibility. We all know who the spin doctors are. They are the nasty, nefarious types, stashed in politicians' back offices, twisting words to mean whatever they want them to mean. They are commonly held to be responsible for the media's mendacity and democracy's decline. They convinced us to go to war in Iraq over weapons of mass destruction that were not there. They declared "mission accomplished" when it had barely begun. They threw the children overboard. Every day they are busy spinning yesterday's denial into tomorrow's full and frank admission. They will say anything as long as it advances the cause of whoever is paying their fees.

But now spin doctors have gone on the counterattack about their own image. Most morning talk radio shows have weekly sessions with spin doctors from government and business explaining how the news of the week has been managed. Of course, these sessions are never very critical of public relations practice and they never tell about the dirty deeds that go on behind the scenes but they do draw our attention to the ubiquity of spin. Perhaps this is the right time to consider the spin doctor's place in the world, particularly as public relations practices now determine how governments do their work and, in particular, wage war.

The Simpsons, that indispensable guide to modern mores, has summarised the spin-doctor situation for all. When a three-eyed fish is found near Mr Burns's nuclear power plant, he becomes desperate to roll back health and safety regulation and decides to run for governor. His campaign team boasts not only a spin doctor, a joke writer and a make-up man but also a muck-raker, a character assassin, a mud-slinger and a garbologist. It is the politics of the bottom-feeders. In the end, despite the spin doctor naming the fish Blinky and coming up with a sterling defence of the creature as an evolutionary necessity, Marge Simpson out-spins them all by serving up the three-eyed fish for Mr Burns's televised dinner the night before the election. It is a spin doctor's nightmare when Mr Burns spits out the fish and destroys his credibility on live television.

The West Wing's communications director Toby Ziegler (played by Richard Schiff) provides an alternative to *The Simpsons* stereotype. Toby is confused, moody, soul-searching and often transfixed in the headlights of another onrushing dilemma, desperately clinging to certainties that turn to dust in his hands, finally saving the day with nothing more than an obscure code of personal honour and recourse to networks and techniques honed through years of failure. Toby, like many spin doctors, is still an idealist. That is why he is working in politics and not making 10 times the salary as a corporate media consultant. But he is an idealist who has come to an accommodation with the pragmatism that successful politics requires in order to achieve what he can.

While spin doctors tend to be more *West Wing* than *Simpsons,* they all want to be *Wag the Dog*'s Conrad Brean (played by Robert De Niro). Created by David Mamet and Hilary Henkin, this character has such a command of the possibilities of the mediasphere that he can create the appearance of a small war with Albania to get a United States president re-elected despite the president's indiscretions with an under-age girl. Conrad Brean is a master at messing with the fabric of reality.

This is the attraction of the position. Sure, the job is despised, the pay is comparatively lousy and the spin doctor will be blamed for any problems, yet be strangely absent when the kudos are distributed. But, in the meantime, the spin doctor has the opportunity to sculpt the terrain on which public debate occurs and to play the puppet-master, crafting the words and images that create the future. And it is a craft because spin doctors are doing more than just spinning a web to catch our minds. The application of spin is subtle work, just ask the spin bowler in cricket or the pitcher in baseball. Ideas of dip, drift, turn and bounce are central to the craft whether you are working with a ball or words.

But where did spin come from? Over the last two hundred years, the representative democracies of North America, Europe and Australasia underwent significant changes. Where once only wealthy men were qualified to be citizens, by the early twentieth century citizenship was extended to all adults, male and female, wealthy and poor. As those democracies became mass societies, the old networks of personal contact no longer held sway and prospective representatives had to find new ways to gather the votes they needed to win election. The advent of new media such as offset printing, radio and television prompted the creation of new persuasion techniques such as advertising and public relations to take commercial messages to the masses and politicians were quick to recognise the usefulness of these media for their own persuasive purposes. US president Franklin D. Roosevelt spelt out his political agenda directly to the citizenry via fireside chats broadcast on the radio. German dictator Adolf Hitler used the radio to spread his mix of hate, hope and hero worship that reinvigorated a downtrodden nation. British prime minister Winston Churchill held Britain together during the darkest days of the Second World War by broadcasting his speeches on the radio. At about the same time social scientists began to use surveys to study both citizens' use of the media and the media's impact on citizens' political inclinations in public opinion research. During the 1950s US presidential candidate Dwight Eisenhower used television to spread his campaign message.

But it was John F. Kennedy's 1960 presidential campaign that showed how a mixture of opinion research and media management could swing close contests and the craft of political campaigning was born. Kennedy's campaign and the three succeeding US presidential elections were closely documented in *The Making of the President* series by Theodore White (1961, 1966, 1969, 1974) who revealed much about the inner-workings of the campaigns. Joe McGinniss carried White's work further during the 1968 US presidential election when he focused on the spin techniques employed by the successful Nixon campaign in *The Selling of the President* (1970). The 1972 US presidential campaign produced three important books that revealed much about the operations of campaigns. First there was *The Boys on the Bus* by Tim Crouse (1972) which showed how the press corps covering the election was manipulated by the party campaigns and each other to produce a sanitised and side-tracked account of what actually happened, a theme theorised by Melvyn Bloom (1973) in *Public Relations and Presidential Campaigns*. Also Hunter S. Thompson's (1973) *Fear and Loathing on the Campaign Trail* captured the temporary and expedient nature of campaigns marked by strategic game-playing and ready compromise.

A number of authors have since documented the rise of the political spin industry that developed to prosecute this new form of political campaigning in the United States (Blumenthal 1980; Dinken 1989; Napolitan 1994; Sabato 1981; Thurber & Nelson 1995), the United Kingdom (Butler 1992; Norris 1999; Rosenbaum 1997) and Australia (Mills 1986; Tiffen 1989). The industry journal *Campaigns and Elections* has documented developing campaign techniques and judged their application in practical conditions as selected articles show (Sabato 1989). The historical development of the political campaign industry is discussed in some detail in chapter

3. The academic discipline of political marketing quickly "colonised" (Wring 1999) this new style of politics. There are now a number of texts that give a technical account of the campaign which, by and large, treats citizens as consumers and democracy as a competition (Kavanagh 1995; Lees-Marshment 2001; Maarek 1995; Mauser 1983; Newman & Sheth 1985; Newman 1994; Newman 1999; O'Shaughnessy 1990).

In response to the growth of political marketing, a strident critique emerged that exposed the hegemonic control of the mass media and the public relations apparatus of the party and state as propaganda designed to dupe the voter (Pratkanis & Aronson 1992; Spero 1980). In particular, this critique targets negative advertising (Ansolabehere & Iyengar 1995; Johnson-Cartee & Copeland 1991) and fundraising excesses (West 2001) to explain the growing apathy and cynicism of citizens (Cappella & Jamieson 1997). Or as Lucaites & Charland argue "Postmodern mass politics... replaces the collective imaginary... with simulacra that remain specular and uninhabitable..." (1989: 33) In short, democracy has become a ghost and a useless parody of its old self.

There is also the connected concern among critics that the spread of political marketing is producing the systematic "Americanization" of politics around the globe (Kavanagh 1996) even though some would argue that this effect is merely a by-product of the "modernization" of societies (Negrine & Papathanassopoulos 1996: 42). The Japanese Liberal Democratic party has taken a systematic approach to campaigning since 1948 (Curtis 1983), though at that stage it relied on a thorough-going organisation of grass-roots support rather than the polling and media management of American style campaigning.

It is reassuring that not all writers fit into these opposing camps. Some appreciate that campaigning is a craft which is something more than marketing (Shea 1996). Some bring the raw experience and urgent enthusiasm of the participant (Johnson 2001; Morris

1997). Many offer a do-it-yourself manual including Shaw & Holstein (1999) for the United States and Richards (2001) for the United Kingdom. There is also the on-going debate about the effect of political campaigns: whether they make a difference or not (Farrell & Schmitt-Beck 2002; Holbrook 1996). The growing number of late-deciding voters with no party attachment but an interest in media campaign coverage (McAllister 2002) makes the question of campaign effects more than an academic issue. It is discussed in more detail in chapter 6. Most significant is the growing sub-literature of those who start out to criticise political campaigns but come to appreciate that they are at the heart of our existing democracy and the formal opportunity for citizens to learn about and participate in political debate (Jamieson 1996; Norris 2000; Scammell 1995; Street 1996).

As campaign logic spreads from elections to government issues management, public education, interest group lobbying and activism, there is a particular need to understand what the campaign is and how it can be democratised to provide the debate, discussion and deliberation on which democracy depends. This project is complicated, but perhaps assisted, by the emerging global regime. The ubiquity and intimacy of emerging media suggest a return to a more personal, and even a more primal, relationship between citizens and their representation. In the immediacy of television and computer-driven opinion research, in the personal contact of direct mail to text messaging, in the centrality of image, in the psychological symphonies campaigns seek to create, there is a clear breach with rational choice theory. As expounded by Anthony Downs (1957), this theory expects citizens will decide their behaviour by making a rational calculation of their optimum economic outcome. Samuel Popkin (1991) was perhaps the first to point out that citizens do not have sufficient time, or certainly inclination, to know all about an issue and depend on competing campaigns to provide the information they need to make a choice.

Emerging already are "viral" campaign strategies using fuzzy logic, ambush promotion and interactivity to infect host populations with arguments towards the debate that goes on during the campaign period (Painter & Wardle 2001). Others argue that greater interactivity, particularly via the internet, will produce a virtuous circle where the more citizens participate in democratic deliberation the better the democracy gets so more citizens are enticed to participate and so on (Norris 2000).

Democracy is held together by a fragile consensus of minds and the creation of that consensus without resort to force or coercion depends on the effective communication of persuasive ideas to a public that is not always interested. A political campaign is not merely the prelude to a snapshot of the "collective will" taken on election day. Rather politics is work that seeks to construct the "collective will" so citizens take particular decisions not just on election day but on a range of issues and in their everyday life as well. The role of the participating citizen is to use all and any means of persuasion at hand to move the collective to actions the citizen considers necessary. Providing effective persuasion is a glorious art, the very art by which democracy functions, survives and even prospers. This raises important questions about the nature of democracy.

Democracy

In *The End of History and the Last Man* Francis Fukuyama famously argues that in light of the dissolution of Communist totalitarianism, democracy has triumphed to become "the end point of mankind's ideological evolution [and] the final form of human government" (1992: xi). While more recent events suggest there might be a bit more life in history yet, democracy, or at least its appearance, is the government of choice even among totalitarian regimes. Paul Hirst agrees that "Democracy is the dominant idiom" of our time and that

"Everyone is a democrat" (1988: 190–193) but he is left wondering if what we have got is really democracy. Hirst argues that the form of democracy that has been victorious limits and contains debate, fails to represent the diversity of interests and opinions in society and is dominated by the concerns of a few institutions. The emergence of disciplined party machines has acted to constrain the operations of democracy in various ways so that, Hirst would argue, it now merely "serves to legitimate modern big government and to restrain it hardly at all" (1988: 190).

So what is democracy and where can we get some? The simple definitions of democracy continue to inform popular discussion: the rule of the many (Aristotle 1946); the rule of the majority (Locke 1966) and; the rule "of the people, by the people, for the people" (Lincoln 1914: 209) are three common formulations. The simplicity of these formulations, as Anthony Birch notes with reference to the final example above, "has rhetorical value rather than logical meaning" (1993: 50) because the simple expectations they engender are problematic in a complex world and even more difficult in a globalising one. These simple definitions do not provide the solid basis required for a thoroughgoing theoretical definition of democracy.

Perhaps the gap between the simple promises of democracy and the complexity encountered in making it work may help explain why the near universal acceptance of democracy is accompanied by a high level of ambivalence, cynicism and disdain towards its political processes. While around eighty percent of citizens express an interest in politics (McAllister 1992) no more than half the adult population follow political and social issues in the mass media (Dahl 1984) and often not more than half and as few as five percent turn-out to vote in elections where they are not compulsory (Chapman and Wood 1984). Citizens regard current democratic practices with "a jaundiced eye" and think "that there should be more to politics than this" (Mackay 1993: 175). A raft of quantitative research bears out these findings: citizens think politicians are too interested in looking after themselves and cannot be trusted to do the right thing. Citizens also believe that politicians do not know what they are doing because they have lost touch with those they claim to represent. This cynicism about politicians is producing a crisis of faith in democracy and adds urgency to the search for redefinition.

The challenge facing democratic theory is to find an approach to democracy that can confront this ambivalence and cynicism by returning the citizen to the centre of the democratic process. Perhaps the best place to start is with the dynamic potential within democracy itself. Unlike most other forms of government which seek to establish an enduring system, democracy actually creates change, adapts to new situations and remakes its own practice continually. The corollary of democracy's dynamic potential is that the search for a definition of democracy can never be concluded, the goal posts are always shifting. Democratic theory requires constant renewal as new conditions, social formations, technologies and complexities arise. Chantal Mouffe argues in her preface to *Dimensions of Radical Democracy* that: "democracy can only consist in the recognition of the multiplicity of social logics... [with] no hope of final reconciliation... the radical impossibility of a fully achieved democracy." (1992: 14)

However the impossibility of completing the democracy project is no reason for abandoning it. The incompleteness of the concept may indeed be the source of its strength because it allows for the malleability that lets democracy be responsive to change. The concept of democracy has its roots in *demokratia,* a word first used by Herodotus to describe the Athenian system of government, particularly from around 507 BC when the Constitution of Kleisthenes came into force and gave supreme decision-making power to the assembly of all adult male citizens (Hyland 1995). The Athenian leader Pericles gave an argument for democracy based not on fairness alone but also on democracy's effectiveness: the city was strong, the quality of life was improving because the democratic system required extensive deliberation before a decision was made: "instead of looking on discussion as a stumbling block in the way of action, we think it an indispensable preliminary to any wise action at all." (Thucydides 1972: s40) Democracy was the most efficient way to transform the multiplicity of interests and views in the society into action because full and free debate generally led to the most beneficial course for the greatest number of citizens. But for the Athenians, democracy was not just a set of institutions; it was an entire mode of life whose "basis was not so much individual material welfare or comfort as communal pride" (Curtis 1965: 23). It was a mode of life dedicated to the pursuit of individual and collective happiness and the realisation of the good life through active participation (MacIntyre 1985). It is important to appreciate for the discussion below that the Athenian "model" was always "indeterminate" (Hyland 1995: 46) and thus open to contest.

Another important aspect of the Athenian model of democracy was its participatory nature. While Athenian democracy did not include women, slaves and foreigners, all the free, native men could and mostly did gather together in an assembly to make decisions about the laws and policies of the city. The participatory model of democracy remains an important element of democratic theory today as a striking and tested alternative to the predominant representative model of democracy. In *Participation and Democratic Theory*, Carol Pateman (1970) argues that participation, both political and industrial, educates and empowers the participant and this is crucial to the health and strength of democracy. In a later work, *The Problem of Political Obligation*, Pateman (1985) suggests that a citizen's obligation to a political process can only develop in the context of a participatory democratic system. There is more to political obligation than the duty of occasionally casting a vote and then providing obedience to the system. There is also an obligation to make the system work by becoming involved in the debate which precedes decision-making. "'Communicative action' is basic to political obligation over the whole of collective life" (1985: 178), as Pateman says, borrowing from Jurgen Habermas (1987). In *Strong Democracy*, Benjamin Barber (1984: 117) continues the work of Pateman by contrasting "thin" representative democracy with "strong participatory democracy with a self-governing community of citizens" who utilise participatory institutions to resolve conflict and decide on action. He accentuates the vital role of debate in participation: "At the heart of strong democracy is talk" (Barber 1984: 173) and points out that for talk to be effective there must also be listening, reflection and a willingness to persuade and be persuaded. Limitations inherent in participatory democracy include the problems of coordinating a large number of decisions from a large number of groups, the difficulties in keeping citizens engaged in going to meetings and the dangers of interpersonal coercion, psychological conformity and leadership cults that small groups may engender.

Representative democracy has developed over the last 400 years as a means of involving citizens of mass societies in their own governance. David Held (1987: 70–102) distinguishes between three general theories of representative democracy: *protective democracy* ensures a social contract where individuals give up freedoms in return for protection from each other and those who seek to rule over them; *radical democracy* where citizens enjoy both political and economic equality to engage with equal freedom in collective decision-making; and *liberal democracy* which protects individual interests and creates an informed citizenry able to use the system to realise their capabilities. John Stuart Mill (1991: 244ff) provides perhaps the most straight-forward rationale for representative government: "since all cannot, in a community exceeding a single small town, participate personally in any but some very minor portions of the public business, it follows that the ideal type of perfect government must be representative... [where citizens] exercise through deputies periodically elected by themselves the ultimate controlling power."

In *Capitalism, Socialism and Democracy,* Joseph Schumpeter (1976: 269) offers a minimalist, "empirical" definition of representative democracy as: "...that institutional arrangement for arriving at political decisions in which individuals acquire the power to decide by means of a competitive struggle for the people's vote." By giving no place in democracy to the citizens and their aspirations except for a numerically insignificant vote in a competition, Schumpeter accepts that democracy generally entails government by elites. Criticism of representative democracy falls into two categories: one, against Mill, points to logical problems in depending on representation to produce policies which reflect the actual aspirations of the electorate and the other, against Schumpeter, points out the propensity to elitism in political arrangements which ostensibly treat all citizens equally. Aristotle, as M.I. Finley (1973: 19) shows, was the first to point out that elections were predominantly aristocratic rather than democratic: the criteria by which the choice of the "best" candidate is made will always be influenced by those who already have power to define "best". Robert Michels (1959: 377–392) developed this insight into a theory of organisations built around the principle of "the iron law of oligarchy": real power always sits with some form of political elite. "Who says organisation, says oligarchy." (Michels 1959: 401) But he does not blame evil oligarchs for the concentration of power but "the very nature of the mass as mass"(Michels 1959: 404).

While there are limitations in various theoretical accounts and practical programs of both participatory and representative democracy, none refute it as an on-going experiment constantly recreating itself by adapting to theoretical developments and changing circumstances. Therefore some theorists suggest that democracy could evolve to make it both more representative and more participatory (Arblaster 1987). Norberto Bobbio (1987: 53) argues that: "between pure representation and pure direct democracy there is not the qualitative leap... [but] a continuum ... [I]n a mature system of democracy both forms of democracy are necessary but they are not, taken on their own, self-sufficient." In conceptualising new definitions of democracy it is important to respond to the critiques of democracy to hand. How can democracy defuse the power of elites while improving the quality of representation and participation it offers? To consider how the citizenry can better control the elite raises, in a mass society, the conduit between them, the media.

The Problem of the Media

It is intriguing that while John Stuart Mill revealed the problem of the media in his theorisation of representative democracy, its ramifications were never pursued. The problem may be stated simply. The representative system allows democracy to extend beyond the single city that characterised Athenian democracy. However to function effectively, representative democracy must be complemented by processes which allow the dissemination of a broad range of views and the opportunity for debate similar to that provided by the Athenian Assembly of citizens. While Mill argued that the press filled this role, he had some unspecified dissatisfaction with its ability to do so comprehensively. He referred to the newspaper press as "the real equivalent, though not in all respects an adequate one, of the Pnyx and the Forum." (Mill 1991: 310) While Mill did not expound on his reservations about the role of the newspaper press, he appears to be pointing to the paradox at the heart of representative democracy: political information is predominantly communicated through the mass media but it is not an effective democratic forum for mass voices. Discussion is dominated by proprietors and advertisers, filtered by journalists and experts and fit into existing expectations.

A number of democratic theorists have made explicit their disquiet about the ability of the mass media to function as a forum. Barber (1984: 197) saw a danger that if deliberation is left in the hands of the media it "quickly degenerates into one more weapon in the armory of elite rule." Similarly Anthony Giddens (1994: 132) holds that his model of dialogic democracy will only work where "differential resources aren't used to prevent views being voiced or for a drastic skewing of the conditions of dialogic interchange." The role of the mass media in providing the forum for deliberation in current representative democracies raises "fundamental questions" for democratic theory and it is easy to share John Keane's concern that "almost nobody asks basic questions about the relationship between democratic ideals and institutions and the contemporary media" (1991: x). The relative absence of discussion of the mass media in democratic theory is remarkable given the way key thinkers such as Mill and Barber have flagged the problem. In his otherwise systematic *Models of Democracy*, Held (1987) makes only one reference to the media in quoting Herbert Marcuse and his dismissal of the media as a tool of coercion. In listing the main forms of political participation, Birch (1993) does not mention activity in the mass media. Even when Giddens (1994) raises the issue of differential resources skewing dialogic interchange he pursues the question with reference to the welfare state rather than media access. In his discussion on the practicalities of citizenship, James Lynch (1992: 51) only mentions the mass media to note a survey that found "television and the mass media have an important and often negative effect on young peoples' values".

The resolution of the paradox relies on the restoration of citizen-to-citizen debate and various theorists have suggested ways to achieve that restoration via "deliberative democracy": "open and uncoerced discussion of the issue at stake with the aim of arriving at an agreed judgement... whereby initial preferences are transformed to take account of the views of others." (Miller 1993: 75) It is difficult to underestimate the importance of debate to the effectiveness of democracy. From Schumpeter's minimal model of representative democracy requiring limited citizen involvement to the complex models of participatory democracy requiring a strong engagement from citizens, the one constant is not free elections or the rule of law but that upon which the whole enterprise depends: free political speech. Free speech is just as vital to Mill's liberal democracy as it is to Mouffe's radical democracy. It is the golden thread from the Athenian assembly to the experiments with new communication technologies. Even Schumpeter (1976: 270) accepts that electoral competition requires opposing elites to put their cases after considering "genuine group-wise volitions". The ubiquity of deliberation as an essential element of democratic practice at so many points along the continuum suggests the crucial roles discussion and debate play in the prelude to democratic decision-making and thus in democracy itself.

John Dryzek (1990) offers a model of deliberative democracy. Rejecting the manipulation, domination, strategy and deception of current representative democracy, he returns to Aristotle to argue for a democracy of practical reason that is not based on complex theory but the common interests we have as a result of our communication with each other. We owe our existence to our ability to communicate with each other and, Dryzek argues, this provides the rational basis from which we can understand how democracy does and should work. He shows that communicative rationality is best expressed in "discursive designs"; these are social institutions "around which the expectations of a number of actors converge... for recurrent communicative interaction... as citizens, not as representatives" (Dryzek 1990: 43). To function effectively "as a site for recurrent communicative interaction" these institutions must allow no exclusions, no hierarchy, no complicity in state administration and no formal rules, while promoting participation in debate governed by informal canons of free discussion, focusing on particular problems shared by those involved and requiring that decisions be made by consensus (Dryzek 1990: 43). Dryzek points to models for discursive designs in the common practices of mediation, dispute resolution, regulatory negotiation, policy dialogue and international conflict resolution and he shows how those designs have been approximated in new social movements. Anthony Giddens (1994) follows a similar path to produce another model of deliberative democracy when he argues that in the "double dissolution of tradition and nature" there is the potential for a "utopian realism" which deals with the rapid pace of social change in a creative way. He points out that "Democratization processes today are driven by the expansion of social reflexivity and detraditionalization" so that while "well established debates pitting participation against representation offer little purchase... dialogic democratization" creates forms of social interchange that contribute to reconstructing social solidarity and further cultural cosmopolitanism by connecting autonomy and solidarity (Giddens 1994: 111–112). In short, while our representative institutions have difficulty dealing with a rapidly changing, globalising world, their decline gives citizens the freedom to create new ways of collective decision-making.

The deliberative view of democracy solves many of the problems of representative and participatory models discussed above by acknowledging the power inherent in the citizen's active engagement in the political process (Cohen 1989). It is important to appreciate the way in which it is the full, free and frank debate that underpins the effective operation of democracy by allowing the reconciliation of individual preferences into a collective consensus and by putting leadership under constant scrutiny to make it transparent. In producing the peaceful movement from the disparate ideas and aspirations held by a group of individuals to a social decision by which those individuals consider themselves bound, deliberation requires the frank exchange of views that allows new ideas to arise. It requires that those views and ideas be intellectually tested with all the skills of reason and persuasion that those individuals have to offer; it allows opinions to mutate and transform until a decision is made to which most participants are happy to be bound – at least until next time – because they have said everything they could to convince their fellows.

How then might the deliberative model of democracy find application in currently existing systems of representative democracy? The answer is difficult because the mass nature of society means that much key deliberation in current representative democracy occurs in the organs of the mass media. This is not to dismiss the importance of interpersonal discussion and small group debate but merely to acknowledge the difficulties in producing authentic democratic deliberation in mass societies. The case of the political campaign is instructive. The campaigns of major parties, government departments or corporations can tell citizens what they want to hear and then insist on their support. Campaigns of this ilk can be successful in the short term but leave unfulfilled expectations in the long term. By way of contrast, campaigns that use opinion research to understand the citizenry's frame of mind and employ the campaign machinery to conduct a two-way discussion with the citizenry that strives for even-handedness and an equality of power can have a remarkable and on-going effect.

Deliberation can legitimate democratic processes, but if and only if those processes can guarantee free speech and an equality of potential participation. These are major provisos and significant stumbling blocks to the achievement of effective democracy. There is a deep-seated and well-justified concern among theorists that the media have the ability to mould and censor debate in mass society. While deliberative democracy seeks to confront the logical limitations of elitism and coercion inherent in representative and participatory models by ensuring an equality of access to debate and discussion in relatively small groups, the power that arises from the centralised role of broadcast media in mass society generally remains a problem that can only be solved by the citizen.

Citizens

Citizenship has come under fire in recent years because it is seen only to achieve solidarity and cohesion by excluding some people from membership. As we saw above, even ancient Athenian democracy excluded women, slaves and those who were foreign born. While modern democracies now extend formal citizenship to women and the poor and foreigners can apply for citizenship after relatively brief periods of residency, there is still a concern that the laws of citizenship deny democratic rights to many active and productive members of society such as illegal immigrants and that there are still practical barriers to the full exercise of their democratic rights on account of gender and class (Barbalet 1988). Further, Hirst is critical of the emphasis that is placed on citizenship in discussion of democratic theory because it ignores the globalising processes which are undermining the nation states to which citizens belong and it disregards the "complex multi-focal politics" which is developing (Hirst 1994: 13). In particular, Julian Thomas and Denise Meredyth (1996: 13) are critical of the emphasis citizenship curricula place on neo-religious "core values" at the expense of teaching "a range of practical and ethical capacities required to negotiate one's various role as a citizen or resident".

Fictional Campaigns

Popular culture's preoccupation with political campaigns from *Pickwick Papers* to *The West Wing* shows that citizens are interested in the campaign and its methods.

Pickwick Papers by Charles Dickens

Chapter 13 Some account of Eatanswill; of the state of parties therein; and of the election of a member to serve in parliament for that ancient, loyal, and patriotic borough: "Both said that the trade, the manufactures, the commerce, the prosperity of Eatanswill, would ever be dearer to their hearts than any earthly object; and each had it in his power to state, with the utmost confidence, that he was the man who would eventually be returned."

Middlemarch by George Eliott
Chapter 51 "Buffoonery, tricks, ridicule the test of truth – all that is very well" – here an unpleasant egg broke on Mr. Brooke's shoulder, as the echo said, "All that is very well;" then came a hail of eggs...

The Distinguished Gentleman
A small-time con man manages to scam his way into Congress on name recognition only – he has the same name as his recently deceased Congressman and campaigns for re-election with the slogan "the name you can trust".

Speechless
Two political speechwriters meet, unaware that they share the same profession... and work for opposing candidates. When they discover the truth, their budding romance gives way to rivalry as they engage in an escalating match of one-upmanship.

The War Room (Documentary)
Watch James Carville, George Stephanopolous and the entire crew of the War Room search out and destroy George Bush's campaign and launch Bill Clinton into the White House in this textbook of modern political tactics.

Primary Colours
We see that Jack Stanton, the presidential candidate in the film, is a flawed charmer with a weakness for bimbos, but we also see what makes him attractive even to those who know the worst: he listens and cares, and knows how to be an effective politician.

Wag the Dog
Two weeks before election day, a scandal threatens to stop the President's bid for a second term. Before the incident causes fatal damage to the campaign, the ultimate spin-doctor is called to the White House and sets out to manipulate politics, the press and the American people.

Spin City
The adventures of the Deputy Mayor of New York City as he spins the news to keep the Mayor out of trouble and the city from erupting.

The West Wing
Saga of a presidency and the adventures of his staff. Includes flashbacks to the original campaign that capture the excitement of turning a failing campaign around.

The boundaries of citizenship will continue to be problematic but in attempting to understand the functioning of democracy from the inside, then citizenship offers firm ground from which to explain the theoretical relationship between citizens and their democratic institutions and to critique the slipping of power away from citizens and towards the institutions. Thomas Marshall (1964) laid the groundwork for contemporary discussion of citizenship with an argument for its reformulation. He suggested that citizenship should ensure not only the civil rights required by the emerging market economy of the eighteenth century (free speech, fair trial etc) and the political rights won as mass consumer markets developed in the nineteenth century (free choice in secret elections etc) but also the social rights that the twentieth century mixed economy could provide (social welfare generally). Mouffe (1992) has argued that citizenship rights do not exist in abstract: "A citizen cannot properly be conceived independently of her insertion in a political community.... (as) an active citizen...who conceives herself as a participant in a collective undertaking." Mouffe (1992: 238) goes on to refuse the distinction between public and private: "We cannot say: here end my duties as a citizen and begins my freedom as an individual.... this is precisely the tension between liberty and equality that characterises modern democracy." This tension not only characterises modern democracy but, as it is worked out in debate and deliberation, has always provided democracy with the dynamism it requires to produce action and change. As we will see in the next chapter, active, arguing hoplites (or self-sufficient farmers) were central to the establishment of Greek democracy.

To create greater deliberative participation in existing representative institutions and to recreate democracy itself, citizens must reclaim their voices in the mass media and in other forums they create. The political campaign, as the pre-eminent form of political organisation in mass society, is the obvious means for citizens to utilise in their work on democracy. It would appear clear that in mass societies direct participation by all citizens in all decision-making is unrealistic but participation in campaigns allows the participation that makes such political systems something more than elective totalitarianism. Election campaigns are particularly crucial moments for citizen intervention. The most significant purpose of regular, free elections is that they prevent elites from becoming entrenched totalitarian dictatorships by providing peaceful opportunities for the exercise of what Hyland (1995: 253) describes as "the law of anticipated reaction" where it is not "the last election that exercises controlling power over the government of the day, but the anticipation of the next election." Even if elections can never quite properly represent the multiplicity of interests in society, even if they always tend to elitism, they are still a key moment for democracy because they do allow for direct citizen participation in the democratic mechanism to create change. The election is the one moment when citizens have a clear and decisive power over government. Politicians dread the electoral backlash and frequently allow electoral considerations to dominate the political processes, as David Mayhew (1974) shows in his study of the US Congress.

Elections are the glue of democracy. They are a real, experiential bond between the government and the governed. The strength of that bond is reflected in research which shows that while a quarter of voters participate in elections out of a sense of duty, almost half vote because of the sense of satisfaction they derive from their participation (McAllister 1992). While any citizen can put him or herself forward for election, while there is free discussion of the issues, while there is no coercion in the polling booth and while the counting of votes proceeds fairly and honestly, then there is the possibility for the people to exercise their will. As the moment of mass decision-making, elections provide the opportunity for direct participation, and election campaigns have the potential to open spaces where new and marginal ideas can be introduced and deployed against established interests. But contemporary politics offers more opportunities for participation than just elections. The spread of campaign techniques from elections to government issues management, public education, interest group lobbying and activism provides citizens with constant opportunities to participate in the political process in a myriad of ways from engineering a global campaign on environmental destruction or African hunger to being a mere book member of an organisation supporting a cause close to the citizen's heart. John Hartley (1996: 43) goes as far as suggesting that the couch potatoes could become "citizens of the media", using TV news as their forum, refusing to participate in established politics but pursuing political ends by creating their own forms of participation from critical consumerism to the formation of virtual republics of fans. The limitations and possibilities of Hartley's citizens of the media are discussed in more detail in chapter 12.

Pericles first pointed out that the strength of a democracy depends on its transparency. Technological change means that politics revolve around "playing the media game", but the game is played fast and intense, in a hot-house atmosphere with a short events horizon, so it is difficult for anyone to reflect on the game being played with them. Deeper analysis of the campaign process is required to reveal the dynamics that underpin democracy, current and future. This close analysis of the content and delivery of political rhetoric in campaigns may also reveal the strategies that can be used by average citizens, just as it is presently used by political machines, to re-set the parameters of debate to produce desired collective outcomes. Increased transparency by its very nature guarantees a more open democratic debate.

Critics are right to be sceptical about the ability of democracies to offer the space for debate and deliberation. Political campaigns involve the rapid construction and adaptation of complex and therefore creaky meta-narratives (a concept discussed in some detail in chapter 4). To be effective campaigns must appeal to the popular consciousness and that process has always made democratic politics a relatively facile and banal activity. The advent of mass society, with greater distance between citizens and their representatives, has only exacerbated this problem. But against the practice of propaganda which seeks to close debate and discussion, contending political campaigns, particularly where there is equality of opportunity to participate in and create one's own campaign, play a crucial role in allowing democratic institutions to come to decisions. Without the outright coercion evident in the 2002 Iraqi election, it is only political campaigns that can produce the majorities required for democracies to take decisive action or any action at all. Thus the political campaign is a necessary condition for democracy in mass societies.

Rather than lament democracy's shortcomings and its failure to adequately represent an alternative or critical or broad range of views, perhaps there is a strategy to understand the nature of modern democracy and work to ensure the representation of other views. This book seeks to review the historical texts that inform current campaign practice, to seek the specifications of effective intervention in contemporary political processes, to delve into the texture of political campaigns that produce "upset victories" and so demystify, and thus democratise, contemporary politics. The challenge for citizens is to do what democrats have always done and grasp the levers of democracy to reform its methods in light of current conditions. Thus our attempt to place the political campaign in contemporary democratic theory leads us to consider how the political campaign is much more than marketing and how a multiplicity of contending campaigns provides the deliberative forum for mass voices.

2
LANGUAGE AND RHETORIC –
FROM THE TRIBE TO THE CITY

The Shaman

While the political campaign is a modern invention of the 20th century, the rhetorical techniques the campaign uses to persuade citizens to action have their roots deep in human evolution. When Winston Churchill or John Kennedy stirred an audience, they were using language to elicit responses that have been hard-wired into human psychology by our evolutionary experience. The most obvious examples are when speeches like Churchill's 'we'll fight them on the beaches...' or Kennedy's 'ask not what your country can do for you...' touch the right buttons to give members of the audience goose bumps. These are extreme cases. Usually the impact of a persuasive communication is far subtler but nevertheless it similarly seeks to touch the right chord in the audience.

To understand how political campaigns work it is necessary to appreciate how the political function of language is embedded deeply in the evolution of human society. The survival of the tribe depended not only on shared language, stories and songs but also on their use to arrive at timely decisions. The techniques for constructing compelling stories and memorable songs were the basis of the practical magic of the shaman. The shaman's work was carried on in early kingdoms by the bard who strategically used language to promote social cohesion and to convince citizens of the need for action. In classical Greek democracies, the Sophists applied rational analysis to the magic of the shaman and bard in order to explain what was persuasive in deliberative assemblies. Aristotle systematised the insights of the Sophists into rhetoric, the science and art of persuading a mass of citizens to an opinion or action. Aristotle established the three categories of rhetorical proof: those from reason, character and emotion. The art of persuasion rests in their comprehensive combination in a convincing style governed by principles of rhythm, harmony and dynamism.

In order to understand what generates the persuasive powers of language, it is useful to consider how the development of human community occurred together with the development of speech and meaning. In the animal kingdom generally, the warning cry of the predator's approach gives an obvious evolutionary advantage but when primates developed an expanded set of manual and verbal signals they created another evolutionary advantage by allowing the relatively peaceful organisation of power within the group (Jaynes 1977).

The archaeological evidence suggests that what distinguishes humans from the other primates is that between 100,000 and 40,000 years ago humans experienced a period of anatomical evolution to "the structure of the larynx, tongue and associated muscles that give us fine control over spoken sounds" (Diamond 1992: 47). These physical changes allowed humans to communicate more delicate nuances via complex languages and thus create new social forms to keep groups together: extended tribes, religion and art (Mithen 1999). While among the primates, clashes over leadership between dominant males often led to the group splitting, among the human tribes there could be consultations governed by the principle of "egalitarian mutuality" (Maddock 1974: 166) where each initiated member could be heard in the discussion preceding collective action. As Tacitus (1970: 111) remarked of the German tribes: "On matters of minor importance only the chiefs debate; on major affairs, the whole community."

Art and religion arose with the similar political purpose of cementing group solidarity and assisting the group to flourish in changing conditions. In the process, the tribe created costumes, paintings, dances, stories and songs that represented deeper, mythological meanings. These meanings were guarded and passed on according to laws usually overseen by the shaman. The shaman was a sorcerer, the conduit between the supernatural and the mundane in the life of the tribe, a priest, a healer and usually a pivotal figure in community singing. Song itself brought a new and increased power to words and fostered the emergence of metaphor because, once they are set to music, words take on new, unexpected qualities: lilt and balance, tone and quality (Bowra 1962: 276).

The application of rhythm, assonance, alliteration and word-play created a melody of words that mimics and builds on the musical melody. The interaction of both melodies in song gives the shaman the power to conjure with the language to first create and then make real the myths by which people live. The power of the song was power over the world, chants had practical magical purposes – to avert the evil eye or cure a disease, to give a person a sense of security against the uncertainties of existence (Bowra 1962; Eliot 1957). The shaman used the mythic resonances of the language to produce greater social cohesion than the threat of mere physical force could ever produce (Berger 1973).

The Bard

The advent of agriculture, the concentration of surplus wealth and the emergence of kings saw the work of the tribal shaman develop into organised religion, often with the king as god. Ritual chanting and repetitive mantras were used to concentrate and control the energies of the population. Language began to play a more coercive role in reconciling individual mental states to acceptance of, or complicity in, social structures. But even all-powerful kings cannot rely solely on appeals to God and a well-programmed population in extreme situations. The timely delivery of words based in and with the inspirational force of socially inculcated songs was a central act of post-tribal leadership. Early literatures from many cultures record how kings formulated appeals to action. *The Epic of Gilgamesh, the Bible, the Iliad, the Odyssey* and *Beowulf* all record moments where a community is welded together and convinced to action by the appropriate words of leadership, often prepared or delivered by the court poet or bard.

In the Viking history King Harald's Saga, the king's bard Thjodolf often uses his linguistic skills to strategic effect. Harald, for example, begins a poem on the pleasures of anchoring in Randers Fjord and calls on the poet to conclude the verse. Thjodolf obliges with: "Next year our cold-blooded anchor/ Will drop in warmer oceans..." (Sturluson 1966: 79) – a call for the invasion of Denmark which Harald then pursues. Similarly when Harald faces certain death at the Battle of Stamford Bridge, Thjodolf sketches out the strategic imperatives with the song: "Though Harald himself should fall,/ Never shall I abandon/ The king's young heirs/... (who) Would soon avenge their father." (Sturluson 1966: 151)

The Bard Reflects

A Welsh bard from the 6th century AD, Taliesin, is credited with the following song. Calder (1983: 101) reads it as "obscure both in meaning and function" but it can be interpreted as the bard's reflection on his work at the juncture of metaphor, magic, myth and the war-machine. The simplicity of style allows the bard to use repetition to build to a stirring climax. Consider how the bard relies on images that still have purchase today. After he claims to be the bubble in beer, it is surprising that he does not claim to be the sizzle in the steak.

> "I was in many shapes before I was released:
> I was a slender enchanted sword... I was raindrops in the air,
> I was star's beam; I was a word in letters, I was a book in origin;

> I was lanterns of light... I was a bridge... I was a path,
> I was an eagle, I was a coracle in seas;
> I was a bubble in beer, I was a drop in a shower;
> I was a sword in hand, I was a shield in battle.
> I was a string in a harp... in the water as foam:
> I was a spark in fire, I was wood in a bonfire;
> I am not one who does not sing; I have sung since I was small.
> I sang in the army of the trees' branches..."
> *Taliesin (quoted in Calder 1983: 101)*

The song reveals the complexity of the bard's role: as political ("a sword in hand") and mythical ("a slender enchanted sword"); and as a leader ("lanterns of light... a bridge... a path") and as a part of the whole ("a drop in a shower... a string in a harp"). Further, while acknowledging the transience of their work ("star's beam... a bubble in beer... a spark in fire"), bards were also aware of its impact on the real world ("a sword... a shield... wood in a bonfire..."). This fragment also suggests the central role of the song in transforming the complexity of existence ("many shapes") through training ("I have sung since I was small") into a political purpose ("the army of the tree's branches...").

The work of the Celtic bard included establishing the king's genealogy, celebrating his victories and lamenting his death (Jackson 1971). The bard was also the repository and interpreter of the nation's history and laws (Hughes 1977; Herm 1976). Bards manipulated not just words but also systems of knowledge as they connected politics to the spiritual and mythical planes of popular consciousness in their utterances as seers and prophets (Freeman 1995).

The political and mythical aspects of the bard's work were intertwined in the bardic style that used a strict metre to combine narrative with stock formulaic phrases, elaborate similes and extended digressions. As Kuno Meyer says of the bardic lyrics: "...they avoid the obvious and the commonplace; the half-said thing to them is the dearest." (1970: 257) By deleting verbs and definite articles, by dispensing with tense and by favouring the unmarked verbal noun, the bards produced an intense, dynamic "spiralling of thought" (Calder 1983: xiii) that inspired commitment to a cause or action.

The "magic" of the bard was in the stylistic techniques which drew inspiration from the fewest possible words. "They took pleasure in... pithy speech which, leaving no space for reflection, would drive a plot to cruel climaxes" (Herm 1976: 251). Whether in the "rushing, torrential, allusive" style of the Welsh or "the clear-cut jewel work of Irish and Scottish composition" (Jackson 1971: 227), the bard utilised "a sparseness, an economy of expression" (Calder 1983: xiii) to twist and turn the language into a powerful weapon for the war-machine.

As the formal intermediary between language and power, the bard plays a key role in post-tribal society by manufacturing social cohesion through the application of communication techniques that constantly connect the political to the mythical and vice versa. Strikingly similar bardic work is carried out today by campaign workers using simple, direct and well-formed words to intertwine politics and image, and manufacture the forms of social cohesion required to produce decisive support in elections and on particular issues. Despite post-modern practices and hi-tech equipment, contemporary campaign workers are essentially doing the work of the bard in a latter day war machine (Stockwell 2000).

Pre-democratic political communication points to the "magical" power that persists in words today so that, as Cecil Bowra (1962: 276) points out: "when, through their sound and rhythm and sense, words exert so strong a hold on us that we can think of nothing else, we still speak of their enchantment".

Derrick De Kerckhove says: "Rhetoric was a sort of democratisation of magical practices" (1983: 186) and in the remainder of this chapter we will consider how, as democratic forums emerged in classical Greece, "magical" techniques of linguistic persuasion were analysed, systematised and developed to produce the art of rhetoric.

The Sophists

A number of developments coincided in Greece from 800 to 500BC which prompted city-states to experiment with forms of diffused and increasingly democratic decision-making (Held 1987). The overthrow of kings, long distance sea trade, intensive agriculture and the introduction of coinage created a wealthy middle class which wanted access to power in those cities (Anderson 1974). These changes coincided with the development of a streamlined alphabetic script which prompted a new precision in thought that sought to penetrate the mystery of myth with exact measurement, rational analysis and the clarification of natural principles (De Kerckhove 1983).

It is not surprising that all this change produced conflict as new classes and new interests emerged. Typically there was conflict between the powerful rich and the relatively poor *hoplites*, the self-armed and largely self-sufficient infantry that formed the backbone of the army in times of war. Where that conflict was resolved by the application of rationality to produce economic justice, constitutional power-sharing and the opportunity for detailed discussion, then democracy gradually developed. In Athens during the sixth century BC, Solon and Kleisthenes introduced constitutions that provided for a participatory form of government which allowed diverse interests to be represented in open debate in large forums that made prompt and binding decisions (Held 1987: 14). But for the Athenians, democracy was not just a set of institutions; it was an entire mode of life whose "basis was not so much individual material welfare or comfort as communal pride" (Curtis 1965: 23). It was a mode of life dedicated to the pursuit of individual and collective happiness and the realisation of the good life through active participation (MacIntyre 1985: 135–136). While the sexist and racist nature of these early forms of democracy is incontrovertible, these democratic debates were the forerunner to today's political campaigns and many of the techniques used to convince citizens then remain relevant today.

Within the open forum of the Athenian Pnyx, and in similar bodies all over Greece, it soon became apparent to keen students that there were more and less effective means of convincing citizens. By applying analysis to debates within political forums, the techniques of effective political communication were revealed and formed into early versions of rhetoric: a science, albeit inexact, which could be taught to citizens who wished to effectively exercise their free speech in those forums (Barrett 1987).

Traversing the fledgling city states of Ancient Greece, the Sophists, or teachers of wisdom, distilled the essential rules for convincing large crowds. Just as other scientists pursued primitive forms of the empirical method, the Sophists gathered examples where an elegantly formed statement swayed an audience or where a speaker used his acute understanding of human nature to get the desired result. They formed these examples into a rough science to assist citizens in pursuit of *arete*, that mix of moral virtue and worldly success won by strong performances in the Pnyx (Barrett 1987).

During the fifth century BC, a group of Sophists set up schools in Athens where they found a ready market not just for lessons on rhetoric but also for the broad general knowledge of human and natural affairs that assisted young men to make convincing arguments in the Pnyx. The key Sophists were foreigners who themselves had limited political rights in Athens but they met a real need as democracy developed and persuasion became a useful aid to advancement.

The first influential Sophist was Protagoras who believed that virtue could be taught and willingly took payment to teach it. He took an avowedly practical attitude to knowledge that is best summed up by his position on religion: "Of the gods, I cannot say either that they exist or that they do not; it is a difficult subject, and life is not long enough." (Diogenes Laertius 1972: 465). Another aspect of his practicality is his humanist (but pre-feminist) notion that "man is the measure of all things" (Diogenes Laertius 1972: 463). This focus on the individual over ideology prepared the way for the audience-centred campaigns of today.

The Power of the Pnyx

About 2,500 years ago, the people of Athens formed a democracy that is still a benchmark for political systems today. Power rested in the hands of the assembly of citizens, or *Ekklesia*, which met in the *Pnyx*, a hillside forum close to the *Agora* (marketplace) and *Acropolis* (temple). Citizens trading in the Agora were rounded up to attend the *Pnyx*. Slaves with police powers wielded a red chalked rope that left a mark on tardy citizens which was a cause of shame.

The Pnyx met for free and fierce debate forty times a year and required a quorum of 6,000 citizens to operate. The agenda for the *Pnyx* was approved by the Council of Five Hundred (or *Boule*) made up of 500 men over thirty years of age selected by lot. The *Boule* was chaired by a president who held the office for one day only. Citizens used logic, emotion and all the rhetorical techniques available to convince their fellows. They had an unconstrained freedom of speech. It was more than a right, it was a responsibility to overcome stage-fright and the jeers of opponents to put a view candidly. The Greeks had four different words for free speech: *isegoria* and *isologia* mean the equal right to be and speak in the *Pnyx*; *eleutherostomou* suggests that a freely given opinion has greatest moral force; and *parrhesia* which meant that brutally frank and direct speech got to the heart of the matter.

Athenian democracy had its limitations. Only free men of Athenian parentage could be citizens, so women, slaves and those born elsewhere or with foreign parents were excluded. Further, citizens often fell under the sway of smooth talkers from wealthy and aristocratic families. Rash decisions were made as when the victorious admirals from the battle of Arginousai were executed at the whim of the *Pnyx* because they refused to risk further lives to search for sailors already lost in heavy seas. Nevertheless, the *Pnyx* steered Athens to economic and cultural greatness, not least because citizens could use free speech to search for the heart of the matter, look for the best solution, challenge accepted wisdom and achieve upsets.

Stone 1988; Held 1987; Anderson 1974

To the question "which man is the measure?" Protagoras, according to Plato (1987: 152), held that "things are to me as they appear to me, and to you as they appear to you". This laid him open to a charge of relativism, that he could not distinguish good from bad. But as he also argued that all sides of any argument should be debated dispassionately, what might appear as relativism is in fact a desire to find the best resolution of each dispute by arguing it out. It is the business of the proponents to each position to make their case by effective use of language and then negotiate the best outcome they can achieve. Protagoras used language to challenge the ideology of society while establishing that debate is the strongest defence available against social disintegration.

"Speech is a powerful lord," declared another of the foreign Sophists, Gorgias (Barrett 1987: 15). He brought to Athens a systematic understanding of the power in political language derived from his experience in the short democratic experiment in his home city of Leontinoi, Sicily. Gorgias appropriated the techniques of poetry to create a new and exciting form of oratory that used rhythm, assonance, pattern and metaphor to engage the audience and carry the argument. In particular, his use of antithesis or contrary oppositions mined the language for the dynamics of similarity and contrast in both the sound and sense of the words. Playing off humour against seriousness was one particularly useful form of antithesis: "the opposition's seriousness is to be demolished by laughter, and the laughter by seriousness" (Barrett 1987: 15). Gorgias's intellectual experiments revealed the play in language: it gives us a broad spectrum of miniscule, elusive differences with which to work and play. It is these fine distinctions that allow us to describe the world and ourselves in enlightening detail (Solmsen 1975). The enlightening power of antithesis can be observed in Gorgias's strong defence of weak causes that led his student, Alcidamas to be the first to challenge the institution of slavery with the statement: "God has left all men free, nature has made none a slave." (Stone 1988: 44)

Gorgias also appreciated the role of psychology in persuasion. He suggested that rhetoric may be an irresistible force that controls the listener's emotions through "witchery" and "sorcery" and that it can have the same impact on the soul that drugs have on the body (Arnhart 1981: 23). Gorgias realised that "the same emotions that may be aroused by speech may also be allayed by it and he borrowed the emotions of poetry to create techniques that might produce "the conscious guidance of another person's soul" (Solmsen 1975: 47). He borrowed from Pythagorean musical theory concepts such as "figure" and "trope" that allowed him to analyse more deeply the dramatic tension produced by repetition and return in a speech and to produce a more complex reading of the persuasive patterns in language (Burnet 1968: 96–7).

Among the minor Sophists, Thrasymachus of Chalcedon pointed out the power of emotional appeals delivered in a low-key style.

Thrasymachus's technique was later called the middle style because it was halfway between grand oratory and plain speech. He found that understating his case often gave it more effect (Barrett 1987). Prodicus of Keos taught that language is the product of human agreement and pursued an intricate understanding of the subtle differences between synonyms to promote the correct use of words (Solmsen 1975). He showed how an understanding of the nuance of language gives the speaker the power to make subtle but telling arguments. Hippias of Elis opposed all specialisation and promoted an enthusiastic self-sufficiency. He was famous for his willingness to lecture on any subject and taught the use of mnemonics to assist the student's memory to retain information and marshal arguments (Barrett 1987).

The Sophists as a group liberated the power of language and made that power available for democratic use. It is the same power that campaign workers seek to harness today and the Sophists' advice to use the subtlety and nuance of language to win the rational and emotional aspects of any debate continues to be valid. The Sophists accepted that any account of the world is incomplete and contradictory. Language can never produce an exact replica of the world but rather language is the tool for communication, the mutual exchange and interpretation of each others' views about the world. The Sophists taught more than a set of technical tricks to manipulate the audience. They taught how to use language strategically to create the open-ended exchange of communications required to produce action in the world which is just what a political campaign seeks to do today.

Aristotle's Rhetoric

The Sophists were roundly criticised by Socrates and his student Plato as agents of self-interest, taking money to corrupt the youth by teaching them to argue convincingly regardless of the truth (Plato

1987). Further, they argued that the rhetoric which convinced the crowd to action was an insignificant pursuit because style not substance prevailed and, as Socrates said, the Assembly could be convinced by skilful oratory that an ass was a horse (Plato 1956).

It was however, Plato's student, Aristotle who systematised the work of the Sophists with his own observations to argue that rhetoric played a crucial role in assisting the assembly to make the best decision. Aristotle took a scientific approach to understanding the techniques used to convince the crowd and in *The Art of Rhetoric* he outlines the speculative, inventive and open process of persuading an audience and producing a result in a democratic forum. The text remains definitive today.

The Art of Rhetoric was one of Aristotle's earliest works and it plays a central role in his overall philosophy. The *Rhetoric* connects Aristotle's *Ethics* to his *Politics*, by giving the citizen the means to seek his own happiness in a forum that may, at the best of times, foster "the good for man." (1953: 27) Happiness, for Aristotle, is work. It is the care of the self through social activity, a free-flowing, ongoing search with one's fellow citizens not for the theoretical truth but for an everyday, practical and probable truth in the given situation. It is a collective pursuit and the practical outcomes of the pursuit bind the city together and then become the city.

When Aristotle begins the *Rhetoric* with the statement that "Rhetoric is the counterpart of dialectic" (1991: 1354), he is making a direct assault on Socrates' account of rhetoric as the counterpart of ad hoc cookery (Plato 1971: 462) and claiming a place for rhetoric in the realm of logical argumentation. By equating rhetoric and logical argumentation, Aristotle demands that rhetoric be taken seriously as a means to pursue the good life in the city state. He has a simple argument for this proposition: that while the purpose of logical argumentation is to discover proofs of the truth, the purpose of rhetoric is similarly to discover proofs, but proofs that lead an assembly or an audience to collectively advantageous action and therefore happiness.

In this common search for proofs, the dialectic touches ground in rhetoric to have a political impact and to play out its social purpose: "for the proofs alone are intrinsic to the art (of rhetoric)" (Aristotle 1991: 1354). The speaker must know the Sophists' tricks in order to be on guard against them and ready to refute them or even use them for the greater good (Aristotle 1991: 1355). For Aristotle however, and here he is at pains to distinguish himself from the Sophists and correct them, the most effective tool in rhetoric is not emotive language or even psychological insights into the audience, but the *enthymeme*, "the flesh and blood of proof" (1991: 1354). The enthymeme may be briefly described as an argument that works with the general citizenry.

Aristotle defines rhetoric as "the power to observe the persuasiveness of which any particular matter admits" (1991: 1355). The work of rhetoric begins with the research and planning that Aristotle calls "invention", the initial discovery of the appropriate premises from which a convincing set of rhetorical proofs can be built. Some proofs pre-exist (for example witnesses and depositions), but the rest the speaker must "invent" (Aristotle 1991: 1355). However, "invention" is not an invitation to fabrication; rather it is a rigorous and rational process of discovering convincing and therefore persuasive arguments.

Before turning to a detailed analysis of the forms of proof, Aristotle analyses the three categories of rhetoric. Legal oratory is used to prosecute or defend a person and convince the courts. Display oratory is designed to praise or blame a person to spectators in any ceremonial forum. Political oratory aims to persuade or dissuade the constituents of a deliberative forum.

Aristotle argued that there were three categories of rhetorical proof: those from character, emotion and reason. The aim of the speech will determine the quantity and mix of categories required.

But reason is the central and conclusive form of rhetorical proof because each minor proof, each step of the way, is subsumed into a rational whole where proofs from character, emotion and reason must match and reinforce each other.

As the use of character and emotion relies on psychological rather than rational insights, these forms of proof do not touch on the truth or falsity of an issue but they should be used effectively because people will judge the speech by them regardless. This is a recognition that rhetoric is more than laying out a rational argument. It is also a psychological exchange: the audience is not just convinced by rational argument but by the argument as it relates to them personally because a conviction is not held in abstract (where one might find a theoretical truth) but rather in the mind of each member of the audience.

Character. There are actually two aspects of character: the character of the speaker (what we would now call image) and the character of the audience (demographics) and while Aristotle systematically confuses them he does outline the importance of both and leads us to consider how they are connected.

In the introduction to his *Rhetoric*, Aristotle explains character as a form of proof he calls ethos – the convincing character of the speaker. It is important to create the appropriate impression of character so that "the speech is given in such a way as to render the speaker worthy of credence" (Aristotle 1991: 1356). He understood that the speaker had to present an impression of themselves to the audience in the same way actors presented their masks in the theatre (Green 1994; Graf 1993). The audience is always looking for the persona; it will construct one regardless, so it is obviously much better to offer a construction that appeals and reinforces the core of the argument rather than take the chance that the audience will find a persona that does not help the argument. Aristotle's theory of tragedy provides useful guidelines for the work of creating the most plausible public persona for the speaker. They should be good, appropriate, real and consistent. Furthermore, characters should "endeavour after the necessary or the probable" (Aristotle 1940: 41–42).

In the body of the work, however, rather than detailing how the speaker might create himself as a character that appeals to the audience, Aristotle (1991: 1388) discusses the equally important question of how to assess the character of the audience: "Let us... go through the characters of men in regard to their emotions, habits, ages and fortunes". Aristotle knew the importance of understanding the audience "demographics". In his tripartite analysis of the speech event that still informs communication theory today, Aristotle (1991: 1358) says: "For the speech is composed of three factors – the speaker, the subject and the listener", but he is quick to point out "it is to the last of these that its purpose is related".

Emotion is the second category of proof considered by Aristotle (1991: 1377) and it is important because it can "bring the giver of judgement into a certain condition". When Aristotle isolated *pathos* or the appeal to emotions as a separate form of proof, he opened what we would call political desire to rigorous scrutiny. While the Sophists had realised the importance of emotions and systematised the technologies of "magic" borrowed from tribal and bardic communication, they had no comprehensive psychological theory. In his book *De Anima*, Aristotle did produce a psychological theory that gave an account of the psyche as, according to Ferguson: "embedded in matter... [so that] mind and body are aspects of the same substance and separable only in thought" (1972: 94). Aristotle sought to reveal how the psychological aspects of a debate might complement and reinforce its logical aspects and how logic might affect the passions. This is the moment when a vast, new terrain of politics is first acknowledged. Previously politics had occurred in the world but Aristotle saw that it also occurs in the mind.

Aristotle confronted the Platonic and Socratic account of rhetoric as a mere appeal to emotion by establishing exactly how important the psychological exchange is in political debate. Aristotle saw how deep into the complex and dangerous web of the human mind the speaker must be ready to go in order to be effective. He wrote in *Rhetoric*: "For things do not seem the same to those who love and those who hate nor to those who are angry" (Aristotle 1991: 1377).

Reason is the third and most powerful category of rhetorical proof. This is not the pure, ideal logic that finds its clearest expression in the syllogism (all ducks are birds, all birds have feathers therefore all ducks have feathers) but the practical, everyday reason of the particular situation encapsulated in the enthymeme, the argument that works. Today we would call this the message. While a valid syllogism moves from true premises to a necessary conclusion, an enthymeme is a simple version of the syllogism that moves with the same rational force from probable, simplified premises to a pertinent conclusion. An example of an enthymeme is: "Given that in exile we fought to return, are we, now that we have been restored, to flee so that we need not fight?" (Aristotle 1991: 1399). It moves from the practical, probable premise via a suppressed premise (it is worth staying here) to a conclusive call to action, packaged as a question designed to move the debate along.

Aristotle was a proponent of empirical reason so he saw that the real work of rhetoric is to isolate just those facts that when communicated in the appropriate pattern for the given situation will produce a convincing argument to a majority of citizens. Rhetoric takes the form of a dialectical argument and makes the most expedient use of the play of possibilities and probabilities revealed by the situation in order to convince the audience to action, while ignoring any elements which are unnecessary to convince the audience. But while rhetoric is seemingly instrumental in purpose, any argument occurs against all the other rhetorical arguments offered on this issue, around this time and so is communicative in function. The interplay of competing rhetorical arguments produces a process of debate that while limited by the practicalities of convincing the audience is nevertheless practical in its effects.

Aristotle (1991: 1404–1414) disdains style, but the audience is the judge and it is apparent that speakers communicate more effectively when the argument is presented using vivid images, explanatory metaphor and engaging wit, with clarity, propriety, purity and rhythm. It is an area that cannot be avoided and so he applies rational analysis "to show how the style and arrangement of speeches can sustain, rather than undermine, the practice of rhetoric as a form of reasoning." (Arnhart 1981: 163) While the enthymeme is the building block of the argument, it is the argument's construction, the way the blocks are put together, that will cause the argument to convince an audience.

Aristotle underlines how rhetoric developed from poetics by way of acting and so is governed by similar principles of dynamics, harmony and rhythm. But these techniques carry heavy luggage: all forms of representation, and the spectacle in particular, require the subterfuges of imitation where "a convincing impossibility is preferable to an unconvincing possibility" (Aristotle 1940: 77).

Aristotle's treatment of style and narrative reveals much about his views on the power of language. To harness that power, as rhetoric seeks to do, requires the speaker to traverse the dangerous field not just between appearance and reality but also between truth and lies. Metaphor epitomises these dichotomies which provide language with its dynamic. Aristotle's ambivalence towards metaphor reveals its problematic function: in his *Logic* "he denigrates metaphorical speech as 'unclear'" (Arnhart 1981: 172), yet in the *Rhetoric* he argues that "metaphor preeminently involves clarity" (Aristotle 1991: 1405). At one level a metaphor is always a lie, a claim that something is other than it is. Yet the metaphor, like the enthymeme, says Aristotle, brings "swift understanding" (1991: 1410) and so is the archetype of communication. Aristotle says active metaphors should link the commonplace to the unfamiliar and the actual to the potential by finding the right levels of wit and vividness, charm and distinction for the particular audience.

Athenian democracy was not without its limitations but the availability of rhetoric played a significant role in encouraging authentic democratic debate in the collective exchanges of practical reason. The teaching of rhetoric tended to broaden the quantity and quality of democratic participation and thus reinforce the democratic nature of the polis. Or to put that in another way, as democracy is an open process, in order to participate effectively in democratic debate, citizens require the skills of rhetorical invention. Thus rhetoric may be understood not as a means to manipulate democracy but as a means to sustain democratic institutions by empowering citizen participants with the creativity required for rhetorical invention while restraining them with the ethical responsibility for informed and constructive participation.

Rhetorical Techniques

- **Alliteration:** repetition of the same sound beginning several words in sequence: **love of land and liberty.**
- **Antithesis:** opposition or contrast of ideas in a balanced or parallel construction: **if war is responsible for present evils, then we should right them by peace.**
- **Aporia:** expression of doubt to draw opponents and identify with them: **I may be mistaken but...**
- **Assonance:** repetition of the same vowel sounds in words close to each other: **no pain, no gain.**
- **Climax:** arrangement of words, phrases, or clauses in an order of ascending power: **lies, damned lies and statistics.**
- **Grammatical break:** omission or transposition of words to create emphasis: **we cannot dedicate, we cannot consecrate, we cannot hallow this ground.**

- **Inversion:** of words, ideas or events to highlight their significance: **renown'd for conquest, and in council skill'd.**
- **Irony:** expression contrary to or understating the intended meaning: **and Brutus is an honourable man.**
- **Metaphor:** words used in a figurative and not literal sense: **iron curtain.**
- **Metonymy:** substitution of one word for another which it suggests: **the pen is mightier than the sword.**
- **Paradox:** an assertion against common sense, but with some truth in it: **it was faster in the slow lane.**
- **Repetition:** repeated use of words or phrases to heighten rhythm and emphasis: **we shall fight on the beaches, we shall fight on the landing grounds, we shall fight in the fields and in the streets, we shall fight in the hills. We shall never surrender.**
- **Simile:** metaphorical comparison using 'like' or 'as': **she was as tough as teak.**
- **Syllepsis:** use of same word in different ways: **hang together or hang separately.**
- **Tautology:** repetition of an idea in a different word, phrase, or sentence: **With malice toward none, with charity for all.**

From the Greek experience, there is an important lesson for current constructions of democratic citizenship. While the notion of robust, free-flowing debate that follows its own logic in search of consensus has been foreshortened by the mass media, a renewed rhetoric designed to counteract the mass media's coercive power offers the possibility that democracy might recreate itself so that all citizens have an equal opportunity to express themselves and so that a more diverse range of frankly stated and freely given opinions can emerge and be contested in collective debate.

3
MANUFACTURE OF FORTUNE –
MACHIAVELLI AND MODERN POLITICS

Machiavelli

Machiavelli (1469–1527) has a bad reputation. His name has become synonymous with cunning, deceit and trickery in politics but he has provided a great service to all humanity by plainly stating what most of those involved in politics do but none profess to do. Machiavelli's empirical approach and application of concepts from military strategy to politics made him the first modern thinker to confront the new formations of political power that developed with the advent of mass society. He introduced a realistic and systematic approach that still informs the strategic use of image and desire in politics today.

Machiavelli saw that the emerging modern state based on manufacture and trade could no longer run on feudal obligation where the populace was obliged to give obedience to the ruler by religious sanction. Rather, the Prince had to win the support of the populace and be ready to repel usurpers. Machiavelli introduced a realism and pragmatism that still informs politics today and that has left an indelible imprint on the practice of political communication. He appreciated that human affairs were not dictated by fortune but could be steered by strategy and skill, that fortune could be manufactured.

Politics was not a passive affair, as far as Machiavelli was concerned: "…it is better to be impetuous than circumspect" (1961: 133) because fortune can be created with dash and determination. This is what the contemporary political campaign seeks to do: to take the world as one finds it but to turn it to the purposes of the campaign.

Machiavelli's own political career was short and brutal. He was a bureaucrat and diplomat for the Florentine republic from 1498 to its fall in 1512. In that time he travelled throughout Italy and to the French court and he was exposed to the new ideas of the Renaissance. When the Florentine republic fell, Machiavelli was sacked, tortured and put under a form of house arrest where he wrote *The Prince* and many other scholarly books which applied the scientific approach of the Renaissance to politics.

Machiavelli recognised that: "Political action took place in a world without a permanent basis for action, without the comforting presence of some underlying norm of reality..."(Wolin 1960: 212) This is a world where the ends can easily justify most means and while power and force were the reigning modes in this moral void, the flexibility of language, particularly when used to play with the subtleties of psychology, made it a useful tool in the process of producing results.

In *The Prince,* Machiavelli explained the importance of image in mass politics and suggested ways in which it can be managed strategically. He argued that people find it difficult to accept the changing world, so they seek out constants in the illusions of religion or, at the other extreme, utopian ideals. They are transfixed by any "spinner of fancies and illusions concealing the true nature of events" (Wolin 1960: 212). He accepted the futility of seeking to dispel well-entrenched illusions, rather he sought to reveal the nature of the illusion in order "to teach the political actor how to create and exploit the illusions" (Wolin 1960: 213).

He pointed out that "contemporary experience shows that princes who have achieved great things have been those who have given their word lightly, who have known how to trick men with their cunning..." (Machiavelli 1961: 99) But while a prince might have to act like a beast, he should not be seen to be a beast.

Machiavelli understood the nature of image: "Everyone sees what you appear to be, few experience what you really are" (Machiavelli 1961: 100).

Despite this pragmatism, Machiavelli was sensitive to "the anguishing elements in the political condition..." but accepted the necessity of immorality because "the imperatives of politics refuse any other alternative" (Wolin 1960: 207–208). A prince "should appear to be compassionate, faithful to his word, guileless and devout. And indeed he should be so. But his disposition should be such that, if he needs to be the opposite, he knows how" (Machiavelli 1961: 100).

Deliberative Forums of the Italian Renaissance

Like the Greek enlightenment, the Italian renaissance occurred in a collection of city-states united by trade and temporary alliances but also subject to in-fighting and foreign attack. Also like Greece, some of those city-states experimented with various forms of collective decision-making that, while excluding women, foreigners and most commoners, moderated the excesses of the leadership and sometimes verged on democracy.

In Machiavelli's own city of Florence, the assembly of the republic met in the Palazzo Vecchio. The Palazzo was originally built in the 1200s to house the government of the Commune of Florence. It contained the Sala dei Duecento where 200 representatives gathered to debate policies for the town and to moderate the influence of the duke (Commune di Firenze 2000). By the late 15th century, the power of the Medici dukes had grown to the extent that the assembly was dormant but when the Dominican friar Savonarola led a revolt against the Medici, the Republic was refounded. A legislative assembly of 1,500 members was created and work began to expand the Palazzo to accommodate the Salone dei Cinquecento. Savonarola was a firebrand who gave prophetic speeches and denounced the Pope until he was overthrown and replaced by Soderini, Machiavelli's patron, who was in turn overthrown when the Medici army retook the city in 1512. After that the Salone dei Cinquecento became the theatrical setting for displays of the duke's absolute power.

In Genoa, an assembly of up to 400 and its committees closely controlled the activities and budget of the duke. Members of this assembly were usually chosen by the duke but to maintain support he had to create a reasonable balance of factions and classes. Government proceeded without formal rules but extensive debate, usually until a consensus could be concluded. The public could object to decisions by councils and if criticism was sufficiently strong, another council might be convened to reconsider the matter (Shaw 2001).

The Venetian republic emerged from communal violence by creating a large assembly that allowed the free exchange of ideas among citizens. Between 7th and 12th centuries, doges (or dukes) ruled by conspiracy and vendetta and five were forced to abdicate, nine were deposed or exiled, five blinded and five murdered (Muir 1999). Around 1200, new families who had made fortunes in trade seized power and transformed the institutions of Venice to counter the political violence that was bad for business. Inspired by the trust required for trade and the collectivity of the convoy where the fastest ship had to accommodate the slowest, the new power established an assembly with 1,200 members, the Maggior Consiglio (Bianchi et al 1997). While this assembly was large, unwieldy and subject to factionalism, it countered excesses of power and could call the doge and all-powerful Council of Ten to account and release those who were unfairly imprisoned. In a bid to limit the violent effects of factionalism, insults, insignia, large banquets and extensive god-parenting were banned, as was electioneering. The possibility of democracy without election campaigns may seem strange to us but doing away with campaigns would put more emphasis on the qualifications, skills and previous activities of the candidates.

This is Machiavelli's legacy for us today: the campaign should be run according to the highest principles but it should always be realistic, be ready for the worst and, while refusing to countenance any illegality, be prepared to do what is necessary to win. Thus we can see the similarities between politics and war. In each theatre, participants must be ready to use parry and thrust, ploy and counter-ploy to achieve their ends. In *The Art of War,* Machiavelli draws out the connections between politics and war and analyses military strategy in ways that show its application to the political world.

Military Strategy

Military strategy provides useful tools to think about campaigns and two forms of warfare have particular relevance to contemporary politics: the strategy of guerilla warfare is useful for situations of offensive insurgency and the strategy of siege warfare has much to teach those in positions of defensive incumbency. If, as Clausewitz says "War is... a continuation of political commerce by other means" (1968: 23) then words are the bullets and images are the bombs, and the rhetorical tools that deliver those words and images to the electorate are weapons systems. To be effective those systems must be arrayed and utilised with the same precision that the military uses to pursue its ends. Machiavelli drew the connection between political and military strategy, but the work of many military strategists is useful to political campaign strategists (Pitney 2000).

Strategy comes from the Greek root *strategia* which means generalship. Strategy refers to the overall planning and conduct of large-scale operations and while it still has its roots in military manoeuvres, it also has enormous relevance to any form of effective action in a mass society. Strategy is the comprehensive organisation of resources to control situations and areas in order to attain objectives. The aim of strategy is to achieve desired results by exploiting the elements of movement and surprise so that one's engagement in conflict occurs under the most advantageous circumstances. The perfection of strategy would be to produce a decision without any serious fighting. The strategist's aim is not just to prevail in battle but to create a situation so advantageous that it must produce the desired result.

In China around the 5th Century BC, Sun Tzu gave one of the earliest and still the most succinct accounts of military strategy: "True excellence is to plan secretly, to move surreptitiously, to foil the enemy's intentions and baulk his schemes, so that at the last the day may be won without shedding a drop of blood" (1983: 20). His observation that "All warfare is based on deception" (1983: 11) may appear to justify systematic lying until the context clarifies that only the opponent need be deceived: when ready to attack seem unable, when busy seem inactive, when near seem far away and vice versa. Further:

> "Hold out baits to entice the enemy.
> Feign disorder, and crush him.
> If he is secure on all points, be prepared for him.
> If he is in superior strength, evade him.
> If your opponent is of choleric temper,
> seek to irritate him.
> Pretend to be weak, that he may grow arrogant.
> If he is taking his ease, give him no rest.
> If his forces are united, separate them.
> Attack him where he is unprepared,
> appear where you are not expected."
>
> (Sun Tzu 1983: 11)

This account and any number of more recent re-statements provide a template for campaign strategy carried out not on the battlefield but in the public debate to influence the actions of constituents. The application of strategic method in military terms seeks to match your strength against your opponent's weakness, and make one's own weakness invisible to the opposition to avoid their strength, and then to move quickly in order to catch them off balance. Being a little ahead of your opponent counts for more than relative power. The importance of timelines were exemplified by Napoleon and his organization of the French army, which marched and fought at 120 paces to the minute, while their opponents stayed at the orthodox 70 paces. This allowed Napoleon's forces to multiply "mass by velocity" both strategically and tactically.

Strategy and Persuasion in Henry V

William Shakespeare's play Henry V tells of the career of a 15th century English king and his attempt to exert military control over France. After winning a long siege, Henry tried to lead his troops back to England via the port of Calais but on 25 October 1415, the numerically superior French forces blocked the road to Calais near the village of Agincourt and challenged Henry's exhausted troops to battle. Henry spoke to his troops and Shakespeare's version of that speech is inspirational:

> This day is called the feast of Crispian:
> He that outlives this day, and comes safe home,
> Will stand a tip-toe when the day is named,
> And rouse him at the name of Crispian...
> Old men forget: yet all shall be forgot,
> But he'll remember with advantages
> What feats he did that day...
> This story shall the good man teach his son;
> And Crispin Crispian shall ne'er go by,

> From this day to the ending of the world,
> But we in it shall be remember'd;
> We few, we happy few, we band of brothers...
> And gentlemen in England now a-bed
> Shall think themselves accursed they were not here,
> And hold their manhoods cheap whiles any speaks
> That fought with us upon Saint Crispin's day.

The French and English faced each other on muddy plowed fields. Henry placed his longbowmen forward on either flank and ordered them to fire. The French cavalry attacked but the mud slowed them down and their horses were easy targets for English arrows. Then the French foot soldiers attacked but they were squeezed together by the narrowing field and the English archers on each side. They could not raise their weapons and were slowed down by the mud.

The English survived three frontal attacks and won the day. Henry's strategy is still relevant today. While refusing to attack, he goaded his opponents into jumping into a quagmire where he used strong positions on either flank to harass them.

Knowledge of the terrain is vital to success in strategy. Some ground is easy to negotiate while other terrain is not. Still other ground may be assumed to be impassable to the opposition but with skilful manoeuvring can be crossed to catch the opposition unaware. In 217 B.C., for example, Hannibal used the ambush to defeat the Roman general Flaminius at Lake Trasimene by making a forced march through marshy terrain considered impenetrable. He appeared unexpectedly behind the enemy, challenged Flaminius to attack and defeated the Romans. By catching the opposition off balance, the outcome may be determined without a contest as they realise the futility of resistance. For example, the speed of Napoleon's offensive across Germany in 1805 caught Austrian forces at Ulm unprepared. Surrounded by the numerically superior French forces, the Austrian army surrendered without a fight.

Two forms of military strategy provide examples of particular relevance: guerilla warfare for situations of offensive insurgence and siege warfare for situations of defensive incumbency.

Insurgency is at the centre of modern electoral practice and the quicker pace of campaign action and reaction made possible by computers and electronic media gives more opportunities to the insurgent candidate or anyone promoting new ideas. (Mills 1986: 87) The old nostrum that "oppositions don't win elections, governments lose them" is no longer true. Oppositions "do not have to cope with the day-to-day demands and compromises of administration and thus can stick closely to a disciplined formula of destabilisation" (Mills 1986: 88). By attacking the enemy's weak points rather than the strong, the rebel refuses to play the enemy's game and instead creates their own.

The concept of insurgency comes from the conduct of rebellions and revolutionary wars. The Romans coined the term to describe the uprisings of the conquered but not subservient tribes of their empire. To wage a successful guerilla campaign, the insurgents must understand the terrain and the people and carefully marshal their forces to attack at the weak points of the established position. They must appreciate the lesson of the Roman general Fabius Maximus who, when confronted with the superior forces of Hannibal, adopted a policy of avoiding open battle and using the terrain to bog down and dissipate the stronger enemy. (Plutarch 1965: 51–83) In modern times insurgency is typically waged as guerilla war conducted by irregular forces within a state and aimed at alienating the mass of the population from the authority of the established government with a view to its final overthrow (Guevara 1969: 384–388).

Che Guevara had both the practical experience and theoretical insights to produce a comprehensive methodology for guerilla war.

[The insurgent] must be equipped from the arsenal its enemy
provides... based on territory favoring their struggle... (use) forces
that lie dormant... (practise) constant mobility, constant vigilance,
constant distrust... The plan, in face of the enemy's general
superiority, is to find a tactical means of achieving relative
superiority in one chosen place, whether by being able to
concentrate more troops than the enemy or by securing advantages
arising out of the utilization of the terrain... bases are points the
enemy cannot penetrate except at the cost of heavy losses....
(Guevara 1969: 384–388)

The propensity of governments to overreact and crack down on the
general populace produces support for the insurgents who are thus
presented with even more weak points where they can attack again
to further destabilise the government. The insurgent guerilla must
know the enemy and terrain so well, that they can find the pivotal
moments to intervene and so turn the enemy back on itself. Castro
is fond of quoting Jose Marti, a Cuban revolutionary who died
opposing the Spanish in 1895: "I have lived inside the monster and
know its guts; and my sling is the sling of David" (Castro 1969: 85).

Sim Rubensohn, the advertising agent lured by future Australian
prime minister Robert Menzies from his opponents to run his
successful campaign, well understood the functions of insurgency:
"...vigorous attack directed against chinks in the other man's
political armour is of vital importance in assuring the effectiveness of
election advertising... non-militant advertising... is ineffective"
(Mills 1986: 89).

At the outset, the insurgents have little going for them but the
terrain and their enemy's weaknesses. In electoral terms, the most
effective strategy is to turn your opponent's weaknesses into your
own strengths and play back, not to their strengths, but to their
weaknesses and in a way that undermines their strengths. By
refusing to play the government's game, the insurgents create their
own game which they just might win. There are a number of

informative examples where well organised "underdogs" have produced upset victories (Beiler 1989, Schmidt 1989).

Siege Warfare has a long history and it offers the incumbent or established position suggestions for strategy in the same way the guerilla tactics are useful for insurgents. The incumbent campaign has little choice over terrain. Their very incumbency has locked them into set positions. The challenge is to use those positions most effectively.

When the village farming communities of Mesopotamia coalesced into the first cities around 4,000 BC, the concentration of food and wealth made them attractive targets for plunder and worthy of protection. "Around every important urban centre rose the massive fortifications that guarded the city against nomadic raids and the more formidable campaigns of neighbouring rulers" (Adams 1994: 18). The walls of these cities were built of stone and brick and defended by bowmen in bastions. While battering rams were used to attack gates, ladders were employed to allow the attackers to scale the walls (Montgomery 1968). Casualties in a frontal attack could be high, so by the Egyptian Middle Kingdom (around 2,000 BC) attackers often besieged the city, cutting off supplies to starve it into submission. Cities dug extensive tunnels to ensure water supply. Stratagems and ruses were also employed to capture cities. "Thot, a general to Thutmose III, captured Jaffa by pretending to surrender and then, when the inhabitants of the city opened the gates, storming it. The legend of the Trojan horse relates to this period" (Montgomery 1968: 45). The Phoenicians invented catapults and the Greeks siege towers. Against this new technology, defenders developed new antidotes – hides to catch flaming missiles, incendiary mixtures against battering rams and towers. "Towns were, still, however, more often taken by the old methods of starvation, fifth column and treachery" (Montgomery 1968: 68). Justinian introduced mining both as a means to enter the city and to undermine walls by filling trenches with explosives. For the next thousand years siege warfare changed little, though Philip Augustus's taking of Chateau Gaillard in 1204 by entry through the latrines is worthy of note (Montgomery 1968), as are the "traditional device" of dumping of swarms of bees on the attackers still used by the defenders of Montalcino in 1553 (Pepper & Adams 1986) and the Dutch practice of flooding besiegers by cutting dykes to let in the sea (Montgomery 1968).

The introduction of gunpowder and metal cannon balls changed the nature of siege warfare. While Charles VIII took Italy in 1495 because brick and stone fortress walls were easily shattered by his metal cannon balls (Montgomery 1968), artillery duels soon became significant, particularly where the defender could outflank the attacker as Monluc did during his defence of Siena (Pepper & Adams 1986: 136–7). Earthworks which would not shatter when hit by a metal cannonball also became important both in themselves and as backing to traditional walls. As more was understood about the powers of gunpowder, it was employed in mines under city walls with spectacular effect and defensive mining became important in the construction of fortifications; "ventilation" was used in an attempt to allow expanding gases of an exploding mine to escape (Pepper & Adams 1986). Vauban refined the art of fortification in the late seventeenth century by using all earth ramparts and building angled bastions so that all parts of the wall could be protected by flanking fire from the walls themselves. "(His) methods transformed this branch of warfare into a geometric exercise" (Montgomery 1968: 293).

The principles of defence that emerge from this brief history of siege warfare are equally applicable to incumbent electoral campaigning:

- Prepare to defend attacks from all salients with geometric precision, preferably by firing on the opponent's flanks.
- Construct defences with common material that withstands direct forceful assault.

- Pay particular attention to weak spots and be prepared for the opponent to go under or over (or around) your positions.
- Be well supplied.
- Beware of treachery and deceit.
- Dump everything available on the enemy (hot oil, swarms of bees, etc).

Incumbents must exert such complete control over the terrain that the certainties they offer seem safe and secure compared to the radical plans of their opponents. Nixon's 1972 campaign set the standard. He took attention away from an unpopular war by highlighting the public's perception of a lack of law and order and equating his mundane and homely opponent with that lack (Thompson 1973).

Campaign Industry

As was seen in chapter 1, the cross-development of political and commercial persuasion techniques over the last century has spawned the political campaign industry in the United States and around the world. This industry uses mass marketing and public relations techniques, statistics, strategic game playing and the early adoption of new technologies to compete for political support. During the 20th century, the old ways of political communication, stump speeches, town hall meetings, closely typed handbills, gave way to marketing, public opinion polls, focus groups, TV advertising, direct mail and computers. This industry is staffed by consultants, often termed spin doctors, who frame arguments and statements to elicit their most persuasive effect on electorate audiences (Maltese 1994; Matthews 1989). While spin doctors are derided as threats to democracy who "try to alter the facts through deliberate and reckless disregard for the truth" (Dilenschneider 1998), this is hardly a new complaint and perhaps they are merely engaged in old-fashioned politics by modern means.

The political campaign industry has its roots in the electioneering of yesteryear. Once the parliament established its independence in the English civil war (1642–51), elections became crucial in deciding the participants in government and the direction of policy. By the mid 18th century, the emerging class of tradesmen, shopkeepers, merchants and professionals began to flex their electoral muscles and the political parties, Tories and Whigs, began to campaign for their support (Nimmo 1999). These election campaigns were relatively unregulated and occasions of drunkenness, corruption, violence and many forms of trickery, as the paintings of William Hogarth show (Bindman et al 2001).

As time went on, campaigns became more sophisticated and began to use the techniques of business to promote political ideals. Liberal John Wilkes was expelled from parliament in 1763 for his strong views but kept his career alive with a campaign through the taverns and inns that included the production of advertising on teapots, snuff boxes, pipes, flyers and many other goods (Nimmo 1999).

As mass democracies came of age with the American revolution and the passage of Reform Act 1832 which broadened the franchise in the United Kingdom, election campaigns became more strategic to appeal to the mass of voters. By 1840 campaigns began to use techniques of image building. For example, the US presidential candidate, William Henry Harrison, was styled as a "log cabin–hard cider" man and war hero though he was from patrician stock and his contribution to the battle of Tippecanoe during the Indian wars is still a matter of debate (Perloff 1999: 25–27). Nevertheless, the slogan "Tippecanoe and Tyler (his running mate) too" was popularised in song and print and on a full range of memorabilia and Harrison defeated the incumbent president, Martin Van Buren.

Systematic marketing techniques were introduced into US presidential elections by McKinley's 1896 campaign which used polling, message development and image packaging so successfully that Theodore Roosevelt remarked that the campaign "has advertised McKinley as if he were a patent medicine" (Perloff 1999: 34–36).

About this time public relations became a business tool and the career of the "father of public relations" Edward L. Bernays shows how these techniques were so easily transferred into the political arena (Stuart 1996). Derided as hype, spin or froth and bubble, nevertheless public relations and particularly its practice of honing the message became an essential part of the campaign's armoury because it provided effective ways to interact with voters in a media-savvy mass society (discussed further in chapter 4). Bernays showed the power, and danger, in public relations in a 1928 stunt when he was employed by a tobacco company to promote smoking among women. Leveraging the work of the suffragette movement, Bernays organised a group of women to flout the prohibition on women smoking in public by lighting up their "torches of freedom" on 5th Avenue in New York. Cigarette sales went up but at a great cost to women's health.

Bernays began to appreciate the political potential of public relations techniques while he served in the US government's propaganda arm during the First World War, the US Committee on Public Information. During the 1920s he tutored politicians on the use of the media and the "engineering of consent". The limitations of PR techniques became obvious when he was retained to humanise the austere and dour president, Calvin Coolidge, and took a group of celebrities for breakfast at the White House only to find the president in a very bad mood. The spin he put on the event nevertheless won the newspaper headline: President Nearly Laughs (Stuart 1996).

During the 1936 United States Presidential elections, George Gallup established the public opinion polling industry when he proved the accuracy of political survey research (Mills 1986; Field 1983). Up to that time the straw polls of the *Literary Digest* were considered the most reliable method forecasting the election outcome. The magazine mailed out ten million postcards to people in phone books and registered as motor vehicle owners asking how they intended to vote. 2.3 million replied and 57% favoured the Republican challenger Landon over 43% for the Democrat Roosevelt. Gallup applied insights gleaned from Kolmogorov's definitive reworking of probability theory (more in chapter 5) to point out two large flaws in this method. In the first place the large sample was useless – Gallup foretold the magazine's prediction by randomly sampling just 3,000 people from the same list. Secondly, there was a bias in the sample – wealthy Republican supporters were more likely to own telephones and cars than poorer Democrat supporters. Then by a door-knock survey of a random sample of all voters, Gallup correctly predicted Roosevelt's return, though because it was done so long before the election, not particularly accurately. From that time on, campaigns began to use quantitative survey research to take the pulse of the public and mould their statements.

Television became popular in the United States during the 1950s and it changed the way that politics is pursued. The ability to blend audio and visual elements together provides a powerful communicative tool. The emotional potency of television was evident in 1952 when the future US President Richard Nixon deflected concerns about improper campaign donations in his famous "Checkers" speech. He went on national TV with his dog, Checkers (which had been supposedly given to his children by a supporter) and appealed for public sympathy because he was operating under a set of rules that would force him to give back the dog and deprive his children (Diamond & Bates 1984). Television is an excellent medium with which to elicit an emotional response that reinforces a difficult political message or distracts from one's own shortcomings. In traditional speechmaking before a large crowd, the production of charisma involved the expression of an over-bearing, almost arrogant, persona. But on television the most effective delivery involves talk directed to the emotions using a soft voice and colloquial language that suggests the candidate is communicating intimately with viewers in the privacy of their own living rooms. Television remains important because it is the major source of political information for people. That information comes in two formats: "free" news and current affairs and paid political advertising discussed in chapters 6 and 7 respectively.

During the 1960s the Rand Corporation developed the principles of game theory (Williams 1966) and they were quickly utilised by campaigns to analyse their position and plot strategy (Blumenthal 1980). Game theory is simply a method of modelling how people interact. It is an effective method for analysing data to understand how we reach decisions interdependently. It is not only used to produce the best strategy but also to minimise bad decisions and to incorporate into our thinking what we learn from our mistakes.

The simplest form of game theory is explored in the Prisoner's Dilemma. Two thieves are arrested and separated. Neither will confess so they have two choices: to stay silent or to agree to give evidence against their accomplice. Without damning evidence from the accomplice, each thief could expect a year in jail. If their accomplice turns against them then they can expect ten years in jail while the accomplice goes free. What is the best outcome for each? Certainly if you implicate your partner you get off scot free... as long as your partner does not implicate you. If you both implicate each other then you both get ten years but if you both stay silent you both only serve one year. By analysing the consequences of actions, game theory gives us the tools to understand how people cooperate, compete, bargain and make coalitions using such notions as fairness, trust, self-interest and power. John Nash, the subject of the movie *A Beautiful Mind* (2002), saw that the best outcome to an interaction was when the participants reached a competitive equilibrium where each achieved the maximum satisfaction they could allowing for all the others to achieve their maximum satisfaction. All models break down because they are only simplified versions of life and cannot control for all possibilities, but nevertheless game theory gives us the tools to dig deep into the strategic potential of any situation in a bid to achieve the best outcome.

Since the 1970s new technologies have remade campaign practice. Computers now power most of the political technologies in use today. Their ability to carry out many computations at high speed provides a valuable tool "to canvass, store and retrieve the interests of the electorate" (Bruce 1993: 17) and also to communicate quickly and effectively with individual members of the electorate. The nature of that communication is truncated when compared to the physical interaction of democratic practice in ancient Greece but it is most effective when it is an exchange. Computers cannot replace the "human" elements in campaigning – the thinking and strategy that sets direction, credibility and performance of candidates, the interaction of ideas necessary to persuade the electorate – but they are a valuable tool that is used for many other jobs besides the standard business applications. They can have an impact in small campaigns (McGillicuddy & Robinson 1989) and are an essential strategic tool in large campaigns (Jensen 1989). Computers are useful tools to automate fund-raising, control campaign finances, manage the phone system for opinion polling then analyse the results, produce direct mail, ensure most effective bookings for advertising, organise volunteers, carry out research on opponents and their policies and even provide assistance in telephone marketing to key voters (Shannon 1994) but "...the core application used during campaigns remains the database coupled with a robust mail-merge facility" (Bruce 1993: 17) to produce direct mail as discussed in chapter 8.

In the 21st century, political campaigns are now orchestrated by *campaign directors*, professional "guns for hire" who employ techniques derived from mass marketing, organisation theory, strategic game play and psychology. They are assisted by recent developments in telecommunications and computers which allow *pollsters* to quickly assess specific audiences' quantitative and qualitative responses to the ideas, issues, personalities and events operating in any political situation. Campaign directors also utilise the skills of *media consultants* to position and re-position their candidate quickly and effectively by "spinning" a favourable interpretation on developments and "massaging" precisely those segments of the audience needed to win an election. *Advertising* and *direct mail*, as well as more traditional forms of communication such as *speeches* and *door-knocking*, are also used to deliver messages designed to elicit an appropriate intellectual and emotional response at the ballot box.

By applying integrated quantitative and qualitative research, spin doctors target and track the reactions of the specific pockets of electors needed to form a majority. They position their candidate to his or her best advantage by using media management and advertising to send carefully scripted messages through the mass media as well as via more personal kinds of contact such as direct mail and telephone marketing and the traditional activities of door-knocking, community networking and speechmaking. Their aim is to deliver a complex but cohesive meta-narrative designed to engage the minds of electors and to elicit from a majority of them the appropriate intellectual and emotional response in the polling booth. To do this, spin doctors instinctively recreate bardic and Aristotelian techniques and adapt them to new technologies with reference to new insights from the social sciences.

The political campaign industry: Structures and Resources

Advertising Strategists
Attorneys–Elections & Compliance
Campaign Management
Data Management Services
Direct Mail: Printing & Processing
Direct Mail: Strategy & Creative
Fax Services
Field Operations & Organising
Fundraising Consultants
Fundraising Software & Computer Services
General Consultants & Strategists
Governmental Relations & Lobbying
Grassroots Lobbying: Products & Services
Grassroots Lobbying: Strategy & Planning
Initiative & Referendum Consultants
Internet Services/Web Site Consultants
Mailing & Telephone Lists
Media & Speech Training
Media Buying & Placement Services
Media Consultants
Petitions & Signature Gathering
Political Memorabilia
Political Web Sites: Online Information
Polling: Focus Group
Polling: Interviewing & List Services
Polling: Pollsters & Analysts
Print Advertising Graphics & Design
Printing & Promotional Materials
Public Affairs: Advertising & Media Production
Public Affairs: Issues Management

Public Affairs: Research & Polling
Publications & Newsletters
Public Relations & Events
Research & Information Online
Research: Issues, Voters & Legislation
Research: Opposition Research
Satellite Services
Speech & Copy Writing
Targeting
Telephone Marketing Services
Video Tape Duplication
Video, TV & Radio Production
Voter Lists
Voter Registration

4
MESSAGE MANAGEMENT –
POSITION AND SPIN

Rhetoric and Propaganda

Political campaigns seek to convince target audiences by managing messages to them. Abraham Lincoln described democracy as "government of the people, by the people, for the people" so it is hardly surprising that the people-oriented techniques of public relations play such an important, if little understood, role in the work of political campaigns. By understanding the political uses of public relations, it is possible to move from experiencing politics as a rush of media items to an appreciation of the underlying mechanics of these events.

Despite Aristotle's enduring relevance, "rhetoric" has become a term of abuse to suggest one's opponents are using glib phrases in the cynical pursuit of their own self-interest. Theorists have given some content to this negative reading of rhetoric: Edward Herman and Noam Chomsky (1988) suggest that public relations, and the mass media generally, are tools used by governments, and corporations, in the *manufacture of consent*. Jurgen Habermas (1989) argues that public relations techniques have closed the *public sphere* to the free-ranging debate that is a vital part of an effective democracy. Postmodernists such as Pierre Bourdieu (1978) have criticised notions such as *public opinion* and *will of the people* as empty ideals which mask the diversity within contemporary societies and the exercise of power over citizens which constitutes the actual practice of government. There is something in these critiques, but they do not explain the possibilities offered by contemporary democracy, which provide for the representation of diverse viewpoints by the Opposition, minor parties, independents, interest groups and concerned citizens. The rule of government is tempered by the plethora of voices heard in the decision-making process.

A useful distinction to make at this point is between the persuasion of rhetoric which seeks to find compelling arguments to convince people and the coercion of *propaganda* which insists people believe certain things or act in certain ways by using communication techniques to end discussion. The term "propaganda" was coined by the Catholic Church in 1622 when it established the *Sacra Congregatio de Propaganda Fide* to respond systematically to the arguments expounded by the Protestant Reformation by propagating Church doctrine (Ward 1995). The term was used in a neutral fashion to denote any political communication until World War Two when it acquired a more negative connotation informed by the practices of Nazi Germany and its Minister for Public Enlightenment and Propaganda, Josef Goebbels.

With an instruction to mould mass public opinion in the interest of the Nazi regime, Goebbels took charge of all mass media in Germany, introduced blanket censorship and provided every home with a radio. He pursued a comprehensive program to ensure that all information flow was in the interests of the regime. He insisted on direct access to the highest level of intelligence so he could tailor propaganda to produce required responses in Germany and among the Allies. On the home front he attempted to steer a path between frustration and unsustainable hope to create "an optimum anxiety level" (Doob 1954: 519). He appreciated that "propaganda cannot immediately effect strong counter-tendencies" (Doob 1954: 521) but realised that by repeatedly labelling people and events with easily learnt phrases and slogans he could touch the audience's existing emotions to evoke the desired response.

This is not to say that Goebbels saw his work as the perpetual production and distribution of political slogans. He knew that "to be perceived, propaganda must evoke the interest of the audience" (Doob 1954: 513). The movies made under his control worked within existing genres, particularly musicals, to spread the Nazi message with some subtlety. He is reported in the documentary *We Have Ways of Making You Think* to have told one producer: "Don't come to me with political films." Goebbels conceived propaganda as the production of a total world-view that, once inculcated in the populace, would naturally produce responses that matched the requirements of the regime.

George Orwell explained how simply propaganda could be constructed. He analysed the content of political propaganda and revealed how easily language could be over-inflated with extended metaphor, pretentious diction and meaningless words "to make lies sound truthful and murder respectable, and to give an appearance of solidity to pure wind" (1970b: 170). In his novel *1984*, Orwell further developed his critique of propaganda through the mass media with his concept of *newspeak*: a language with a shrinking vocabulary designed for use by the media to make heretical thoughts, particularly against the state, literally unthinkable.

To combat the totalitarian certainty of propaganda and the "dumbing-down" of the media that Orwell foretold, active citizens can make use of rhetorical persuasion to offer alternative arguments and extend the debate. The subversive potential of rhetoric has long been recognised. The Roman experience suggests that the power of rhetoric was not lost on the "thinly disguised oligarchy" (Stone 1988: 6) which ruled that city and its empire. The Roman Senate banned the teaching of Latin rhetoric in 92 BC although it still allowed the teaching of Greek rhetoric. A facility in Greek was an upper class accomplishment and so while children of established families could learn the techniques of rhetoric, the lower classes and particularly its upwardly mobile members, the nouveau riche, could be denied access to the effective use of language in a political context (Stone 1988: 43). The point of the speech in the ancient Athenian Assembly, and political campaigns today, is to persuade the citizen-audience to points of view that allow majorities to be formed and ideas to be turned into action. Rhetoric seeks to approach this persuasion in a scientific, or at least systematic, way and is thus a necessary condition for the effective operation of a healthy democracy.

Honing the Message

Messages are more than words. They combine into a multi-level, multi-channel meta-narrative that uses words, images and emotions to position ideas that persuade the people needed to produce the desired outcome. The formal speech which Aristotle analysed so comprehensively continues to play an important role in politics, perhaps because it provides the opportunity for "the old-fashioned virtues of reason and evidence and logic" (Watson 1995). But beyond the speech, Aristotle's *Rhetoric* still exerts a key influence in the construction and communication of political campaign meta-narratives that use all the possibilities of the full range of mass media to communicate a complex web of messages to diverse groups of citizens. Aristotle saw the importance of integrating the logical components of an argument with complementary emotional and character components to create an over-arching "body of proof": the grand enthymeme of the whole speech (Arnhart 1981. 37–38). As a proponent of empirical reason, Aristotle saw that the real work of rhetoric is to identify the patterns of facts and emotions, which will, in appropriate circumstances, produce a convincing argument for a majority of the audience. One thing that new technologies and techniques cannot alter is that the crucial rhetorical exchange is still, as it was for Aristotle, "mind to mind" at the moment of persuasion.

However, the Assembly which informed Aristotle's accounts of rhetoric and politics is not presently available in mass society. Political decisions are no longer determined after all interested citizens have had the opportunity to put their case in a forum where all citizens are guaranteed equal access. Nevertheless, even though messages are communicated through the mass media, Aristotle's categories remain particularly pertinent. Regardless of the complexity of the argument or the technology and strategies used to transmit it, character, emotion and reason or image, desire and message are still the main constituents of a persuasive case offered in the process of citizens convincing fellow citizens to action. Below, the modern political campaign's reworking of the Aristotelian categories are considered.

Character/Image is an important part of the message of the political campaign even when there is no candidate and just a concept because every rhetorical exchange requires some level of interpersonal interconnection to create the "mind to mind" experience needed to produce persuasion. Further, the perception of close personal contact created by the electronic media has promoted Aristotle's argument from character to the forefront of contemporary electoral politics where the theatrical presentation of the ethical persona has been recrafted as image-building. The "image" problem for an election campaign is that in a mass democracy most citizens do not have the opportunity to know the candidate or spokesperson intimately. Therefore they will construct their own "intimate" relationship with the candidate based on the observations they make of the candidate's persona, fitting the relationship into their own personal system of relationships as best they can. To address this problem the campaign creates the opportunities to highlight the characteristics of the candidate's persona to which swinging voters, as well as stalwarts, will be attracted. In doing this, the campaign is merely seeking to create an intimacy between the candidate and the citizen despite the limitation of mass democracy.

Regardless of what the speaker says, clothes, hairstyle, speech, posture and attitude will be read by the audience as statements about the kind of person the speaker is. Communicating the persona has always been an important element in democratic politics. In ancient Greece, gesture and stance communicated important political messages (Bremmer & Roodenburg 1993). Tracing the history of imagery through United States presidential campaigns before television, Melder (1989) comes to the conclusion that campaigns of old were packaged and managed more completely and simplistically – and in some cases more misleadingly – than any modern-day political consultant could ever engineer.

Daniel Boorstin (1962) identifies what he considers the key characteristics of the image. Firstly he argues that the image is created and constructed to achieve certain goals. Then, for the image to be effective, it must appeal credibly to the values and common sense of the audience. Finally, he argues, the image so constructed is vivid and concrete but still ambiguous enough for viewers to supply their own interpretations and to draw their own conclusions about the image's meaning that is not too far from the creator's intention. Images are devices of shorthand identification in a symbolic universe which are not complete until they are received and processed by the audience. Perhaps the most useful way to achieve an understanding of image is to consider the conditions of failure. What is the effect when the image is faltering? A sure sign of an image problem is when the public and, even worse, the media report that there is "no there there" (Diamond & Bates 1984: 31). Political advertising may be turning style into substance but it clearly fails when, after all its efforts, there is no substance apparent.

While the speaker may possess or project an image, it means nothing until it is perceived: "Each image exists as the person's subjective understanding of things... an image is a human construct imposed upon an array of perceived attributes projected by an object, event or person" (Nimmo 1999: 119). That act of perception contains cognitive, affective and connotative elements and while it is relatively easy to supply the informational and emotional facets to an image, the third facet is equally crucial. The realm of the connotative indicates how citizens see themselves in relation to the speaker, their position on the issues and ideas vis a vis the speaker's position. These considerations point to the limitations of the media campaign: the speaker cannot just be images on a TV screen. There needs to be substance to the speaker, and preferably substance consistent with the media image. The challenge for the campaign is to draw from the speaker a character that has both substance and appeal. There is more to the communication of image than simple presentation. The image also ideally carries consistent logical and emotional messages that appeal to both the reason and desires of the target audience.

Emotion/Desire is another important part of the message because it is crucial in eliciting an appropriate psychological response at the moment of decision. Technological change has provided powerful means to touch human emotions: personally-addressed direct mail, radio, computer-assisted telephone marketing and, most significantly, television. Where once TV producers used loud, raucous repetition to attempt to lodge the message in the subconscious of the audience, they now look for an instinctual feeling of resonance in selecting music, lyrics, words and images that prompt appropriate responses as they gently "stir" the subconscious. The symbolic dimensions of politics rule. That is why many advertisements mirror dreams. While individuals cannot express the impact of these advertisements verbally, it can be observed in their behaviour (Emery 1987: 37).

Television producers, Merrelyn Emery argues, have cast off the mechanistic view of perception as rational inference from sense-data, to embrace the naive realism of direct perception which holds that humans just extract the meaningful knowledge which they decide they require direct from their environment. In preparing their emotional enthymemes, campaigns use research to define the audience's desires and so crystallise moments of meaning that address their concerns. The campaign is attempting to "strike a responsive chord with the reality... the viewer experienced" (Diamond & Bates 1984: 119). The affective nature of television dictates much about the presentation of the speaker's persona via that medium. The emotional potency of speakers talking quietly and candidly about their own private life has been exploited to reinforce a political message, or at least to distract from some shortcoming. While Aristotle's categories of emotions remain a useful guide to the production of an affective response by the contemporary campaign, a mass society requires a much more subtle approach to the layering of responses to the desires of various segments of the audience as will be discussed below.

Logic/Message is the core of any campaign. As Ron Faucheux (1993: 261) puts it: "The Message is the central strategic rationale as to why a speaker or issue position is the right one at the right time and is preferable to other alternatives." The message may be summarised as a slogan which is simple, concise and direct, yet with enough narrative texture to allow the citizen-audience to produce their own complex readings. Despite the importance of character and emotion in crafting a persuasive message, a campaign needs to be based on compelling, logical arguments. The statements of a campaign require their own logical consistency so that opponents cannot portray inconsistency as a sign of weakness and confusion. Politics is more than a dream; it is about effectively tending society, dealing with people and their problems, creating a material future from a material world and drawing real conclusions from real premises. The rationality of rhetoric is always truncated and expedient but it must always be there: anchoring the campaign, focusing "the message", establishing the speaker's credentials, working in tandem with image and emotion to engage and persuade the voter.

Messages are devised with regard to the research and the same message may have a variety of forms designed to appeal to different target audiences. Those messages are placed in a variety of media consumed by the target audiences. Thus the campaign, day by day, seeks to build this array of individual communications into a meta-narrative that persuades the citizen-audience to act or think in a particular way. While debate within the campaign is an important element in ensuring that the campaign's message continues to be rational and relevant to the citizen-audience, all media messages from the campaign are ideally consistent and mutually supporting. Ideally the message of the campaign is also consistent with, and reinforces, the image of the speaker it seeks to promote. As the campaign progresses, the message needs to be refined and reinterpreted in response to developments from other campaigns and political life generally. This is not to say that the campaign can afford to shift ground erratically. It should seek a level of consistency as it develops new forms of its arguments which are the logical outcome of the speaker's image and the campaign's previously communicated messages. So in the 2000 US presidential election, though George W. Bush started the campaign with the message Compassionate Conservative, the reformist challenge of John McCain prompted him to shift to Reformer with Results which he carried off by pointing to his conservative reforms that achieved compassionate results.

Message Management Strategy

Strategy provides the broad principles by which the campaign will construct the meta-narrative that sends a multiplicity of variations on the key campaign message to a variety of targeted audiences in various configurations by assorted media over the length of the campaign. The media campaign strategy is the crucial connection between the objectives of the campaign and the day-to-day tactics the campaign uses. Strategic development of the message focuses on these key points:

- Define your objective – what exactly are you trying to do?
- Key selling proposition – what is the key idea that will be most persuasive and convincing to your audience? This idea should be included in every message throughout your campaign.
- Key statement – the message must be kept clear and simple. Aimed directly at your objectives, it communicates your position to the desired audience without any confusion or misunderstanding.
- Research – understand the situation, appreciate the alternative possibilities and be aware of the target audience's attitudes.
- Planning – prepare for all eventualities.
- Action – pursue the planned strategy rigorously while always being ready to adapt to meet new situations with a spin that reinforces your key statement.
- Communication – ensure your messages are getting through to the target audience.
- Evaluation – use constant tracking research to adapt your strategy and messages to better achieve the desired effect.

The most effective message is something that is simple and true. Once you've designed your message and tested it to ensure that it is appealing to the target audience, use it consistently. This is crucial to getting the message across. Work it into all media contact. Use it in all your communications, direct mail, telemarketing, speeches and personal contact.

The crucial thing in campaign work, the thing that makes it a campaign, is a commitment to consistency and strategic effectiveness: all campaign activity should be cohesive with the central message and directed towards achieving the desired result.

Position

Product researchers conceptualise new products by analysing consumers' perceptions of products already in the market. In doing this they look at the responses of different segments of the market marked by age, sex, occupational status and educational status. Product researchers then evaluate those new products by investigating how different market segments rank their preferences for new and existing products. Good product research can then suggest the most effective market position of the new products. Look at breakfast cereal in the supermarket. There is a product line for every age bracket. Some are pitched to women, some are pitched to men, most are pitched to children. Some tout their health advantages, some promise prizes. Each of these product lines is designed and promoted to attract a particular market niche. If you were trying to sell a new kind of breakfast cereal, then you would design your packaging and advertising to position your product where it would attract the biggest market share.

While there are differences between marketing a product and persuading people of a political idea, political campaigns have borrowed the notion of position from concept evaluation techniques utilised in product marketing. One major difference is that while a new product can be designed from the beginning as something that appeals to the target audience, the speaker always brings the baggage of their history and their own personal convictions. While the deliberation required by democratic politics is substantially different from the commercial discourses which surround the marketing of a product, politics and marketing both presently occur to a significant degree through the mass media, so certain techniques are mutually applicable. As Mauser (1985: 107) suggests: "Concept evaluation procedures permit candidates to evaluate alternative postures and positions that they are considering so that they may determine the campaign themes and slogans that would best position them in the political contest."

Political campaigns seek to target and communicate with particular segments of the audience whose support they require to achieve a goal. To win the US presidential electoral college, a candidate needs the support of just those states which will provide a majority. Therefore presidential campaigns don't waste their time on states that they will win easily or which they are sure to lose, rather they battle it out in the states that will decide the election and appeal just to those segments of the electorate who are undecided or prone to swinging. Similarly in parliamentary elections where leadership rests on gaining a majority of seats, campaigns will target the undecided and swinging voters in just those seats it needs to win.

This approach sits outside the traditional left/right, liberal/conservative analysis of voter preference. Perhaps this model of political behaviour was always over-simplified, a result of the adversarial culture of politics ignoring the complex realities of an electorate of individuals, each with their own history and their own particular world view. Persuading the swinging and undecided voter is about more than edging the campaign across some imaginary left-right spectrum, it is about identifying the themes that concern the audience and reinterpreting the campaign, its image and its message, in that light. Blumenthal (1980: 5) explains: "...each candidate is a dream problem, a problem that must be solved consciously (by) stimulat(ing) the public's wish fulfilment for the candidate through the manipulation of symbols and images, enticing voters to believe that the candidate can satisfy their needs." Positioning a speaker involves everything from deciding on the appropriate glasses frames or elocution lessons to the fine detail of particular policies. There is no exact formula in this area – it depends on the electorate.

Research into the audience helps the campaign understand not only who it is addressing but also what is important to that audience and to various segments of that audience. Then the campaign can position itself to appeal to the logical and emotional world-views of that part of the audience required to prevail. The campaign seeks to present messages that find sympathy and respect from the target audience. This demographic research is still the foundation of political campaigning and the challenge remains to ensure that the campaign sends messages that are true and consistent with each other and with the campaign's image and overarching message.

Ronald Reagan made an art form of positioning. He veered between the friendly TV host and the guy next door, never the President responsible for the excesses of government. His achievements may have been limited but he was always electorally successful because he reinterpreted the Horatio Alger truism – that a person can be anything you want to be – for the video age: "you can *position* yourself anywhere you want to be" (Matthews 1989: 214). While no speaker can position themselves as something they are not, they can certainly position themselves as something they could become, and with a little skill, the campaign can position the speaker to appeal to their natural supporters as well as targeting the swing voters. Thus, for example, Green candidates opposed to industrial development may position themselves to win the vote not only of their "dark" green core constituency but also of a more conservative group of citizens who simply do not want their environment to change. Similarly anti-abortion activists referred to themselves as pro-life and thus stake out the high moral ground. If they were pro-life, then that made the other side pro-abortion and anti-life. In response, the women's movement began to promote itself as pro-choice while positioning their opponents as anti-choice, a grievous complaint in consumer-oriented capitalist competition.

The crucial thing in campaign work, the thing that makes it a campaign, is a commitment to *consistency* and *strategic effectiveness:* all campaign activity should be cohesive with the central message and directed towards achieving the desired result.

Spin

In the flow of the campaign, external events and opposition efforts challenge the campaign to spin debate back to its core message. The application of spin is key work for the campaign. The idea of spin comes from ball games such as tennis, baseball and cricket where players seek to put a spin on the ball so that it bounces or even moves through the air in ways that are disadvantageous to the player's opponent. The "spin doctor" has become a key player in the media's campaign mythology, as if every politician has a panel of wise witch doctors in the backroom, turning their dross into useful sound bites. Spin is really about framing issues to fine-tune position through the management of expectations and selling to the media the version of events most advantageous to the campaign. It is the campaign's interpretation of events and so it should be part of everything the campaign does.

The great Australian master of spin is Prime Minister, John Howard. The start of the 2004 federal election coincided with new revelations about the PM's handling of the Children Overboard affair where he had moulded the truth to win the previous election. The opposition Labor Party said the election was going to be about trust and Howard straight away responded that only he could be trusted to deliver continuing economic well-being. In campaign parlance, Howard "Hung a Lantern on his Problem". His problem was that he was losing public trust because of Children Overboard, his promise that there would "never, ever" be a Goods and Services Tax and then introducing it and 25 other alleged lies that the Labor Party was publicising. There was no future in denying that he was a serial liar, so he did the next best thing, which was to redefine trust in terms much more suitable to his needs and providing the opportunity to hammer home his economic credentials by asking the question "who are you going to trust to keep interest rates low?"

Labor, in a complete miscalculation, missed the opportunity to turn the debate onto their positive economic agenda and instead were seen to be signing a big piece of cardboard promising to keep interest rates low, something they could not actually deliver because the control of interest rates is in the remit of the independent board of the Reserve Bank. Labor tried to fight the election without a position on the one big issue that Howard established by his deft spin and they were soundly defeated.

While often portrayed as the problem with contemporary democracy, spin is not a negative practice. It should not involve obfuscation because that comes across as bluster; nor should it involve lying because that is too easily found out and liable to turn into a bigger problem. It should involve interpreting and defining issues in the campaign's own terms to assist the speaker to communicate the campaign message to the target audience. It is an important part of all political work and indeed the substance of the contest for electoral support.

Campaigns commence framing their issues from the beginning. Early message development prepares for all eventualities along the way and practises addressing them with a constant tone and campaign message. Succinct, relevant statements focus attention on the campaign message while generalisations or unsupportable statements do not. There is always the danger that the opponent, or the media, seeks to define the campaign's message but the campaign does not have to respond to every question using the parameters inherent in the intervention. Rather, the campaign seeks to restate the question to give an answer that goes back to its core message and its version for the day.

The mass media is liable to be constantly opening up new avenues of debate between competing campaigns and providing the citizen-audience with the space to offer feedback to the campaigns. To be involved in opportunities for deliberation afforded by the electoral process, each campaign should ideally be reviewing their meta-narrative constantly in order to refine it so that it can engage more effectively in the rhetorical exchange between itself and the electorate.

Spin – Some Modern Enthymemes

Spin is the substance of the day-to-day work of any political campaign trying to promote its message and undermine the opponent's. Some methods have proven their effectiveness at this work. These methods are equivalent to the topics of Aristotle's enthymeme – set pieces to deal with standard campaign occurrences.

Don't Get Mad, Don't Get Even, Get Ahead

Campaigns can get dirty, accusations and allegations fly in all directions and skeletons come out of cupboards. It is easy in the closed, internal space of the campaign for intrigue to assume major dimensions. It is important that the campaign keeps these things in perspective and remembers its main objective: to win. Rather than responding to the substance of the charges against it, the campaign must use the opportunity to tailor its response to promote its positive messages and highlight opponents' negatives.

Hang a Lantern on Your Problem
The most effective strategy to deal with a disaster is based on the simple fact that: "...it is always better to be the bearer of your own bad news" (Matthews 1989: 156) because that gives the impression that the situation cannot be too bad because there is no hush-up. The pre-emptive strike also provides the opportunity to interpret the problem in the campaign's own light. So when Ronald Reagan was faced with a concern about his age in the polling, he defused the situation by volunteering: "I will not make my age an issue in this campaign. I am not going to exploit, for political purposes, my opponent's youth and inexperience" (in Matthews 1989: 158).

Keep Your Enemies in Front of You
While in elections the campaign's opponents nominate themselves, all campaigns have the opportunity to define their enemies. The fewer they are, the more effective the campaign's work will be. Where the incumbent has strong support from the wealthy development "community", the opposing campaign might hold an event specifically for developers to announce their development policy. The developers became a little more comfortable with the campaign, know that they can speak productively with the candidate and no longer feel obliged to put any extra into the incumbent's war-chest. As Lyndon B. Johnson observed: "Better to have 'em inside the tent pissin' out than outside pissin' in" (Matthews 1989: 158).

Leave No Shot Unanswered
It is never wise to leave a negative charge against the campaign without response. Often there is the hope that if a problem is ignored it will go away and the fear that a response will keep the issue alive. It is better to put a simple denial on the record, perhaps at a busy news time when it will not gain much prominence, than to let it fester in the minds of the journalists. If the situation cannot be

turned into a positive then the least that can be done is to counter-attack with a more heinous charge: catch the opponent in a lie, ridicule them, use their argument against them (Matthews 1989: 122–128).

While day-to-day spin involves tinkering with policy pronouncements, the situation will also arise when it is required to deflect disaster and turn it into an opportunity. This is damage control, "the need to manage a crisis, to minimise a problem that suddenly raises its ugly head and can't be ignored" (Stewart 1994: 24–29). To do this, the campaign needs to be flexible, ready to admit its shortcomings where necessary and to promote those shortcomings, or at least the admissions, into a positive thing about the speaker and the campaign. The aim of spin is to deflect problems presented by the media by turning those problems into opportunities to communicate the core campaign message.

Positive vs Negative Campaigning

Another facet of the meta-narrative arises because all political campaigns involve a mix of positive and negative messages: what is good about the speaker or proposition and what is bad about the alternatives. The challenge is to get the mix right. If campaign A is all positive, then it is leaving the opposition in campaign B to create its own story about itself that will be much more advantageous than what campaign A might offer. If campaign A is all negative, then it might be seen as cynical, nasty and vicious and, while providing plenty of reasons not to support campaign B, it fails to provide a reason for voting for campaign A. It is all in the mix.

Negative campaigning has been blamed for the malaise of democratic politics. Ansolabehere and Iyengar (1995) point to laboratory experimentation and analysis of real campaigns to claim that negative campaigning favours conservatives over independents, favours men over women and turns away independent and swinging voters so that only the most partisan voters stay interested in the election. Unfortunately, as Ansolabehere and Iyengar admit, negative campaigning also works better than positive campaigning and that is the reason it remains an important part of any campaign's armoury. In the 2004 US presidential election, Democrat John Kerry opened with a strong, positive claim to military leadership based on his record in the Vietnam War. This ostensible positive also contained a big negative for Bush whose war record involved avoiding his Reserve responsibilities. The Bush camp effectively stymied Kerry's position with ads of doubtful veracity undermining Kerry's war record by suggesting it was manufactured which in turn highlighted positive perceptions about Bush's frank speech. Skilfully, the Bush campaign turned his opponent's biggest positive into their own positive.

Mayer (1996) argues that negative campaigning is a legitimate and necessary part of a democratic discussion because it provides citizens with essential information about the issues and choices at stake. Despite their disdain for the viciousness in some negative campaigning, people know that there are two sides to every story and they just want to know what they are. Thus we can see that every time Bill Clinton came clean about his sexual indiscretions, he was forgiven. His mistake in the Lewinsky affair was that he should have admitted everything sooner. People already knew that he was a man who had trouble saving his affections for his wife. Clinton's mistake was in attempting to deny it.

The interplay between the positive and negative sides of all campaigns is the ground on which the whole campaign is played out. Use of positive and negative techniques is most effective when combined coherently to restate the campaign's key message and undermine the opponent's message. The campaign should aim to recreate the opponent in negative terms that highlight its own speaker's positives and produce positive policies, which highlight the opponent's negative attributes. That is, in developing the campaign message, the campaign considers not only its own strengths and weaknesses but also the strengths and weaknesses of the opponents and seeks to maximise the benefits of the opponents' weaknesses by promoting their reverse as just those strengths exhibited by their speaker. Negative attacks on opponents and their policies work best when they are honest, fair and implicitly reinforce the campaign's own positives. The campaign is always seeking opportunities to spin the comparison back to the opponent's negatives and the campaign's own positive agenda. By way of contrast, the campaign seeks to minimise its own weaknesses by showing that its opponent could not improve the situation or that the campaign's weaknesses are the reason for its positives, that the speaker's arrogance is the reason they can push things through and get them done.

Message Delivery

While following chapters look at the particular channels for delivering campaign messages (free media, advertising, direct contact), it is important to consider here that message delivery is a holistic process that seeks to recreate traditional forms of message delivery through contemporary channels. It is useful to consider four forms of traditional message delivery that still connect with audiences today: the slogan, the speech, the mantra and the myth.

The slogan seeks to summarise the message in words which, in the bardic style, should be simple and direct, a clear and precise narrative moment with the power to turn events and yet diffuse enough and with enough narrative texture to allow members of the audience to produce their own complex readings. As William Safire says: "Good slogans have rhyme, rhythm and alliteration to make them memorable. Great slogans may have none of these, but touch a chord of memory, release pent-up hatreds, or stir men's better natures" (in Faucheux 1993: 26).

A strong slogan encapsulates the campaign message and is easy to identify with the campaign. For example, slogans such as Bill Clinton's "There's a place called Hope" or Tony Blair's "New Labour' or in Australia, Gough Whitlam's "It's time..." all manage to state the core message of their campaign in ways that could only be identified with them. Some would argue that identification of the slogan with the campaign can only be guaranteed if the slogan names the speaker or proposition such as "I Like Ike" or "Kennedy Cares".

Any slogan should first be tested by qualitative research to ensure that the intended message is getting across to the audience. In fact testing a raft of slogans and seeing if the test group has anything further to offer can ensure that the campaign arrives at the most effective slogan. Finally, it is important to stick with the slogan. It should be incorporated in all material sent out by the campaign: on letterhead, at the top of press releases, in direct mail and all advertising. Adopting a new slogan as a quick fix or as part of a temporary campaign is to be avoided, though it is sometimes necessary to develop the slogan to respond to some fundamental shift in the campaign.

Great slogans from around the world

Harrison 1840: *Tippecanoe and Tyler Too*
McKinley 1896: *Patriotism, Protection, and Prosperity*
Roosevelt 1932: *The New Deal*
Churchill 1940: *We shall never surrender*
Eisenhower 1952: *I Like Ike*
Kennedy 1960: *Kennedy Cares*
Johnson 1964: *All the Way with LBJ*
Goldwater 1964: *In Your Heart You Know He's Right*

Anti-Goldwater 1964: *In Your Guts you Know He's Nuts*
Nixon 1972: *Re-Elect the President/Now More Than Ever*
Whitlam 1972: *It's time...*
Fraser 1975: *Turn On the Lights*
Whitlam 1975: *Shame, Fraser, Shame*
Reagan 1980: *Renew America's Strength*
Reagan 1984: *Morning in America*
Clinton 1992: *There's a place called Hope*
Howard 1996: *Warm and comfortable government*
Blair 1997: *New Labour*
Gore 2000: *The New Democrat*
Bush 2000: *Compassionate Conservative/ Reformer with Results*
McCain 2000: *Straight-Talk Express*
Chirac 2002: *Vote for the crook not the fascist*

The speech is the oldest form of political communication but still one of the most powerful ways to get a message across. The interaction between speaker and audience, the two-way flow of information as they face each other in the flesh is the aim of the whole campaign so it is useful and informative to test out that interaction in the form of a real speech. While many campaign speeches are now set pieces, testing the campaign's lines on a real life, non-partisan audience is the best way to find out if they are working.

Like all narratives, the speech functions best with a beginning that establishes a theme, a middle that carries it to a climax and an end where the whole is wrapped up and summarised. A good introduction captures attention and introduces the speaker and their theme. Unlike other narratives, the speech must not only state the case but also demonstrate it, so the middle is also divided into a further three categories: narration – the statement of the facts; proof – to establish the speaker's case; and altercation – the use of (often ironic) ripostes to rebut the adversary's case. The epilogue is a brief, comprehensive restatement of the argument from character, emotion and logic that leaves each member of the audience 1) with a clear idea of the difference the candidate could make and 2) inclined towards one's case.

In preparing for the speech it is important to consider the audience. Who are they? Why are they here? What are their interests? What do they already know? The more you know about the audience, the more prepared you will be and the more effective the speech will be. Next, consider the campaign's message and how it can be best put to this particular audience, how the speech can most productively interact with the interests of this particular audience and how it flows from the general to the specific in a way that can carry the audience along. The best speeches sound spontaneous and conversational because the speaker memorises the outline and practises key lines but gives their own inflection and rhythm to the body of the speech, engaging the audience and building to a strong finish.

When it is time to give the speech, the speaker arrives early to get a sense of the space and test the technology. Before they speak, the speaker ensures that they breathe deeply and have the time and space to focus. As the speaker addresses the audience they should turn to people in all sections of the room and stay aware of the time limit.

The mantra is traditionally a word, phrase or verse repeated over and over as a sacred formula. The practice is taught by the Hindu and Buddhist religions to assist meditation on the way to enlightenment. In the contemporary political campaign, repetition is similarly the key so lines which have tested well in the research are developed into tight, cohesive argument that encapsulates the key message and that argument is repeated by the speaker in all available forums as a mantra. The message is not even starting to get through until the campaign is bored with repeating it. Ensuring that the mantra continues and that it is repeated by all possible means requires a high degree of discipline from the campaign.

The myth of the campaign, its development and presentation, require a deft and astute hand. This is not to suggest that the campaign can spread fairytales but rather that it must face the reality that its work is manipulating not just words but also systems of knowledge and belief. The world is a complex place and to manage the information coming at them, people resort to interpreting it through the filters of their expectations, the archetypes they have experienced and the narratives they know, in short the mythology by which they live. Joseph Campbell (1991) has analysed myths from around the world to isolate the recurring themes that appear to be deeply entrenched in the human psyche. The campaign is more than smart lines, it is about connecting with the audience's belief systems and myths and placing the campaign within those systems to the best possible effect.

5
RESEARCH –
QUANTITATIVE AND QUALITATIVE

The Role of Research

Aristotle emphasised the importance of understanding the character of the audience in framing the speaker's rhetorical inventions (Aristotle 1991: 1388b–1391b). The speaker in the Athenian Pnyx knew the opinions and attitudes of many members of the audience from personal contact and listening to them speak. A practised speaker could, as they still can now, just look around to sense the mood of the crowd and judge its characteristics in terms of age, class, wealth and power. This allowed the speaker to adapt the speech to the crowd, to "invent" appropriate arguments for the particular occasion. By contrast the political campaign in contemporary mass society needs to employ more complex research strategies to understand the impact it is having on the minds of the audience so that it can develop its messages and better persuade them to a particular action.

Demographic, historical and background research are important parts of campaign work and are discussed in detail below but quantitative and qualitative opinion research are at the very heart of the campaign because they offer the only opportunity for the campaign to understand what is going on in the minds of the mass audience. Of course the campaign will get feedback from organisations and individuals but opinion research, using techniques that ensure a high degree of statistical probability, gives the campaign a systematic account of what the whole audience is thinking. Opinion polls are produced from and read against a model of citizen behaviour that acknowledges not only the importance of intention, issues and policies but also the relevance of speaker imagery, social imagery, current events, emotional feelings, personal events and the epistemic issues inherent in the citizen's own system of knowledge and belief (Newman & Sheth 1985). Under this model of opinion polling, a broad range of issues and events are investigated which might contribute to the citizens' decisions and which indicate where they may be open to persuasion. Polls serve the useful purpose of establishing the mood of the electorate, finding which issues are important and which positions have appeal to the citizens. From this work the campaign can develop and refine the "lines" which constitute its message. One pollster summarised his contribution to campaigns: "The main part of our work was the central campaign structure, the rhetoric from the leaders and ministers, the concentration of the issues, identification of regional emphases and all that PR stuff" (Lawson 1993: 1).

But opinion polls can never achieve the same level of connection and accuracy as was achieved in the face-to-face contact of the Athenian Pnyx. As John Dryzek points out: opinion surveys, by constantly seeking to categorise people and their opinions, reduce those studied to objects with bundles of attributes in order to produce an instrumental result (1990). Pierre Bourdieu (1978: 124) suggests "public opinion" is a specious category because not everyone has an opinion, not all opinions are of equal value and there is no consensus about whether the right questions are being asked.

Further, polls are unreliable for predicting who will win an election because while they purport to measure the level of party support if an election was held at that particular moment, in fact the election is not being held *then* but at some later date. Those polls actually cannot predict the outcome of the election when it is held because a large number of citizens do not decide how they are going to vote until the last few days of the campaign (Totaro 1995). Polls cannot tell the future. The polling organisations' practice of merely distributing undecideds in the same proportions as the decideds tells us less than nothing about citizen intention. It is a dangerous practice that disguises the real situation. Further, as citizens understand the role of the poll in the campaign, there is the possibility that they begin to frame their answers to send a message to politicians and the media. Published opinion polls that crop up constantly during an election are a case in point: "they are measuring something, and it is probably something quite interesting, but whatever it is, it's *not* how people intend to vote in the... election" (Secombe 1992: 41).

The validity of polling is also under question in the debate around the efficacy of polls commissioned by and published in the media. In the first instance there are phone-in polls. These "polls" have become a staple of the media diet because they are a good way to give the appearance of interactivity that actually makes money for the media outlet because callers bear the cost of having their say. But participants in phone-ins are self-selecting – they are consumers of that particular medium, they are motivated by the issue and they may even be making multiple calls at the behest of a campaign – so the outcome of these polls have no claim to represent the actual state of public opinion. Then there are vox pops where half a dozen passers-by are asked their opinion on a current topic. This is a cheap way to pad out a story by giving it another angle and showing the human side of the debate but the participants in a vox pops are a minuscule sample and the information that results has no claim whatsoever to scientific validity.

Even polls commissioned by media outlets from reputable research companies can be subject to suspect interpretations. Journalists are interested in beefing up their stories with conflict and surprise. Management spend a lot of money on these polls and they are usually intimately involved in making sure that they get value. The polls are analysed in a pressure-cooker atmosphere so it is not surprising that they are subject to all manner of editorial twists. One journalist notes in a reflective commentary piece: "Even pollsters would never dare postulate on their findings the way journalists do" (Secombe 1995: 25). In short, news polls should be treated cautiously. They are read by the audience as persuasive so the campaign must respond to them: claiming credit for the good news and discounting the bad news but the campaign should not read them as true or use them as the basis for planning.

If democratic politics was reduced to nothing more than the production of decisions in response to opinion polling and that polling was measuring nothing real, then democracy would be debased because opportunities to debate through the detail of any issue would be limited. However, access to a representative sample of the citizenry offers some opportunities for campaigns to engage in a set of statistically probable rhetorical exchanges with the citizenry. The scientific nature of polling is discussed in the section on quantitative research below but on the practical question of how to make democracy work in a mass society, Bernard Berelson (1952–3: 313) argued that: "opinion research can help a democracy to know itself, evaluate its achievements and bring its practices more nearly in accord with its own fundamental ideas." Orwell also thought: "some mechanism for testing public opinion is a necessity of modern government and more so in a democratic country" (1970a: 167–8). Polling is certainly a key tool in keeping campaigns relevant to the electorate. As Mills (1986: 64) observes: "One State Government minister commented polls were valuable to him because they helped break down his isolation from the electorate."

The political campaign does not use polling to close the debate but rather to understand how the mass of citizens are responding to the candidate and the campaign's contribution to debate. While voter polls may be little more than indicators of electoral mood, campaign teams read them closely to see what is working and what is not and particularly to ascertain the level of the undecided vote because that indicates the field of opportunity to persuade swinging voters to support the campaign (Fenwick et al 1985: 38–41). Thus market research is a tool to assist Aristotelian "invention" and offers campaigns the opportunity to extend their "mind-to-mind" rhetorical exchange with the citizenry of a mass democracy.

So the campaign then needs to retain the services of opinion pollsters who have quantitative and qualitative models and access to the computer programs and banks of phone lines required to assess the electorate's response to the ideas, issues, personalities and events operating in a campaign. To be effective, the pollster should operate within the principles of targeting and tracking (Mills 1986: 8–13).

Targeting in campaigns involves developing campaign messages directed in particular towards the citizens who are most important in achieving the campaign's goals, the swinging and undecided voters in the marginal electorates required to win the election. Targeting also has an application in other political campaigns where the aim is to convince particular demographic groups to a point of view and subsequent action because all political work seeks to increase the campaign's supporters by sending messages to those who are not already committed to the campaign's point of view.

While television and radio advertising and direct mail provide the opportunity to target key citizens directly, those citizens rely significantly on news coverage to inform their decisions. The campaign must use the news to send messages that research has suggested will be effective in persuading the swinging and undecided in the necessary electorates to the campaign's cause. Coolly targeting the message at a handful of electors is difficult in the bustle of a campaign where the expectation from the media and even many campaign supporters is that the whole electorate is the target. Irrelevant issues will take on a life of their own, opponents and interest groups will push your campaign on to their terrain and agenda and colleagues will come up with great ideas but persistence in pursuing targeted citizens is what wins campaigns. Ideally the campaign will create a synergy between its targeting and tracking: by appealing to precisely those demographics that are required to win, then tracking how their opinions develop so the campaign can create the material that will affect targeted citizens in ways that will show up in further tracking research and so on.

Tracking involves continually retesting the undecided and swinging citizens in key marginal electorates, so the campaign can get an accurate understanding of the effect of its work and just where the debate stands. Tracking the impact of the campaign on the minds of the citizens suggests further strategy for the campaign. Just as a skilful speaker in the Athenian polis could sense the mood of the crowd and tailor his presentation so that he could "work the crowd" to persuade them to a particular point of view, the contemporary campaign similarly "works the audience" around to a point of view that results in a particular decision at the ballot box. In the 1993 Australian election, it was evident from the government's tracking research that their attempts to put a positive spin on economic news were pointless because swinging and undecided voters knew how bad the economy was. But those same people said they harboured deep reservations about the opposition's plan to introduce the Goods and Services Tax. They did not think a new tax would improve the economy. The government gave up mentioning the economy to concentrate solely on attacking the GST and astounded political scientists by winning what should have been an unwinnable election in such dire economic straits.

All research has its limitations when it is used just to guess the campaign's success rather than as a tool to create the next phase of campaign activity. As some practitioners say: "Good researchers are observers, not oracles" (Adams 1993: 36).

Campaigns that are poll driven are doomed to failure but when the campaign uses the polls to fine-tune the delivery of the message they were going to give anyway, then they are on the road to success. Good citizen research is reading the mind of the audience as it is being persuaded. It not only records the current state of citizen opinion but is also a simulation of the campaign, testing the effectiveness of various strategic feints. The campaign must use the polls to reposition itself, not by changing its policies, but by choosing which ones to emphasise and then reinventing, reinterpreting and repackaging them in the ways that maximise their appeal.

Demographic Research

In the pre-campaign phase, the campaign researches the demographic statistics and past voting habits of the electorate. Government statistics offices and electoral oversight bodies have a wealth of information that assists in understanding the target audience and their past activities. The campaign also reviews the recent press looking for local issues that have already been identified by concerned residents and organisations. All this material is consolidated in a document that provides a comprehensive overview of the terrain so the campaign can understand with whom it is dealing, what is important to them and the dimensions of the campaign and its logistical requirements.

By closely studying previous results, whether they are voting outcomes in elections and referenda or analyses of the impact of an information campaign, the campaign can assess which geographic areas are supportive and need only maintenance and reinforcement, which areas are opposed and need only basic information and which areas may be fertile ground for the campaign's arguments. By matching this geographic information with census data, the campaign can start to build a demographic profile of the age, sex, education, occupation, earnings and other social characteristics of the target audience. Of course individual census data is confidential but government statistics offices prepare summaries of that data in geographic areas from the whole country down to zip code or post code areas and even small districts which contain just a few hundred people. By putting together the demographic data for targeted precincts, the campaign can begin to understand who they have to convince.

The campaign has to move from seeing their audience as some massively homogeneous whole and start thinking of them as numerous small pockets of distinctiveness, each needing its own unique approach. Market segmentation has been criticised for breaking up the unity of nation and class but perhaps that unity was only ever an ideological product. Accepting difference and working with its complex agglomerations of those differences is the only practical way to approach personal characteristics, and communicate with individuals, in a mass society.

There is a always the danger that unrestrained segmentation may lead to an unsustainable number of variables, introducing so much complexity that analysis is impossible. Therefore the process of demographic segmentation should be restricted to a simple set of evaluative criteria. Criteria for assessing potential segments are discussed below:

Age – groups will have distinctive histories, ideas and expectations related to their physical age. Young people are more likely to be involved in, and therefore interested in tertiary education while people in their 30s and 40s are more likely to have young families and so are interested in maternity benefits and school education while older people are liable to more sickness and so are interested in health issues.

Sex – each gender has significant differences; men tend to be more interested in defence and workplace issues while women tend to be more interested in education and health issues. Of course, some women are interested in defence and men in health but analysis is only possible because the researcher is looking for gross tendencies. Also there are differences in the types of magazines, newspapers and television programs consumed by different gender groups, a factor often modified by age and social class differences so young women may have quite different values to their mothers.

Socio-Economic Demographic Segments

A High managerial, administrative or professional
Employ others in large organisations or take a high degree of responsibility: Chief executive officers, general managers, company directors, lawyers, doctors, builders, developers, farmers, legislators and government appointed officials.

B Intermediate managerial, administrative and professional
Service relationship with employer or client, planning and supervision responsibilities: Scientists, engineers, social workers, tertiary teachers, middle managers, accountants, artists, physiotherapists and other health professionals.

C1 Supervisory, clerical, junior administrative or professional
Manage small groups or with moderate responsibility for personal actions: Small business operators, school teachers, technicians, nurses, data processing operators, executive secretaries, clerks, sales representatives, bank tellers.

C2 Skilled manual workers
Tradespersons with extended training: Carpenters, plumbers, electricians, metal workers, painters, plasterers, tilers, printers, mechanics, chefs, hairdressers and horticulturalists.

D Semi-skilled manual workers
Workers requiring licensing: Truck drivers, taxi drivers, train drivers, ambulance drivers, plant operators, machine operators, police and firefighters.

E Unskilled manual workers
Workers without qualifications: Builders, labourers, mine labourers, trade assistants, factory hands, process workers, cleaners, farmhands, shop assistants.

F Pensioners, widows
Dependent on a relatively high level of state support.

G Long-term Unemployed
Dependent on a relatively low level of state support.

Note: The short-term unemployed are classified by their last job; full-time students and home-makers are classified by the family's main breadwinner. This table is a compilation of British, German and Australian standards for occupational classification.

Class – social status is a difficult concept to determine and analyse. Earnings provide some indication of class but do not allow for the manual worker with a high demand trade or the impoverished aristocrat. Education is another useful indicator but it does not allow for the self-made person or under-paid academic. Occupation generally has a strong relationship to income, educational level and attitudes and research indicates that the employment category of the main wage earner in the household is a good indicator of the whole household's social status or class. The breakout bo⁻ sets out the standard classification of socio-economic demographic segments that are useful in analysing the interests of particular classes and contacting those classes through the newspapers, magazines and television that they typically consume.

Neighbourhood – the complexities and systematic irregularities of occupational classification have led to analysis of social class by neighbourhood. Researchers have identified neighbourhood types based on area (inner-city, suburban, rural), prevalent types of property (detached houses, apartments) and characteristics of residents (single, young couples, large family).

Ethnicity – may be extremely important on some issues or in some situation where, for example, the party or candidate has strong ties to particular communities and may have represented them well in the past. Ethnicity may override the operation of other determining factors or allow family influence on decision-making. Communication with ethnic groups may be facilitated by newspapers or magazines in their particular language.

Psychographics – previously mentioned methods of segmentation may be too simple to describe the numerous variations in behaviour and outlook within the population. Psychographics seek to cluster citizens into groups based on common interests and attitudes which tend to determine their political opinions and actions (Shama 1985: 10–14). This method can be useful because attitudes to welfare or abortion, for example, cut across age, sex and class boundaries but can become crucial in deciding the outcome of a campaign where that particular issue has become central.

Geo-Demographics – new computer software and available databases have prompted advances in mapping technology that allow the campaign to map out citizens in the electorate for more effective information analysis (Hoskin 1989). This new software graphically portrays where the citizens are and then colour-codes them according to defined characteristics. Thus the campaign can visualise strategies and ensure all areas are covered and no groups of swinging voters are missed. Further, "groups of untargeted or loosely targeted voters can be collected into new subsets of the voter lists…" (Sachs 1993: 59). The software can then be manipulated to produce lists for direct mail and phone contact efforts.

Segmentation parameters need to be reviewed periodically to ensure they remain realistic. Changing social roles have lessened the importance of the man as the head of the household and now women and children, many of whom are staying at home longer than in past generations, exercise a greater degree of power and autonomy. Every campaign is a challenge to understand the citizenry in its complexity at that particular time. The segmentation process is made up of the following steps:

- define parameters for segmentation and isolate relevant segments
- analyse the segments while considering the consequences of their composition
- develop strategy to target required segments
- prepare positioning strategy for each target segment, ensure overall consistency
- implement media strategy for each target segment.

New information technology means segmentation can be based on small amounts of information about large groups (address, age, occupation) or large amounts of information consolidated into profiles about individuals.

Segmentation allows citizens to be treated as individuals and also put together into meaningful groups that the campaign can address systematically and cost effectively. From the campaign's point of view, the game is to identify segments accurately and to communicate information about the candidate and policies in ways that invite a response from individuals.

Quantitative Polling

Within campaigns, the results of polls can become a form of currency, spent to bolster internal morale or impress journalists, flashed about when they predict victory, hidden away or re-written when they presage defeat. But, as was seen above, polls are about the current situation when they are taken and subject to respondent manipulation so they are unreliable as predictors of campaign outcomes. However, polls serve a much more useful purpose in gaining an understanding of the mood of the electorate, finding what issues are important, what positions have appeal and what language is effectively communicating to the citizens. Four kinds of polls may be considered by the campaign: exploratory polls to investigate the lay of the land before a decision has been made to commit to the campaign; benchmark polls to establish the state of public opinion as the campaign commences; trend polls to measure movement and change about half way through the campaign; and rolling polls taken to determine day-to-day trends where four hundred responses are analysed with one hundred added each night and one hundred dropped from five days previous.

To grasp the complexities and nuances of the electorate's mind, the campaign needs to retain the services of an independent opinion poll researcher who has statistical models, computer programs, banks of phone lines and a staff that can elicit unbiased responses. The pollster has to be capable of putting these elements together to assess the electorate's response to the ideas, issues, personalities and events operating in a campaign. While there are national and even regional differences in the language, emphasis and manner of the interviewer, polling techniques are similar all around the world (Worcester 1983).

To be useful the polls must be produced from and read against a model of citizen behaviour that acknowledges not only the importance of issues and policies but also social imagery, emotional feelings, candidate image, current events, personal events and epistemic issues (Newman & Sheth 1985). This model covers the broad range of issues and events that might contribute to the citizen's decision and shows the areas where they may be open to persuasion. In elections a good pollster probes the strengths and weaknesses of the campaign's arguments among undecided and swinging voters in marginal seats. Thus they reveal the field of opportunity to persuade those key voters to support the campaign. Polls are best used as tools for setting the future direction of the campaign.

As was discussed in chapter 3, opinion polling came of age in 1936 when George Gallup applied Kolmogorov's new work on probability in statistics to the political field (Mills 1986). Andrei Nikolaevich Kolmogorov was a Russian mathematician who was in his twenties when he was appointed a professor at Moscow University in 1931. His book on probability theory was published in 1933 and it built up probability theory from first principles as Euclid had done with geometry. In working from first principles, Kolmogorov provided a rigorous definition of conditional expectation and took a systematic approach to accounting for the role of probability in statistics.

Statistics is the science which deals with the collection, classification and use of numerical facts or data. Before Kolmogorov, statistics had been a fairly haphazard affair. While the census, which sought the same information from everyone in a state, was a valid instrument to describe the real world, various forms of surveys and straw polls attempted to describe the world without being, as Kolmogorov showed, conclusive as to the actual situation. In short, surveys and straw polls might be right but just as easily they might be wrong – they were shots in the dark.

Probability theory studies the relative frequency of given events. If you asked everybody the same question you would have 100% probability of their position (as long as they did not change their minds), but asking everybody is time-consuming and expensive. The question is, how many people do you have to ask to have a high degree of certainty as to their position? Kolmogorov's work established that one could estimate the probability that a random survey's results were correct, based on the number of respondents and the spread of their responses. The sample had to be randomly selected to have a high probability of being representative of the whole but surprisingly you only needed a thousand respondents, regardless of the size of the whole, to have a high degree of probability that one's survey results are accurate to within one or two percent.

Achieving a random sample of everybody in a particular area is not easy. Gallup began by sending agents into randomly chosen neighbourhoods with instructions to knock on randomly selected doors. With the growth of telephone ownership, Gallup's method of randomly door-knocking clusters of voters has been replaced with computer-assisted telephone interviewing of voters randomly selected from the electoral roll. The potential for bias is apparent – some people still do not have phones, the rolls are often out of date and include those who have passed away and moved on, some people keep their phone number unlisted and transients often only register in their new electorates at the last moment. One method of allowing for these last three categories is by contacting randomly generated phone numbers and then questioning the respondent as to whether they are eligible and likely to vote. The only method for catching those without phones is a door-to-door survey but the phone poll is the cheapest effective means of assessing the electorate's mood.

Another source of sampling error that can affect randomness concerns the question of who is most likely to answer the phone. This is addressed by asking to speak to the person who last had a birthday in the house. Another problem can arise when no one answers the phone and pollsters re-call the number up to five times in order to make contact. When no one answers the phone and where the randomly selected respondent refuses to answer the questions, these non-response errors can produce the over-representation of some groups and the under-representation of others. The pollster should match the demographic composition of interviewees to the demographic composition of the whole population and compensate for any differences by weighting or adjusting the results so they reflect the actual population. Then there is the problem of surveying the appropriate population – where voting is not compulsory, on average about half the eligible voters do not turn out on election day, and while the campaign is interested in finding triggers to turn out voters to support them, they must concentrate their energy on those most likely to vote.

Even when polls are random they can be wrong. Sources of error include: "prior prejudices and question bias; the construction, analysis and interpretation of the polling instrument and results... and a host of problems with the interviewers and respondents" (Sabato 1989). There are a number of ways for campaigns to combat polling error. Great care needs to be taken with the framing of questions to ensure that they elicit an unbiased result. The wording of questions and their order can lead the respondent to certain answers. While the campaign will have particular questions it needs answered, it is best for a non-partisan researcher to write the questions to avoid special pleading. Further problems can arise where interviewers let their personal biases intrude on the interview. The campaign should insist on quality control measures to ensure that the pollster's training and oversight of the interviewers produces a standardised administration of the questionnaire.

Briefing a second polling company is an expensive way to check on the validity of the first polling company's work and if their findings vary markedly then confusion may reign. The only real protection is for the campaign director to insist on an objective stance when briefing the pollsters and so steer the development and interpretation of the polls to answer the questions that the campaign needs answered while ensuring the neutral tone required for their validity. The campaign director should also insist on access to the raw data so they can analyse the numbers themselves with a critical eye.

While Gallup specialised in measuring the opinions of whole populations, campaigns today are more interested in gauging sentiments among target demographics and honing in on their decision-making process. This strategic form of political polling was developed by Lou Harris for John Kennedy's presidential campaign in 1960 (Mills 1986). The polls are a reading of the mind of the electorate as it is being persuaded. A good poll not only records the current state of citizen opinion but is also a simulation of the campaign, testing the effectiveness of various strategic feints to create "... microcosms rather than unreal abstractions of the campaign" (Harrison 1980: 8). The campaign must use the polls to reposition itself, not by changing its policies, but by choosing which ones to emphasise and then reinventing, reinterpreting and repackaging them in the ways that maximise their appeal. Polls "provide the strategy to communicate the reasons behind positions and decisions in such a way that more support for your views might be generated" (Meadow & von Szeliski 1993: 49).

Research Terms

Aided recall: respondent recollection prompted by researcher.
Analysis of variance: explaining statistical variation as product of several variables.
Awareness: respondent recall of information, either spontaneous or prompted.
Back check: supervisor contacts respondent to confirm interview properly carried out.
Bias: anything that causes survey findings to differ from the actual situation.
Callback: further attempt to contact a pre-selected respondent when first attempt failed.
Cartoon test: respondents asked to fill in speech balloons in comic-strip relevant to issues.
CATI: computer assisted telephone interviewing.

Cluster: group with similar attitudes or characteristics, neighbourhood.

Coding: process of allocating codes to open-ended questions after fieldwork.

Contact sheet: record of the calls, attempted and completed, made by an interviewer.

Correlation: interdependence between attributes or variables.

Coverage: reach of media outlet to target audience.

Data collection: gathering information by interview, group discussion, questionnaire etc.

Debrief: informal verbal report soon after data collection, before printed report.

Grossing up: scaling results of a survey to the whole population.

Indirect question: qualitative technique to uncover ideas respondent reluctant to reveal.

In-house research: conducted by organisation wanting information, liable to bias.

Mean: average, sum of responses divided by number of respondents.

Median: middle of set of numbers, point where half of numbers larger and half smaller.

Mode: most frequent response in a set of responses.

Moderator: individual who facilitates interaction in a group discussion.

Penetration: proportion of a population who have a certain characteristic, seen ad etc.

Telephone centre: central office housing telephones for research or other contact.

Verification: check during data coding and entry undertaken by a second person.

Mills almost gets it right when he says: "Politics still needs judgement and skill to determine when and if poll advice should be accepted..." (1986: 64). Effective politics is a matter of skill but the skill is not in instinctively knowing when to accept or reject poll advice, rather it is in hearing what the target audience has to say to the campaign through polling and responding to that (and nothing much else) with the words and images that the campaign produces.

Qualitative Research

While quantitative polling reveals the big picture, it is not so effective in monitoring the minutiae of motivation. Another, more qualitative form of research is useful to probe beyond the cognitive and statistical manifestations of opinion, to the values, emotions and feelings that will determine a citizen's opinion. Qualitative research is based on a small number of more intense interactions than quantitative research. Practitioners characterise qualitative research as: "an imprecise science which seeks to understand, through discussion, observation and analysis, the psychological motives that underpin consumer attitudes and behaviour in a given market" (Adams 1993: 36).

Focused interviews were first used in early sociological investigation of the media. Paul Lazarsfeld was investigating what made radio popular at Columbia University in 1941 when he asked Robert Merton to assist in tabulating audience responses. Merton gave depth to this process by inviting the test subjects to gather as a group to explain their positive and negative responses to particular programs (Merton et al, 1990). As quantitative research developed, many researchers saw that a focussed interview revealed much about why people had the opinions they reported in the quantitative survey.

Group dynamics prompted participants to draw out discussion and ideas from each other and produced more insights than the facilitator could ever elicit on their own. It is generally accepted that women are more successful as facilitators because both men and women are not as willing to bare their souls to a man. Ideas often emerge more easily with groups of the same gender. The positive aspects of group interaction include synergy, snowballing, stimulation, security, and spontaneity (Hess 1968). Of course, as in any group, there are dangers of members falling out and arguments becoming bitter and part of the role of the facilitator is to note the intensity that the issue raises and move on to rationally look at the causes of that intensity.

While some researchers are using one-on-one interviews in shopping malls and on the internet to explore qualitative issues, the most common form of qualitative research is the small focus groups of individuals targeted by the campaign: undecided voters from marginal electorates or demographic groups at which the campaign is aimed. While this form of qualitative research is no substitute for the thorough-going deliberation which would ideally be debated in a democracy, it nevertheless provides campaigns with the opportunity to observe political discussion among the citizens and to appreciate their arguments. Groups contain up to a dozen participants and they are generally recruited by random phoning to find members of the target segments such as young women or older men.

To achieve a maximum benefit from research, quantitative and qualitative work feed off each other: qualitative research asks questions raised by the last round of quantitative research and develops questions to be asked in the next round of survey work.

The success of small group research is dependent not on statistical validity but on the abilities of the facilitator to foster debate with casual but incisive questioning that probes people's motivations and develops solutions for the campaign's problems. "The art of the focus group is born of the skill of asking questions" (Herbert 1994: 42). Whenever possible campaign staff should also observe discussion, reading body language and tone of voice first-hand, to find the lines and positions which ring true and produce strong reactions. Another important use of qualitative research is in testing the effectiveness of advertising by showing it to small groups and observing their responses before it is broadcast.

Background Research

A final form of research is that required for negative campaigning on your opponent's shortcomings. It is a dangerous area that can all too easily backfire on a campaign. It should be based on rigorous opposition research of the opponent's public record to identify hard information that shows contradictions between their statements and actions or that highlights other reasons why they should not be elected (Persinos 1995: 20–23). It is most effective when it attacks an opponent's policy positions but it can also be useful in repositioning the opponent's character. It is also useful to do opposition research on the campaign's own candidate so it is prepared to respond to adverse material that will probably turn up some time during the campaign.

Some would argue that the growth of negative research reflects the laziness of journalists. In the past they would have used shoe leather to background the candidate but they are now so spoon-fed that campaigns must do the work for them (Persinos 1995). The most effective opposition research is the most obvious: is the opponent on the electoral roll? Perhaps they are not eligible to nominate, perhaps they do not live in the electorate. Are their nominators eligible to sign the nomination form? Was the nomination in on time? Perhaps the opponent can be knocked out of the race before it begins. Similarly all statements and material put out by the opponent's campaign should be carefully fact-checked to see if they can be caught out lying.

The availability of computer databases makes it very easy to trace someone's public record through their appearances in newspapers, company and court records and legislative debates. Everyone has enemies and a campaign would be remiss if it did not talk to the enemies. Where criminal, credit and tax records are not publicly available (and therefore cannot be used by anyone involved in the campaign), such information does much to flesh out the campaign's understanding of the opponent and may be brought to light by unassociated third parties.

Needless to say, the candidate should never be associated with negative campaigning. It is best leaked to a journalist who can check the information for themselves and take responsibility for it. If that is not working, then it should be left in the campaign director's hands or those of a sympathiser. However it is released, full documentation should be available for journalists. Particularly nasty material should not be dropped on election eve because it may have the effect of garnering sympathy for a candidate perceived not to have the opportunity to answer. Further it is crucial that the same charges cannot be made against the campaign's candidate. There is no point in spraying around opposition research indiscriminately. It should be used sparingly, in the context of key targeted issues to position the opponent as someone not worthy of election. The campaign should aim to recreate the opponent in negative terms that highlight its own candidate's positives.

It is very difficult to fight a well co-ordinated negative campaign. As George Stephanopoulos has said of attacks on former President Bill Clinton: "...as long as you can keep a rumour in play it doesn't matter if it is true, because the fact of the rumour creates a dynamic which makes people more willing to investigate and more willing to print stories that wouldn't otherwise be news. It's not enough to dispute the rumour – you have to disprove it. The burden of proof is shifted..." (Blumenthal 1992: 32). Nevertheless, as Clinton's victories show, by hanging a lantern on your problem, by accepting blame and spinning back to the policy issues that really concern the swing voter, a campaign can fend off the most comprehensive negative attack and still earn a victory.

Overall, what the polls tell the campaign is secondary to what the campaign does with them. Polls "provide the strategy to communicate the reasons behind positions and decisions in such a way that more support for your views might be generated" (Meadow & von Szeliski 1993: 49). Mills (1986: 64) points out that: "Politics still needs judgement and skill to determine when and if poll advice should be accepted." The skill however is not in instinctively knowing when to accept or reject poll advice; rather it is in hearing what the polling has to say and responding to this in the words and images that the campaign "invents".

6
MANAGING THE MEDIA –
PRODUCING EFFECTS

Mass Media Effects

In Aristotle's *Rhetoric*, direct speech is the only form of communication considered. In contemporary society there are many channels which the campaign can use to communicate its message. While, as will be seen in chapter 8, forms of automated personal contact such as direct mail do have a persuasive effect, in a mass society the most obvious way for the campaign to connect with the audience-electorate is through the mass media. But rather than dispersing a random selection of messages and images into the media-sphere, a good political campaign seeks to develop a strategy that positions the candidate to most effectively appeal to targeted voters. It then communicates with that group through every available means: free editorial coverage and paid advertising in the mass media and more personal contact through direct mail and door-knocking. As Shirley Leitch (1992: 36) suggests: "absence from media products is absence from the public arena and the public agenda of debate."

To participate in the processes of democratic deliberation offered in currently existing representative democracy, the campaign must effectively communicate through the "noise" of the mass media by understanding the processes and turning them to the campaign's advantage. Political campaigns seek to communicate their message in a manner which utilises the speed and complexity of contemporary media to their advantage. To this end campaigns are constantly deploying the practical techniques of media management to place persuasive arguments before targeted audiences. In the next chapter the role of advertising is discussed and later in this chapter the mechanics of presenting a message through "free" editorial space are analysed. Before moving on to the practicalities, it is useful to question what effect the mass media has on the citizenry.

During the course of the twentieth century, theorists have sought to explain the "effects" of the mass media, particularly on the political process. Larry Bartels (1993: 267) claims that the inconclusive state of research in the "media effects" area is "one of the most notable embarrassments of modern social science". After many years of study and experiment in effects theory, Bernard Berelson (quoted in Diamond & Bates 1984: 347) was philosophical about his findings: "some kinds of communication on some kinds of issues, brought to the attention of some kinds of people under some kinds of conditions, have some kinds of effects." Attempting to understand the complexities of effects theory may appear to be a futile endeavour lost in the minutiae of individual cause and effect but as the aim of the political campaign is to have an effect on the citizenry, then it is important to continue to explore why those effects occur and how they are achieved.

In the 1920s, early theorists of the mass media such as Harold Lasswell (1927) advanced what is now summarised as the "bullet" or "hypodermic" account of media influence: the skilful propagandist could so mould the content of a broadcast that it unerringly stimulated the audience's dispositions and preconceptions to produce a desired response. This "strong" effects theory held that the mass media was a vehicle through which selected content could "shape opinion and belief, change habits of life, actively mould behaviour and impose political systems" (McQuail 1981: 263). The rise of the Nazi Party in Germany and its use of the mass media to broadcast overt propaganda were seen as confirmation of the strong effects of the mass media (Ward 1995).

By the early 1940s "strong effects" media theory was under empirical challenge. Paul Lazarsfeld and associates's (1944) study of voting behaviour showed exposure to campaign information communicated through the mass media had only "minimal effects" on citizens. Voters mostly had long-term party allegiances that were reinforced, he concluded, by the campaign material of those they supported while the material of those they opposed was ignored. Word-of-mouth communication with community "opinion leaders" was found to be a more significant source of political information than the media. Through the 1940s and 1950s, Lazarsfeld's findings were extrapolated and expanded into a general theory of "minimal" media effects: that the media had only a slight impact on people's behaviour and beliefs. One interpretation Lazarsfeld offered was that the media only had a minor effect because they did not have the ability to deliver political messages with any predictable effect. This reassuring interpretation was unearthed in research funded by the media industry. It carried the proviso that skilful research could assist in producing advertising that gained the attention of enough of the audience to become the subject of word-of-mouth discussion which could still produce a significant market share for a product. This strand of the "minimal effects" thesis led to a plethora of empirical work in the United States in the 1940s and 1950s that confirmed the view that the media were relatively harmless to democracy and mostly reinforced the pluralist views of the society in which those media were produced (Stevenson 1995: 37).

Minimal effects theory began to be contested in the 1970s by a number of theorists who suggested that the mass media did have a "relatively strong" effect on public opinion. Four empirical interventions in particular refocussed media theory on the effects produced by the way the media organised its work. Maxwell McCombs and Donald Shaw's (1972) observations on agenda setting indicated that the rank order of issues voters nominated as important in an election closely correlated with the rank order of issues raised in the press. Elisabeth Noelle-Neumann's (1974) "spiral of silence" theory suggested that the suppression or amplification of viewpoints in the media produces a decrease or increase in the willingness of citizens to express those viewpoints. George Gerbner and Larry Gross's (1976) "cultivation hypothesis" identified the way the public's perceptions of a crime "problem" were shaped and cultivated by how the media reported and portrayed criminal violence. Stuart Hall's (1978) *Policing the Crisis* theorised the processes involved in the media construction of a "moral panic" about mugging to suggest a theoretical link between the operations of the media and the closure of discussion. Taken together these writers suggest that while the media do not have a uniform or decisive effect on people, they do set the scene and affect what people talk about.

However, another of Lazarsfeld and Merton's (1948) interpretations of Lazarsfeld's data argued that the media only had minimal effects because the flood of unrelated fragments of news constantly bombarding citizens did not encourage them to participate in political deliberation but rather acted to "narcotise" them. Thus the minimal effect of the media was produced because its form so overwhelmed the audience that they were rendered powerless, which one would have to agree is a major impact. With the advent of television, critics began to find major effects in the way television works to limit the potential for viewers to rationally analyse its output: "(t)elevision works as a positive effect" (Emery 1987: 36). These critics argue that television is used to arouse the emotions because it can thus evade perceptual filters to communicate directly to the subconscious. Television, argues Derrick De Kerckhove (1983: 197), "is now translating our past visual biases in terms of a direct access to the central nervous system." Its frenzied presentation of fragmented images "cut to the music" render it visually meaningless "when we consider that our visual validation of the world consists of continuous scans of a slowly changing environment" (Emery 1987: 36).

Further, there appears to be a scientific consensus emerging that television viewing slows brain electrical activity, particularly in the left hemisphere where information processing and analysis occur (Emery 1987). While this effect limits the ability of the viewer to recall information, at the same time "TV programs artificially manipulate the brain into paying attention through the use of frequent visual and auditory changes" (Juan 1992: 14). This hypnotic effect ensures that viewers retain experience in the unconscious which they can recognise again and even perhaps act upon, most profitably for the advertiser, at the point of sale: "A coherent dynamic is established between viewer, advertisement and point of sale... TV's power is seen to lie in exploiting our unconscious ability to recognise while reducing our ability to consciously recall." (Emery 1987: 35) Thus this second strand of "minimal" effects theory leads back to a different account of "strong" media effects: specific pieces of content may be insignificant, but the psychological impact based in the form of television exerts a powerful negative influence on deliberative processes.

Edward Herman and Noam Chomsky (1988) have given a detailed analysis of how the mass media operates to produce the "manufacture of consent", a concept first introduced by Walter Lippmann (1932). They argue that while the media in a democratic society should be "independent and committed to discovering and reporting the truth", the reality is that "the powerful are able to fix the premises of the discourse, to decide what the general populace is allowed to see, hear, and think about and to "manage" public opinion by regular propaganda campaigns" (Herman & Chomsky 1988: xi). They detail how the concentration of media ownership, the influence of corporate advertisers inherent in the media's reliance on advertising revenue, the privileged and uncontested position of experts and the homogenous world-view produced by the media all act to limit the potential for new voices to be heard.

Thus we can see that versions of strong media effects have made a comeback and while they do not suggest the close connection between message and effect that the old bullet theory promoted, they nevertheless hold that some relatively strong correlation is there. It would be hard to imagine that advertising could become a billion-dollar business if there was not some strong correlation between message and effect.

The important thing for campaigns to learn is how to manage the complexities to produce the desired effects: how to set the agenda, cultivate relevant issues, promote one's own issues up, and opponent's issues down, the spiral of silence and produce and defuse moral panic as required. This involves not only delivering the argument by images and texture direct to the citizen's subconscious but also playing the game to manufacture the campaign's own brand of consent: suborning owners and advertisers, finding one's own experts, explaining one's position in light of the reigning world view and managing relations with the media in ways that fit with their needs and deadlines.

Free media

The day-to-day media work of the campaign involves the constant repetition, refinement and redevelopment of the candidate's positions in light of the latest statements from the opposition, external developments and, most importantly, research. This is how the spin discussed in chapter 4 is applied. Every campaign teeters constantly on the edge of disaster and to turn each day into an opportunity to improve public support for its position, the campaign needs to promote its positive agenda enthusiastically while remaining flexible in its media strategy, ready to admit its shortcomings where necessary and able to turn those shortcomings, or at least the admissions, into positive things about the campaign.

There are many useful accounts of the techniques of media management and public relations (Evans 1987) and analysis of the impact these techniques have on news production (Carey 1995). There are some useful journalistic accounts of the minutiae and mechanics of media management in specific campaigns (Thompson 1973) and even detailed work studies of journalists during election campaigns (Kerbel 1994) but little has been written about the practicalities of media management in election campaigns except for simple "do and don't" instructions (Kellems 1994). While no campaign will comprehensively subvert all the filters applied to political events in the process of news production, it is important to recall that the production of the news is work and, like most human activity, is a process of expedient actions dictated more often than not by the limitation of resources and the demand for product rather than by management preferences and institutional agendas.

To communicate its messages through the mass media, it is incumbent on the political campaign to understand how the news is made so it can mould messages to the parameters by which the media operates. There are numerous cases to attest that "strategic use of limited resources and clever tactical skill can overcome intimidating odds" (Schmidt 1989: 191). By presenting journalists with images and messages they can easily comprehend at convenient times, the campaign improves the chances of its message being communicated through the mass media. The campaign must be aware of journalists' deadlines and work to them. The campaign has to also use the news cycle. Ten years ago the news cycle was daily. Campaign teams met in the early morning to review the evening TV news and morning papers and set the media agenda for the day. But now as morning, lunchtime and late evening TV news becomes more prevalent and personalised news services are delivering stories around the clock, the news cycle is speeding up. The campaign has to be quick to react and always focused "on message".

The role of personal contact in news production should not be underestimated. Personal contact ensures that the campaign appreciates the conditions under which journalists operate: "... daily news demands and imperative news schedules that they must meet" (Herman & Chomsky 1988: 18). Other commentators have given an even more harried account of news production: "So speed and quantity substitute for thoroughness and quality, for accuracy and context. The pressure to compete, the fear that somebody else will make the splash first, creates a frenzied environment in which a blizzard of information is presented and serious questions may not be raised..." (Bernstein 1992: 21). The news created in this environment is superficial, speculative and obsessed with simple extremes (Crichton 1993). The situation will only get worse as technology allows the introduction of one-person news crew: a journalist constantly on the road, responsible for all the technical details, reacting to news without the time, energy or resources to understand it (Shapiro 1993). These are the parameters within which the campaign must seek to create the news it wants to hear and that is achieved most effectively by giving journalists what they need, when they need it and in the language that they can use (Bell 1991). While the journalist always has last say, there is always a chance that the campaign which develops itself as a reliable and consistent producer of news can help out the journalist and at the same time, fly under the radar of the powerful forces that seek to mould the news.

The rules governing this area are fuzzy. There are constraints to the timing and forms of media contact. There are practical considerations that make outright lying hazardous: in most circumstances, there is the strong possibility that the lie will be found out before the election (Kellems 1994: 34). But beyond that, the only rule is that there are no rules. Even independent inquiries have shied away from suggesting limitations to the role of government media advisers even though they are on the public payroll (Electoral and Administrative Review Commission 1993: 123–4). Creativity and chutzpah are everything. Various journalists' Codes of Ethics bind them to honesty, fairness, professionalism and to respect the confidences of their informants but nothing formally binds their informants. This is the field in which the campaign has to operate and to do that it has no alternative but to use the media as it finds it and for its own ends. This is the press agentry end of public relations but it is the work of the media campaign.

Monitoring the media is the first step of the media campaign. Knowing what is happening and where the media mind-set is at is the first prerequisite of dealing productively with the media. It is most important to closely analyse the media consumed by the targeted demographics. Newspapers and magazines are procured, analysed and stored. Clippings are added to issue files. A bank of audio and video recorders attached to radio and television sets is a useful tool in monitoring not only the statements of opponents but also the effectiveness of the campaign's own efforts. Access to "wire services" which feed news to multiple outlets has become cheaper in recent years. These services are a major news source and should be regularly monitored to see the opposition's plays and how the campaign's own plays are interpreted. The systematic and timely analysis of the media is crucial to the operations of the campaign. Commercial operators offer not only the traditional clipping service but also detailed monitoring of not only electronic news services and talk-back radio (Wright 1995: 4).

A media contact system is the next step of the campaign. The campaign needs a system that allows it to quickly contact all media outlets. It needs to generate a list of all relevant media, their phone numbers, deadlines and journalists' direct numbers and even their home numbers. By its nature this list needs to be constantly updated. It is a key document in ensuring a comprehensive approach to the media. It is of further assistance if the media is also grouped in subsets that allows the campaign to contact specific audiences by region, issue, age, sex etc. The programmable facsimile machine, the email address book and text messaging program are useful tools for just this job. Each allows for the rapid dissemination of press releases and other campaign information direct to news rooms and journalists thus avoiding the necessity, though not the desirability, of ensuring coverage by the wire services. At opponent's press conferences, campaign operatives now text message questions and prompts direct to journalists in attendance. Text messaging gives the campaign the ability to impart spin about an event as that event happens.

As the contact system develops, it becomes a model of how the press works and the weak spots in the news cycle where entry may be possible, become apparent. For example: Saturday, Sunday and public holidays are slow news days when journalists are looking for stories. Getting stories up on Fridays is very difficult as journalists seek to finish stories they were sold earlier in the week. Thursdays are not much better except for journalists on the Sunday papers who will be locking in stories. Breakfast radio is a soft target because journalists have to work so quickly with few resources other than the newspapers and wire services. The press release on the top of the pile, sent by a pre-programmed fax machine at 4am, might catch the breakfast journalist's attention if it suggests some breaking angle or local colour, particularly if the campaign rings in at 5.30am with a sparkling sound-bite. From there the story might be picked up by the station's morning talk-back show, monitored by television news and given a shot at the six o'clock slot. If not, print journalists may hear it over breakfast and get a story idea. The campaign must become a close observer of media dynamics in order for it to create its own chances.

Media events are designed, promoted and run by the campaign to give the news media what they need: an arresting image and an interesting quote (Ward 1995: 55). The campaign needs to provide such images and quotes that send the message it wishes to send. The safest and most effective way to do that is for the campaign to hold a media event where it has some control over what the journalists record. Edward Bernays invented the media event in the 1920s by staging "overt acts" to desublimate and redefine public perceptions, mostly about commercial products (Blumenthal 1980: 21–22). The campaign utilises "props", backdrops and physical interaction with third parties to provide the strong images that the media find useful, "pictures that complement the story line" (Ward 1995: 55). It also needs to present a sound bite, a short, pithy, evocative message for the moment. In its simplest form, the media event may be just a door-stop press conference. Research indicates the average length of sound bites from US presidential candidates on network news had dropped from 42.3 seconds in 1968 to 9.8 seconds in 1988 (Glover 1993: 40).

The very act of gathering the media together makes the event news. Finding themselves in the one place, the journalists are bound by self-interested solidarity to give the story a run – they would not want to miss out on something that everyone else is running. Media events may be counter-productive if not carefully planned and preceded by well-researched advance work. Campaign operatives stay one step ahead of the campaign, preparing the way for events, to ensure that the message comes through clearly and the campaign is not embarrassed. They are also concerned to ensure that, when travelling, the media have access to the means to send their stories back: phone lines for radio, data lines for print and satellite up-links for television. While organising and running a media event is a relatively simple logistic exercise, the content requires creativity because it is with the sound bites and images the campaign produces at these events that they pursue debate in the highly mediated processes of the mass media.

Media releases are discounted by some commentators: "In writing scripts, journalists made little use of press statements issued by parties and political leaders. As one journalist noted, press releases

are too wordy and not suited to TV news which is chiefly visual"
(Ward 1991: 55). Nevertheless, the media release is a key strategic
tool and the cornerstone of the media campaign. It sets out the
message for the day in clear terms for not just the media but for the
campaign itself. To be effective, the media release should not be too
wordy. It should never be more than one page. The first paragraph,
the only one likely to be read, must simply, clearly and succinctly set
out the image that symbolises the message for the day, preferably in
a colloquial fashion. As one study on the language of news reporting
says: "Contemporary language style in television news is "poetic"
and "emotive" rather than strictly conative and referential" (Powell
1993: 1). That study also notes the common use of combative and
adversarial metaphors and "isms" in political reports, an effect that is
also evident from a cursory scan of newspaper headlines. These
considerations inform the construction of the image contained in
the first paragraph.

Media Release Tips

The campaign should issue at least one media release each day
setting out the message, image and media event for that day in clear
terms.

- Identify it as a media release, date it clearly and include contact
  details.
- Write a clear, short headline and have only one idea per
  paragraph in journalistic style.
- The most important information should be presented first.
- Use double spacing and large margins. Make it easy to read.
- Include indications of photo opportunities or good, clear stock
  photos.
- Remember the media release should be news and must include
  new information or at least a new angle.

- Check that it answers the basic questions: Who? What? When? Where? Why? How?
- It must reach the correct gatekeeper on deadline.
- Keep it short and simple: no complex constructions, no jargon, no long words when a short one will do. No more than 25 words to a paragraph.
- Keep it clear and concise: be direct, local and personal.
- Use active not passive verbs and short, "bouncy" sentences.
- Make the first paragraph count.
- Direct quotes in the release are the basis of a 20-second grab for radio and TV.
- Follow up by lobbying key journalists and political reporters at wire services.
- Ensure that journalists have phone numbers to reach the campaign for comment at all times.
- Develop contacts with opinion leaders active in the media – proprietors, management, editors, commentators, chiefs-of-staff and radio announcers.
- Pay attention to detail. Go over your story at least three times to make sure that it makes sense, that it flows, that you can substantiate all facts.

While the faxed or emailed media release remains an important building block of the campaign's media contact process, the increasing cheapness of audio and visual production gives campaigns the capability to produce and distribute electronic media releases. While the media always prefer to gather their own grabs, sometimes cost and availability mean that this option is just not possible and it is better for the campaign to supply the audio and vision required for a story to go to air rather than to see it not go to air at all. The growing use of campaign financed satellite links carries this strategy to its natural conclusion: part of the campaign's work is to ensure that the candidate is available with an appropriate grab just before deadline. At the other end of the scale is the practice of pumping grabs into radio breakfast news: relevant sound bites are phoned directly to regional radio newsrooms early in the morning when journalists are traditionally scratching for stories for the high rating breakfast news.

Media conferences are held to give all media access at the same time, to give journalists the chance to ask follow up questions and to ensure a story receives the greatest possible exposure. A simple door-stop interview merely offers a talking head against a nondescript backdrop and while that can be useful for a quick comment, the media likes and deserves an extended opportunity to talk about the story. By holding the media conference in a room, the campaign can exert more control over the backdrop to reinforce the message that the candidate is giving verbally. A colourful display with a clear message might find a long shot of the candidate against the backdrop used as a cutaway to cover the jump when the journalist splices together two quotes from the candidate. Similarly any device that illustrates the story will attract extra media prominence – many campaigns have used the large, free-standing gauge that shows the increasing cost of opponents' promises or advertising. The gauge becomes a recurring media story until it reaches some goal shortly before the election when it is topped with a flashing red light. Even more effective is holding the media conference outside at a symbolic site where the candidate is not only pictured against the colour and movement of an appropriate setting but may also be filmed showing an interest in a problem, getting hands-on experience in the issue and meeting people concerned with the matter. Material such as this will gain added prominence for the story on television and in the similarly image-hungry print media. The conference should be well organised, punctual and short. Statements should be short and to the point, not laboured or like a lecture. Check and double check.

No one will notice the things that go according to plan, but they will notice and remember omissions or mistakes. The media do not have to stay. But a well-run and productive media conference will convince journalists that they are dealing with a professional campaign that understands the process and therefore might have something worthwhile to say.

Major events such as candidacy announcements, campaign launches, addresses, rallies and debates need to be even more meticulously planned than simple media events. Media coverage is the key objective, so the event should be planned to fit into media schedules, the candidate's message should be clear and easily understood and the media should be given all possible help to cover the event sympathetically. Campaign launches are key events in setting the tone of the campaign, positioning it for the big pitch, defining the candidate and sending the key message of the campaign, particularly to the targeted segments of the citizenry. The media should be fully briefed about the mechanics of the event and the contents of the policy speech so they can have the cameras rolling at the appropriate times. The location depends on the circumstances of the campaign – a lowly community hall in a marginal electorate might best suit a government trying to lose an image of aloofness while an up-market concert hall may suit an opposition campaign trying to assume the mantle of government. Whatever the location, the room should be full so enthusiasm for the campaign is apparent to the media consumer. Supporting entertainment should be carefully selected to send an appropriate message – dancing girls will get a run on television but a string quartet may be better to suggest the sobriety and substance suited to government. Careful preparation and practice with the candidate is required for all major events so they don't produce a "slip up" which itself becomes the news and so obscures the message. This is particularly true in debates where the candidate must be prepared to turn all manner of questions into opportunities to get key messages across. The debate has become a central moment of election campaigns because voters make assessments about candidates from watching them (Kraus 1999: 391). The campaign "rehearses" the lines and images that need to be communicated in the debate and ensures that the physical and procedural formats of the debate allow the candidate to get the required messages across (Faucheux 1993).

Talking to journalists and media executives is perhaps the most important step in the campaign. A media release by itself is just dead trees and wasted effort if it is not followed up, and this is where the personal relationship with the journalist becomes important. By doing something as simple as ringing up "to make sure the fax has arrived", the campaign has commenced a personal relationship with the journalist. From this introduction the campaign can lobby the journalist for coverage of its story. The relationship can be built further by social contact and casual backgrounding of the journalist off the record, explaining the "real story" of the campaign. Tuchman is right to highlight the personal element in news construction: "news is an interchange among politicians and policymakers, newsworkers, and their organisational superiors, and... the rest of us are eavesdroppers on that ongoing conversation" (1978: x). The point for the campaign is to get into that game. The campaign should pursue these personal relationships that encourage journalists to ring the campaign for comment on the opponent's statements or if they are just looking for a story. Journalists should have the phone numbers that will reach key campaign staff at all times.

It is also important for the campaign to develop similar contacts with opinion leaders – proprietors, management, editors, chiefs-of-staff and radio announcers as well as other commentators, church leaders and key community figures. In this way the campaign can ensure that it will be the subject of discussion among those with power and influence over the media and so create the potential to edge further up the media agenda.

Dealing with the media requires a particular attitude: the campaign must exude confidence, develop a thick skin and always be positive about its chances. The candidate should never be nasty or mean, particularly to journalists themselves. It is pointless to complain about coverage unless a journalist's unfairness is threatening the campaign itself. If complaint is necessary, then it should be carefully planned, well-detailed and arrive with such force (simultaneously complain to management, other media, oversight bodies and the journalist union ethics committee) that the journalist is too busy to cook up a nasty reply for publication (Kellems 1994).

Alternative Forms of Free Media

It is easy for a campaign to become obsessed with its appearances on the evening TV news and the daily papers. These are the major sources of news for the citizenry and the ones that will be most carefully analysed by the commentators, but they are not the only sources of news. We saw above how breakfast radio was an alternative means of entry to the news cycle. Other alternatives include cable/pay TV, local and community newspapers, letters to the editor, talkback radio, TV talk shows, community TV and radio and the internet. They are all useful, and sometimes more effective, means of getting the campaign message across to the target audiences.

Pay TV, whether it comes via cable or satellite, analog or digital, offers new opportunities to identify with particular audiences and to circumvent the constraints of the network news' world view (Labiola 1993). As the electronic media diversifies into new channels and formats, the power of the traditional news sources will decline and new points of entry will be available to campaigns which stay aware of what their target audiences are watching. "The new technologies seem to dictate that the pyramid structure of communications will continue to flatten out..."(Sirius 1994: 48). However, most pay TV channels do not even make a pretence of reporting the news, so the campaign has to adapt its message to fit the format and give the channels what they need or be ignored. Clinton's appearance on MTV and 1992 US presidential candidate Ross Perot's use of 30-minute advertorials on cable barely hint at the diverse and perverse possibilities ahead to deal with the increasing pace of the campaign (Wark 1993).

Local and community newspapers often provide campaigns the opportunity to talk directly to targeted geographic, psychographic and ethnic demographics. Local newspapers, supported by local advertisers and often distributed for free, are read by a significant proportion of recipients and should be addressed with stories and angles relevant to their locality and their readers' interests. There are also community newspapers, again often free, designed to appeal to particular demographics such as gig guides for young people and the gay community. Ethnic communities also produce their own newspapers and a presence there, translated into the appropriate language, can earn support just for caring enough to address that community. The dynamics of a campaign are always developing and a good performance in the local media might earn the campaign not only the support of swinging voters and undecideds it needs but also the respect of the central media who consume local and community media as part of their general media consumption. While 1950s United States anti-communist Senator Joseph McCarthy's political position may have been too fanatical for a democratic society, it is instructive to see how he built his campaign from outside the mainstream, in local and regional newspapers (Bayley 1981).

Letters to the editor and talkback radio offer the campaign and its supporters access to the mainstream media. While these forums are mediated by editors and producers with an eye to what their audience wants to read and hear, the campaign can make inroads by organising and training groups to relentlessly relay the campaign message, in their own voice and in the style of the particular forum.

Norma Verwey gives a detailed account of the history, impact and political dimensions of talkback radio and recognises its potential: "...the general public, and especially housewives, had found a new, and perhaps for the first time, permanent voice. And what a political and potentially important voice it could become" (1990: xi). Bolce et al (1996) report findings that indicate that talkback audiences are attentive, engaged and politically conservative. Getting a message across in the letters pages and on talk-back radio requires a band of stalwarts who are willing and capable of monitoring the media and finding opportunities to deliver the daily message. They won't all succeed every day but armed with the names and addresses of other supporters and instant re-dial phones they maximise their chances of getting the campaign message through. They should be briefed each day on the current campaign message and how they might put their own personal touch to it. They should not appear to be mindless partisans but perplexed and concerned citizens trying to come to a conclusion that, inadvertently, favours the campaign. These forums are monitored for their political content and have become a crucial part of the back play for campaigns (Wright 1995).

Talk shows have become useful vehicles for candidates to develop their images. Bill Clinton playing saxophone on *The Arsenio Hall Show* changed the way that people viewed him. He moved from being a straight politician to a human being with his own set of talents and foibles. Clinton and Perot's use of *Larry King Live,* at the classy end of the talk show spectrum, gave them the opportunity to present a mix of their personalities and policies in depth (Wark 1993). Similarly, personality based radio talk shows are an oblique entry point to the media scrum (Stewart 1993).

The internet is a relatively open system that provides campaigns with the means to communicate with wired audiences. Internet access continues to grow but its decentralised nature resists forming audiences in the same way that traditional broadcast media do. The use of email to build communication lists will be discussed in chapter 8, but the worldwide web offers campaigns speed and mass interactivity that make it a useful tool for campaigns to find new constituencies and new ways to build an organisation and keep it informed (Conrad 1994). The campaign cannot afford to just put up a web site and hope for the best. It has to engage the audience by giving it what it wants: "... as more and more people get a voice, a voice needs a special stridency to be heard above the din. 'Excite or get lost' is the message of the medium" (Sirius 1994: 48). Policy-laden web sites are reassuring for supporters but sites to swing across undecideds need to use the interactivity functions. Calculators to work out tax savings can be quite involving at a personal level (Johnson 2001: 142). The aim is to create a personal piece of persuasion for that particular citizen and provide the opportunity for the campaign to respond on the themes about which the visitor is interested. Spoof sites and sites launching negative attacks are uses of the web that have been particularly effective (Johnson 2001: 143–4).

Alternative campaigns can subvert a range of media management techniques to open new areas for debate. In the case of the "McLibel Two", a couple of vegetarians wrote and published a small pamphlet critical of the environmental, health, industrial relations and culinary practices of the McDonald's hamburger chain. McDonald's responded by initiating a libel action against the authors of the pamphlet who fought the case both in the courts and mass media but, more significantly, also on the internet where they used the opportunity to focus on the corporation's conduct (http://www.mcspotlight.org/). After ten years of debate in the courts and the press, McDonald's eventually won the court case but not before they made a number of damaging admissions and endured adverse findings by the courts against the corporation's treatment of animals and young workers. In McDonald's own terms, they lost the public relations battle (Higgins 1997: 17).

The media is a tough game but by making contacts and networking, the campaign can build its coverage. A rigorous, professional approach makes its own opportunities. The campaign must always aim its messages through the channels that communicate with target audiences. It is relatively easy to carry the debate in the quality papers and on *Meet the Press* but still lose the battle with people on the ground that the campaign needs to convince.

7
ADVERTISING –
FROM DREAM TO REALITY

The Role of Advertising

Besides the processes of media management by which campaigns communicate their messages through "free" editorial space, the other crucial work of the campaign in the mass media is the production and distribution of advertising. Advertising has become the most significant campaign site because it is there for all to see in the dominant media forms, it is a chance for the campaign to put its case directly, but most importantly, it is effective. For greatest effect, the free media message should be coordinated to complement and cohere with the advertising. The range of advertising styles for different media, their appropriate combination and media-buying methods to maximise reach to target audiences are discussed.

The irony of advertising is that although it is consumed by everyone, it is directed only to the target segments of the audience. Whether communicated by television, radio or newspapers, political advertising seeks to bond the matrix of ideas, images, policies and arguments together to elicit a moment of "emotional exchange" (Diamond & Bates 1984: 10). Ads aim to crystallise moments of meaning which address the concerns of the target audience and leave them more inclined to the campaign's goals (or less inclined to oppose them). The ads are doing the same work as the "free" media campaign and so it is vital to the campaign's success that both are coordinated so that they combine to produce a synergy above and beyond their individual contributions.

Critics of political advertising focus on two key areas: cost and the diminution of rational political debate. In the first instance: "The burden of funding (TV advertising) inevitably exposes parties to the undue influence which their financiers will seek to wield" (Ward & Cook 1992: 21–2). While ads can be created on the cheap, it is expensive to air them. Television stations are almost entirely dependent on their advertising revenues and to put an ad precisely where the campaign needs it to reach a particular demographic can be very costly. In the United States, legislation forces television stations to charge political campaigns at the lowest rate they have charged in the preceding 45 days but this has done little to limit ballooning campaign budgets (Wertheimer 1997). One solution would be for governments to insist that television stations, which are licensed to use the public airwaves, have to provide free airtime for the transmission of political advertising during election campaign periods. Already some stations carry political debates without charge and provide free air time for charities.

Robert MacNeil (1970: viii) is just one of the critics unhappy with the impact of television advertising on rational debate in political campaigns: "television advertising was turning election campaigns into clashes, not between ideologies or policies but between rival teams of Madison Avenue experts, spending millions of dollars to manipulate the visceral reactions of the masses." Other critics argue that TV advertising "forecloses rather than improves the prospect that elections will be decided by informed voters making reasoned judgements at the polls" (Ward & Cook 1992: 22), and that it is shallow, superficial and manipulative (Ansolabehere & Iyengar 1995: 7). The absence of dialogue at first appears to be in the nature of television advertising. It is a one-way street pumping heavy traffic from the television station into people's living rooms. The critics can see no way back. These are strong criticisms and some would argue that they require the banning of political advertising (Ward & Cook 1992).

It is not necessary here to argue the pros and cons of free speech except to note that the kind of "rational public debate" which proponents of banning extol is much more likely to be found in academic journals than in bars or over kitchen tables where most political debate takes place. The model of debate suggested by critics of political advertising misunderstands where the important dialogue is going on: not in the privileged space of some ideal debating society but in the heads of the citizens. This has always been the site of the most important debate in democracy because this is where people are persuaded. Like all professionals, academics and newspaper journalists supporting the ban on political advertising privilege their own activities and degrade the power of people to know their own mind. Political advertising is an unavoidable element in election campaigns today, protected by freedom of speech provisions, and so it is useful to appreciate its role though somewhat more difficult to appreciate how to make effective advertising.

Campaign TV Ad Types

Witherspoon (1989: 61–74) provides a catalogue of some forms of campaign TV advertising.

Attack: negative attacks on opponents and their policies which work best when they reinforce your campaign's positive positions.

Biography: documentation that establishes the candidate's achievements, character and family situation.

Comparison: contrasts the policy positions and characters of various candidates and the voter is invited to choose between them.

Complaint: a member of the target audience shares their complaints about the opposition.

Issue definition: informative material positioning the campaign on issues that have been shown in research to be important to the audience.

Response: attempt to counter and defuse negative attacks on the campaign by responding directly to the allegations of opponents.

Slice of Life: dramatic but realistic portrayal of the doubter being convinced by the believer. Conflict between them creates interest.

Theme: positive images accompany the campaign's musical theme to "paint" the emotional trajectory of the campaign.

Vision spots: candidate summarises character, themes and issues in a statement of their aims and objectives.

11th hour blitz: in the final phase, the campaign must be ready to respond quickly and effectively to developments, shifts and the final tracking research.

West (1994) adds another:

Identification: name/face recognition to establish the candidate's presence in a campaign, particularly useful when candidates are not well known.

The author would add the following to this catalogue:

Negative to positive: Ads that start out with a strong negative on the opponent but then turn to a relevant positive from one's own campaign.

Factual: using newspaper headlines and other independent sources to establish the campaign's position.

Even if its role is understood, no one can say what makes effective advertising until after the campaign is over. Diamond and Bates (1984: 389) conclude *The Spot,* their detailed analysis of the rise of political advertising on television, by calling it a "problematic art". Robert Root (1987) has analysed advertising as a form of

Aristotelian rhetoric advancing arguments of character, emotion and reason as a persuasive message in the exchange between advertiser and audience. Any political advertising that sought "not to persuade, but to control; not to stimulate thought, but to prevent it" (Corcoran 1979: xv) would quickly doom the campaign that commissioned it to irrelevance because the citizenry is very sensitive to any suggestion that they have no alternative. Further, if any campaign thought a politician or political idea could be "sold like toothpaste" (MacNeil 1970: viii) they would soon learn that citizens expect an argument and while they can accept it, and even prefer it, when it is short and to the point, they nevertheless expect both logical and emotional content.

As was discussed above, effective tracking research questions a sample of the electorate to monitor public opinion and tell the campaign what is going on in the electorate's collective mind, their reactions and response to the campaign's arguments. David Sawyer argues that the whole process, polling, focus groups and advertising together, achieves the Aristotelian goal of "genuine dialogue with the voter" (Diamond & Bates 1984: 6). It is perhaps not as authentic as a face-to-face meeting, but then the original Athenian democracy was more like 1:6,000 rather than 1:1 anyway. The criticisms that advertisements do not engage viewers in dialogue, that they are intended to create an emotive response and that they are mediated by advertising agencies all point to realities that the campaign has to face in fashioning its advertisements. To be effective, election advertising must be based on an appreciation that "ads are condensed images of wish fulfilment" (Blumenthal 1980: 5) and crafted so that those wishes develop from the campaign's key messages.

Television Advertising

TV advertising, in particular, is a development beyond oral and literary forms: "far more dynamic and flexible... dramatic or cinematic rather than promotional" (Root 1987: 60). Despite these differences, the purpose of TV advertising is still to persuade, using all expedient means. The opportunity to blend audio and visual elements together provides a powerful communicative tool that can carry messages and stir emotions at the same time. The campaign must always remember that it is dealing with an electorate that has very high levels of TV literacy. By the time they are old enough to vote, people have probably already watched a year of television. They instinctively understand the grammar of production language, they appreciate the narrative import of zooms, pans, cuts and pace. They are attuned to the stock characters, plots and twists of a dozen genres. They appreciate the ironic possibilities of such a "cool" medium. They know how the form works and ads must be created that reflect that sophistication. Direct quotation is an effective entree into the sophisticated world of the electorate's TV literacy and the charge that the campaign has plagiarised some concept, genre or style carries little weight with an audience familiar with *The Simpsons* and its constant quotations from TV, movies and the full gamut of popular culture (Greer's new Ad 1991: 4–6).

Image is the substance of television, not just the pictures but the whole experience of the audience processing what they see and hear through their understanding of the world so that they stand in relation to what they see and hear on TV. The act of perception contains cognitive, affective and conative elements, to put it simply: what the voter knows, feels and thinks about the image received. While it is relatively easy to supply the informational and emotional facets to an image (see below), the third facet is equally crucial but somewhat more difficult to provide. The realm of the conative covers what the audience thinks about the campaign: "... how close a voter perceives himself to the political object, ie his proximity along specific dimensions (or with reference to specific matters) of sufficient salience to trigger for him an idea of what he proposes to do about the object" (Nimmo 1985: 122). Where the campaign has the research, it will know who it is talking to and what they are thinking about, but what comes next as the campaign turns to produce the television ads is that moment of creativity where the next step is taken to conceive and plan the ad.

These considerations point to the limitations of the media campaign – the candidate cannot just be images on a TV screen, in the final analysis there has got to be a real person there, preferably one consistent with the media image and promoting policies in which they believe and, above all, one that can relate to target segments of the citizenry and move them to action. As Camille Paglia (1992: 101–3) says: "Man is not merely the sum of his masks. Behind the shifting face of personality is a hard nugget of self, a genetic gift." How then can this "gift", the effective aspects of the candidate's character, be communicated? Where that event is not authentic, where the dialogue is less than genuine, where for example there is "a dissonance between the candidate's advertising image and his actual demeanor" (Diamond & Bates 1984: 32) then the campaign is doomed to failure. No one knows what good political advertising is until after the election but strict conceptual discipline allows the campaign to draw the images from reality in a creative fashion to further the discussion with the targeted citizens.

Emotion is the key to motivating action as a result of any ad. Television "makes it possible to transport emotions" (Bergmann & Wickert 1999: 460). Getting the right mix of emotions throughout the advertising campaign and in any particular ad is the challenge. Anger and concern, self interest and respect need to be deployed in just the right combination to carry the message and convince the targeted citizens to action. Emotions do not occur in abstract or just in someone's head, they occur as people act in the world. Where the ad can touch something real, whether it is put at risk or a possible achievement, then the emotions raised by the ad are much more likely to be effective. One useful technique is the complaint ad where a member of the target audience shares her complaints about the opposition. Sometimes known as whining (or in Australia whingeing) Wendy, the person delivering the complaints looks straight at the camera as this challenges the viewer to share the emotion of the complaint. The aim here, as with all emotion in ads, is to point the audience towards catharsis where they purge these emotions by performing the desired action, desired first by the campaign and now by the citizen. It is not surprising in this bardic work that appropriate music or other sound effects can provide strong reinforcement to the emotional message.

Message is the third crucial factor in the TV ad mix. Despite the primacy of emotions, no campaign will be successful if it merely seeks to stir emotions in a void. The ads must relate not only deeply but also convincingly into the swinging voters' practical concerns because politics is something more than toothpaste. The campaign is doing something more than selling a product. It is asking the electors to entrust the candidate with their votes for something more than momentary satisfaction. They trade their vote for a share of a better future, for the person and the plans that can impact on the real world for their benefit. Of course, policy statements must be absolutely correct and have their own logical consistency so that opponents cannot portray inaccuracy and inconsistency as signs of both intellectual and character weakness. The campaign must institute a regime of fact-checking and have the documentary proof to back all claims. Opponents will attack the ads, so be ready for them with strategies to spin their attacks back at them and onto the campaign's positive points. But beyond that, we return to Aristotle's formulation of rhetoric as the counterpart of dialectic. Politics is more than a dream, it is about effectively tending society, dealing with people and their problems, creating a material future from a material world, drawing real conclusions from real premises. The rationality of rhetoric is always truncated and expedient but it must be there, anchoring the campaign, establishing the candidate's credentials as a politician, working synergistically with image and emotion to engage and persuade the voter.

Negative Advertising Television advertising has proved an excellent vehicle for negative attack ads. A few graphic images and some alarmist facts read out in a sober voice over strike hard into the audience's subconscious. One of the first political ads during the 1952 US presidential election campaign saw Dwight Eisenhower attack the amount of federal debt, the high tax rates and US involvement in the Korean war. In the 1964 US presidential election the Democrat incumbent Lyndon Johnson decided on an early attack on his Republican opponent, Barry Goldwater. The Daisy ad below was only aired once on one network and did not name or even allude to Goldwater but the word of mouth, assisted by Republican complaints that he had only pointed out that the US could not use nuclear weapons, convinced a lot of people that Goldwater was likely to start a nuclear war. Johnson prevailed.

Daisy 60 seconds

Video

Audio

0.00 A young girl is picking petals off a daisy in a field as the camera tracks in to her upper body

Background sound effects of birds and insects. Little Girl: One, two, three, four, five, seven, six, six, eight, nine, nine

21.00 Girl looks up and camera zooms in to an extreme close-up of the girl's eye.

Loud man's voice counting down: Ten, nine, eight, seven, six, five, four, three, two, one

31.0 A nuclear explosion

Explosion noise

35.0 Explosion continues

Johnson from a radio address: These are the stakes – to make a

world in which all of God's
children can live, or to go into the
dark. We must either love each
other, or we must die.

52.0 Black background with
white letters: "VOTE FOR
PRESIDENT JOHNSON ON
NOVEMBER 3."

Voice over: Vote for President
Johnson on November Third.
The stakes are too high for you to
stay home.

The 1988 US presidential campaign saw the Republicans under
campaign director Roger Ailes become very astute in turning
information from their focus groups into negative television
advertising. Vice President George Bush Snr was trailing Democrat
challenger Michael Dukakis by 16 points. The Bush campaign held
focus groups in states that had previously been won by Republican
President Ronald Reagan but which were now veering back to the
Democrats. A couple of the groups were led through some of
Dukakis's more liberal decisions: opposition to capital punishment
and the pledge of allegiance being recited in schools; allowing
murderers to have weekend passes from prison. While some
participants could rationalise individual positions, the cumulative
effect produced a strong reaction from the groups with half the
members switching allegiance by the end of the session (Moore
1992: 237). The Republicans ran a series of negative ads on the
issues including one featuring Willie Horton, a black murderer who
had re-offended while on leave and another with black actors in
prison garb going repeatedly through revolving doors. Without
formally playing the race card, Bush's campaign had introduced a
moral panic about black crime into the campaign and while Dukakis
explained that the legislation that allowed Horton out was a
Republican initiative, his efforts were futile in the face of the force of
Bush's TV ads.

Willie Horton 30 seconds

Video	Audio
0.00 Photos of Bush and Dukakis with "BUSH & DUKAKIS ON CRIME" subtitle	Bush and Dukakis on crime
03.0 Photo of Bush with "Supports Death Penalty"	Bush supports the death penalty for first degree murders
06.0 Photo of Dukakis with "Opposes Death Penalty"	Dukakis not only opposes the death penalty
08.0 Photo of Dukakis with "Allowed Murderers to Have Weekend Passes"	He allowed murderers to have weekend passes from prison
12.0 Photo of Willie Horton, a black man with a beard looking down at the camera with "Willie Horton"	One was Willie Horton who murdered a boy in a robbery stabbing him 19 times
17.0 Photo of Horton with a prison officer and "Horton Received 10 Weekend Passes From Prison"	Despite a life sentence Horton received 10 weekend passes from prison.
21.0 Same Horton photo with "Kidnapping"	Horton fled, kidnapped a young couple
23.0 Adds "Stabbing"	Stabbing the man and
24.0 Adds "Raping"	Repeatedly raping his girlfriend.
26.0 Photo of Dukakis with "Weekend Prison Passes"	Weekend prison passes.
28.0 Adds "Dukakis on Crime"	Dukakis on Crime

Advertising agents are paid to be "creative", however the campaign must keep a tight grip on not only costs but also the content of ads.

The advertising agent's goal is to create great advertising while the campaign's goal is to win. Great care must be taken to ensure that the ads address all the tracking research, not just the one point the advertising agents find compelling. An ad must make its points cleanly and clearly and integrate with the wider campaign. As was noted above, all ads should be pre-tested in qualitative groups to gauge their impact, ensure their effectiveness and find out if change is necessary. Campaigns can rarely afford to let advertising agents make ads to be shelved but qualitative research does allow the campaign to concentrate their resources on ads that work and weed out any with undesired or even disastrous consequences. Campaigns cannot afford to leave advertising solely in the hands of agents who are used to selling products and are not attuned to the imperatives of political campaigning, so campaigns find it necessary to ride their advertising agents to make them produce the best, most effective advertising possible. Close supervision of media buying is also required to ensure the advertising campaign is pitched to areas where there are marginal seats and to demographic segments where undecided and swinging voters are concentrated.

Coordination and Imagination

It was seen above how crucial consistency is to the campaign. That consistency is obtained through the discipline of the campaign. There is a need for firm central control to ensure that all messages cohere as they are developed from the tracking research. All advertisements, print, radio and television as well as free media, direct mail and personal appearances must hammer the same message. The close coordination of advertising with publicity work produces synergies that give the campaign something more than the sum of parts (Schnur 1999). One useful way of ensuring integration is for the campaign to organise a media launch of every advertisement. Television ads are particularly influential when the news media amplify ad messages through their coverage (West 1994). If the campaign can make all new ads newsworthy then it establishes itself as a player in the media's eyes but, more importantly, it gains extra screenings of the ad to the very attentive news audience who otherwise might avoid watching ads at all. Always consider that criticism of opponents' advertising is a cheap way to spin their efforts back against them where the campaign can show that they are beholden to special interests, playing fast with the truth, have offended minorities etc. Bill Clinton's 1992 campaign manager James Carville even uses the strategic dissemination of ads designed purely to mislead the opposition: "We would put ads on the satellite that we weren't going to run," just to freak them out. Fake spots, so they would have to put some time and money together and respond to it." (Jamieson 1996: 503)

Target Audience Measurement

Once the campaign has identified its target segments of the audience, researched the issues that will attract their support and produced ads appealing to them, the next step is to ensure that the messages are getting to the audience and that the campaign is getting value for its advertising spend.

Television and radio stations aim for particular demographic groups as their target audience: 18–25, 45+, housewives during the day, men during sports, the high socio-economic AB category during in-depth current affairs and yuppie (young urban professional) women during *Ally McBeal*. The station's aim is to sell those audiences to the advertiser. The campaign's aim is to communicate particular messages to particular target audiences and no one much else.

Thus the campaign seeks to play its ads on stations and at times that maximise the number of connections it makes with the target audience. To do this, the campaign has to make the right media-buy and fortunately the advertising industry already has the consultants, ratings data and software to assist the campaign in spending its advertising budget. Their job is to best match the campaign's target audience with the appropriate stations to achieve the highest possible TARP (or Target Audience Rating Points).

TARPs are a survey-based estimate of the size of the target audience listening to a channel or program calculated as a percentage of the potential target audience.

$$\frac{\text{Average Target Audience}}{\text{Target Audience}} \quad \text{x } 100 \quad = \text{Total TARP (\%)}$$

Media buyers have a range of other indicators to understand what audiences are being reached:

gross impacts – the sum of audience for each spot in the schedule. There is a danger that a high gross impact means a few members of the target audience have experienced the ad a lot and most others not at all.

cumulative audience – the total number of different members of the target audience who experience the ad. The danger is that some members of the target audience have just seen the ad once.

gross ratings points – the cumulative TARP delivery of an advertising campaign measured using both reach and frequency analysis.

cost efficiency – the relationship between the cost of placing the ad and the target audience reached. CPT or cost per tarp is a common measure of cost-efficiency.

Radio advertising provides a relatively cheap alternative to TV. It allows direct appeal to particular groups of potential supporters among the target audience of the particular station. Radio has its own history of political advertising, preceding television and then developing against the new and dominant medium. The centrality of the word to radio made it an effective forum for formal rhetoric. In the 1920s campaigns bought air-time for the broadcast of speeches and by the 1930s they were producing spots and even dramas promoting their candidates (Diamond & Bates 1984: 88–94). Now radio has a much different role in people's lives and so political advertising has changed too. It must be designed to fit the demographics of the particular station where it is played, using the language and even the humour relevant to the listeners. That fragmentation of the radio audience, along with the medium's third rank status (behind television and the newspapers) and its "hot" emotive power means that radio allows the campaign to make an "invisible" tactical move on key segments of swinging voters which "an opponent, political insiders and the news media will remain totally unaware of until its impact has already been achieved." (White 1993: 45) Whatever the campaign does on radio must reinforce the television advertising and some experience suggests that radio advertising is perhaps best used to hammer home key themes from the television advertising to particular demographics. This was certainly the experience of the Australian Labor Party's 1993 campaign, when they bought large slabs of radio time to keep playing the campaign's key line against the Goods and Service Tax: "15% on (name any product)" followed by the sound of a cash register ringing. The ads were purposely targeted at particular stations' demographic by mentioning products heavily promoted on the station: CDs on youth stations, beer on sports channels etc. "Each ring of the cash register was another nail in their coffin" (Curry 1994).

Print advertising is also most effective when reinforcing television advertising. Where voting is voluntary, there is evidence to suggest that committed newspaper readers are more likely to vote than heavy television viewers (Rust et al 1985). There is always the temptation to use the newspapers to place detailed, lengthy arguments but unless the candidate needs to establish that they have detailed policies, one clear image and a series of short points is the best way to get a message across. Use of print-intensive ads can sometimes make the counter-productive suggestion that the campaign has something to hide behind all those words. Desktop publishing means that campaigns can design their own print ads and discounts for bulk newspaper bookings make print advertising a relatively inexpensive tool. Print ads are particularly useful for listing endorsements, documenting television ads, particularly negative attacks on opponents, comparing policies point by point and getting out the vote (Faucheux 1994c).

Other advertising formats should also be considered where they have applications for particular purposes. Billboards are good for building identification ratings and are also a useful way to mark out the campaign's territory where that territory is geographic. They also offer good reinforcement for television advertising though they are subject to alteration by opponents, which sometimes produces a humourous message against the campaign that sticks in peoples' minds more effectively than the original. Yard signs and posters on firm backing are also effective ways to build identification. Relatively cheap to produce, signs can be easily spread across the target area to suggest the campaign's breadth of support. Leaflets and pamphlets are another cheap campaign tool but they will not get much attention if they are just stuffed in a letterbox. Hand delivery increases their readership. Trucks and buses can be converted into travelling ads that can be moved to gain maximum attention outside major events and at different locations during different phases of the rush hour. In the past, amplified voice might spruik up the campaign but citizens have become much more sensitive to noise pollution in recent years. Internet banner ads have recently become another potential campaign tool but before the campaign commits its budget to this new form of advertising, it should have a high degree of certainty that the ads will appear before the target audience in ways that will positively attract their attention.

Production is the process that takes the ad from concept to realisation. The campaign should sketch out the ad itself. Television advertising starts with a storyboard or just a sheet of paper with a line down the middle and audio on one side and vision on the other. Remember that the ad should be driven by the research, not telling people what they want to hear but responding to their ideas and inclinations with an intervention that leads them to a greater inclination to support the campaign's cause. It is important to test the ad before releasing it and with expensive television advertising, the producer shows a set of storyboards and reads the voice over to the focus group or shows it a simple version of the ad produced on Powerpoint. Quick and easy access to production facilities is an important requirement of modern campaigning. Print materials can be produced on the most primitive home computer but expertise in rapid production and an understanding of the "grammar" of visual messages are also important elements in the effective design of print materials. Similarly while audio and video production can be done on relatively cheap equipment, the key requirement for effective advertising is the ability to quickly produce a simple, clear message that sways the viewer and usually a professional with experience is the best person to achieve this end. While advertising can be expensive, small campaigns can make cheap ads on home video-editing and desktop publishing equipment and run them at low cost in off-peak times or cheaper parts of the newspapers (Franzen 1994).

The future of advertising is reliant on changing media formats. The means of delivery to the audience are in constant flux and the campaign has to be constantly updating its media methods to make sure it is communicating via the channels that its targeted audience is consuming. Media convergence and the advent of not just the internet, but other forms of electronic communication such as text messaging personalised agents will produce a totally different relationship between the media and the audience. But advertising will not disappear, it will change. Not as much will be interspersed in television programs like a tax on the viewer. Already people are zipping (recording programs and then fast forwarding through the ads) and zapping (using the remote control to change channels during the ads). Advertising will have to earn attention from an empowered audience with a lot more subtlety. Perhaps the advertiser will have to pay for the audience's attention. Most likely the advertising will simply become the program (product placement is already pushing programs to this now). Advertising will use psychological and physiological discoveries to seek more immediate access to the decision-making centres in the brain, "...to burn a sales message directly onto the synapses..." (Schrage et al 1994: 73). Political campaigns have no alternative but to embrace the new media as the audience does and rise to the challenge of "memetic engineering" (Schrage et al 1994: 176).

8
DIRECT CONTACT –
FROM DOOR-KNOCKING TO THE INTERNET

Door-Knocking and Grassroots Activity

Direct contact is still the most persuasive form of political communication. Interpersonal contact at meetings, events and the doorway develop a personal relationship between the campaign and the citizen. The problem is that, if not well planned, these contacts can be time-consuming and ineffective at convincing the target audience. However audience segmentation and canvassing can generate lists of targeted individuals who can then be engaged in inter-active communication by direct mail, telemarketing, e-mail, door-knock visits or special purpose meetings or events.

In the frenzy of modern campaigning, personal contact is often overlooked as an effective means of establishing a relationship with the voters. While, in elections, the campaign is working the electorate on a macro scale, the candidate's most effective contribution is to work at the micro level by getting involved on local issues, speaking to community organisations and local opinion leaders and door-knocking the electorate. Similarly in campaigns by all forms of interest groups, it is crucial to have a body of supporters ready to turn up to a rally, demonstration, meeting or media event or who are at least willing to sign a petition and perhaps make a monetary contribution. Every opportunity should be taken to build grassroots support and communicate the campaign's message to the target audience personally.

Evidence to hand on which forms of voter contact have the greatest impact on election outcomes suggests that incumbents and insurgents benefit differently from different forms of contact (Kenny & McBurnett 1997). Newcomers tend to get more effect from

152

personal contact in general, probably because they are less well known than incumbents who have had the opportunity to establish some sort of relationship with the citizenry. Incumbents appear to be able to use contact through the media to maintain their advantage which indicates that incumbents who reach a large percentage of the electorate via the media are difficult to beat.

Clothing and grooming send messages whether the candidate wants them to or not. It is much better for the campaign to take control of the candidate's physical image to ensure they are sending messages consistent with the campaign's key messages rather than allowing an eccentric personal style to send conflicting or confusing messages. Clothes, hair and make-up all require attention to suggest that the person behind it all can exercise self-control, knows what they are doing and can provide leadership where required. Black, dark grey or navy blue suits, either plain or pinstriped for either men or women carry the message that the person wearing the suit is committed has a professional approach. Brown suits, particularly for men, are notoriously liable to clash with skin colour. Glasses can obscure the eyes so large, clear, non-glare lenses with thin frames are preferred (Brown 1994: 40–2). Posture and gesture also merit consideration. Bremer & Roodenburg (1993) trace the history of authoritative comportment back to the ancient Greeks who have left Western society with the impression that anyone standing up straight and not flapping their arms around can be trusted. Presentation and attitude will be read by the citizen-audience as it decides what kind of person the candidate is. Honing a candidate's image involves everything from deciding on the appropriate tie or brooch to elocution lessons. There is no exact formula in this area – it depends on the electorate. In some electorates candidates should never be seen without a suit, in others they might succeed *because* they do their door-knocking in sandals and t-shirt. The symbolic dimensions of politics rule.

Door-knocking is still the best way for candidates to meet the voters in election campaigns, particularly if it is done in a systematic way (Duquin 1989: 41–45). Government statistics offices can supply information on social indicators for clusters of about 200 family homes. When cross-referenced with booth or precinct turnout rates, profiles of swinging voters from quantitative research (and information about registered voters in the United States), the campaign can pin-point areas where door-knocking will be most effective. Persuadability of each booth, precinct or seat can be calculated by averaging the split vote (the percentage of voters who voted for different parties) and the switch vote (the percentage of voters who shifted their allegiance from one election to the next). Additionally, the candidate does not have to knock at every door. A telephone canvass or alternatively a small group of campaign workers canvassing ahead of the candidate identifies supporters (who are invited to meet the candidate at a local home or park), opponents (who are left with a pamphlet extolling the advantages of the candidate, framed to highlight the opponent's negatives) and swinging voters (who receive personal attention from the candidate). Volunteers are given a script and trained to talk to the public. Each contact with a supporter or swing voter should generate a direct mail that focuses on the campaign's position on the issues that are important to the citizen. Intensive canvassing will also turn up people who are not on the electoral roll and the enrolment of likely supporters, along with a welcome from the candidate, can produce beneficial results. In particular, it is vital that the candidate canvass apartments, caravan or trailer parks and newly built areas to enrol likely supporters and establish a personal relationship with newcomers. Many politicians owe their success to timely and assiduous work in caravan and trailer parks.

Community leaders give the campaign a useful conduit to the public. Just as the campaign establishes good relationships with the owners and editors of local newspapers, it should also contact local opinion leaders: religious and community leaders, school principals, police commanders, publicans and any other local identities with a high profile. Seeking out people whose opinions are heard and valued by others is an important part of campaign work. Research indicates that "opinion leaders have the potential to cause significant shifts in public opinion" (Omura & Talarzyk 1985: 95). They will not all warm to the campaign but at least there will be a personal contact, so if the opinion leaders have a problem there is a chance they will come direct to the campaign rather than spreading the problem to everyone they meet. On the positive side, they may talk up the campaign because they have been convinced or because the campaign has shown an interest in them.

Interaction with community groups on local issues "fleshes out" the campaign's image by giving it the opportunity to actualise the one-on-one relationship that mass media activities strive for but can never completely deliver. Every attempt should be made to address community organisations within the electorate. This is where the campaign deploys the traditional skills of speechmaking as discussed in chapter 4. Speaking to meetings is a craft that can be learnt. The psychology of large groups suggests that it is better not to make eye contact with each and every member of the audience because it makes the speaker look shifty. Rather, it is better to divide the room into three zones (left, right and centre) and address the speech equally to one person, camera or spot in the middle of each of these zones. Thus "people near that focal point will think that the speaker is actually looking at them, and feel the strength of one-on-one communication." (Alexander 1994: 54) Powerful public address systems mean candidates can use a conversational volume and tone but still be understood by the audience. This produces a much more empathic relationship with the audience than shouting at them. Where practicable, the speaker should attempt to "work the room" to meet everybody there.

Direct Mail

Direct mail has become a very significant site of political rhetoric in recent years. The production of direct mail is made possible by merging lists of targeted citizens into computer word processing software to produce a letter to each of those targeted. Direct mail appears to be a particularly effective method of soliciting support from targeted sectors of the electorate, combining "sophisticated political judgements and psychological, emotional appeals with the most advanced computer and mailing techniques" (Sabato 1989: 88). Direct mail differs from leaflets and pamphlets a campaign might put in a letterbox because it is addressed by name and sent to specific targeted recipients rather than being delivered using a blanket approach. Unaddressed campaign materials do have a place in a campaign – to trawl for postal and absentee voters, for example – but most unaddressed mail is merely showing the flag and relatively ineffective.

Criticism of direct mail centres firstly around the advantage it gives to incumbents who can use their taxpayer funded offices, computers and mailing privileges to ensure their re-election (Arieff 1979: 1446). While this issue is a matter of concern, it is unlikely that incumbents will ever give away their advantages. Therefore the tasks for the challenger are to raise the money required to compete with the incumbent and to focus the message for the target audience more cogently and precisely than the incumbent, weighed down by their voting record, can. Other concerns with direct mail revolve around the fear that by targeting the persuadable in general and the marginal seat swing voters in elections, the process of direct mail is debasing the mass debate that should be the centrepiece of democracy (Gosling 1996: 21). In particular there is a concern that while associations connected by direct mail techniques may be successful early and in national campaigns, in the long term and at a local level associations based on social networks and institutions have greater success (Godwin & Mitchell 1984: 839). These concerns go to the heart of the question of how to do democracy in a mass society. While the campaign must present a public face for all, direct mail is good for establishing a relationship with people important to the campaign.

The overriding principle of direct mail is personal intimacy: the campaign should not only personalise letters so they are addressed to the intended recipients, but also the text of the letter should contain references to the recipients ("Dear John and Mary... as I'm sure you will agree, John and Mary") and their street and suburb. Signatures and postscripts should be in the candidate's hand writing and be printed in fountain pen blue. Direct mail works because while "...people do not really believe that substantial effort has been invested in reaching them ... the delightful illusion persists, for technology has become fraudulently adept at lending a personal gloss to a mechanical and remote process" (O'Shaughnessy 1990: 94). While direct mail is more expensive per contact than television advertising, it can be much more finely targeted to make a connection with just those who need to be convinced to achieve a particular outcome. Of course, direct mail works most effectively where it reinforces and is reinforced by the advertising campaign and all other campaign messages.

While first developed in the United States for fund raising purposes, direct mail was used by US Republicans for persuasive purposes as far back as 1972 (Arieff 1979: 1445–7). Issues-based, vote-grabbing direct mail was increasingly utilised in California and other urban areas during the 1980s (Luntz 1988: 155). Because direct mail arrives at the voter's home as a personally addressed piece of post, it is an invitation for activity within the codes of correspondence: "an epistolary discourse between two people" (Root 1987: 28). Contributing to the perception that the campaign really does care, these 'personalised' messages are capable of producing a strong impact. The aim is not to win arguments nor to impress with eloquence; the purpose is one of direct communication that builds a relationship with the citizen yet to be convinced, by utilising basic rhetorical modes that will be convincing in the decisive moment (for a comprehensive analysis of the Aristotelian basis of direct mail see Root 1987, chapter 3). While there is some point in mailing to dedicated supporters of the campaign to reinforce their position, there is little point in expending money or energy on confirmed opponents (a move which in effect delivers details of the campaign directly into the hands of the opposition). Most direct mail should be sent to targeted citizens. As much care should be taken in deciding who the campaign contacts as is given to the contents of the mail-out.

Writing Direct Mail

Keep it simple: Use short, simple words that a ten-year-old can understand. If in doubt get a ten-year-old to read it and it will soon be apparent where it works and where it fails. No Latin roots, no complex constructions, no jargon, no long words when a short one will do and no showing off. The point is to communicate simply, clearly and effectively. "Expenditure" is hard, "spending" is easy.

Keep it short: One sentence and one point per paragraph will keep people reading. Never put more than three lines to a paragraph. Deliver important points in one line paragraphs. If you have a complex sentence then see how you can split it into two simpler sentences. One page is plenty unless you need to make it clear that you have a substantial position on some particular subject.

Keep it positive: People want to hear positive things from their politicians. They will stop reading if the letter gets too negative so leave attacks to the last half of the letter and then put them in terms of contrast with your positive attributes. Leave the mudslinging and personal abuse out all together. Keep it positive and the voters will keep reading, feeling better about the candidate all the time.

Be emotive: "...direct mail consultants have long known of a secret ingredient to stir the soul: emotion." (Sabato 1989: 88) Good direct mail, like all effective rhetoric, seeks to complement its rational arguments with strong emotional appeals. The writer should not be afraid to "pull at the heart strings".

Be direct: Use active not passive verbs and short, "bouncy" sentences. Use punctuation to highlight your message and be ready to break the rules of grammar to give key points impact. Jolting sentence construction and even typing errors can effectively emphasise the message.

Be local: The technology of direct mail allows the campaign to address small segments of the electorate with specific messages that highlight the candidate's involvement in the local area. This technique can be used most effectively to communicate that the candidate is part of the community and so aware of the issues that affect individual voters.

Be personal: As Byron wrote: "'Tis pleasant, sure, to see one's name in print..." and this is where direct mail gains its power. The direct communication to the voter reassures them that the candidate has them in mind. To maximise effectiveness, direct mail has to be something personal from the candidate. Personal experiences like family interaction or things likely to be shared with the voter (eg sitting in the traffic) build the one-to-one relationship.

Stick to the message: Just two or three messages should be refined from research and the mail should concentrate on hammering them home simply and clearly. They should be consistent with all other media and from letter to letter (Shea 1996: 210). There is a tendency to be expansive because of the form. The codes of correspondence do allow for the gratuitous aside. These temptations must be resisted because they can all too easily cloud the message and point to other issues which the campaign does not need to raise.

Make the first paragraph count: "The opening paragraph, the most crucial part of the entire letter, is usually succinct and breathless. It is designed to rivet the reader's attention and pique his interest immediately, explaining in an intimate or momentous way why the letter is written, what the common ground with the reader is, or how the candidate's election will be vital to the recipient's own welfare" (Sabato 1989: 96). This is the only paragraph likely to be read so it should carry the key message, preferably in a strong image that will stay with the reader.

Check everything: Spelling, dates, content – make sure everything is accurate because a lot of people, including the campaign's opponents, are about to receive this information and all will be reading it with a critical eye. As we have seen, this is a very personal medium so it is just as easy to put people off-side as win them over. Make sure that the campaign is not about to alienate sectors of the electorate that it needs for victory.

Where the campaign can afford to canvass the entire electorate, either by phone or foot, it can then delete opposition supporters and produce separate lists so that appropriate material can be tailored for the campaign's confirmed supporters, third party supporters and undecided swinging voters. Responses to surveys, incoming constituent phone calls and candidate contact may provide the basis for in-house lists which can be used to mail letters on specific issues.

Too often individual voter contact with the campaign is treated as a nuisance by campaign workers, whereas the application of computer technology and a systematic approach to this contact from highly motivated constituents can provide useful lists for mailings in the final weeks of a campaign (Tobe 1989: 136–144). Issues lists may also be supplemented from the mailing lists of sympathetic organisations or by lists purchased from commercial suppliers.

If the letter cannot be properly dated because of scheduling problems then it should bear a universal designation such as "Sunday afternoon". The letterhead should include the campaign address, phone numbers and a photograph of the candidate. It should carry the key message of the campaign – eg, "a local who cares" – and be properly authorised with disclaimers ensuring that it was produced from recycled materials and not at the public expense (where these things are true). Colour is an important consideration and should be determined by psychological considerations rather than party tradition (Ward 1992). Similarly, party affiliation need only be highlighted where it is a clear positive (Knight 1988: 28) as the party connection could otherwise be seen as an intrusion on the two-person world of direct mail contact.

The letter is only one element in the communication and the complete package should be carefully developed. According to Guber (1997: 83), the majority of people "read campaign literature en route from the mailbox to the trash can," so the mailing envelope should not turn off the recipient. A return address is required by postal regulation and it is perhaps safest to leave external adornments at that. A window-faced envelope with the address printed on the letter is the cheapest approach and gets around the problem of double-checking that each letter is in the right envelope. Another solution is to send the material in postcard format.

Enclosures can be an effective tool for driving home the candidate's message. Issue surveys that call for a mail-back response help build the candidate-voter relationship (pre-paid postage will maximise returns). Booklets with dense print can send the message that the candidate has detailed policies, but do not expect them to be widely read.

Sabato admits that "the art of direct mail is still inexact... (and)... that last week's magic may not work for this week's candidate." (1989: 99) As we saw above, practitioners are not sure exactly how or why television advertising works and the relative lack of research on direct mail means the situation is even worse. There are numerous examples of where direct mail has or has not worked but, in the rude empirical tradition of the Sophists, practitioners have found that some things work better than others. By its personal nature, direct mail requires a deft hand, creative but careful, to be effective. It must be produced from deep analysis of the research and with a close empathy for the targeted sectors of the community. Ideally it should be tested in qualitative research groups as part of the production process or, where time and resources permit, by test mailings and follow-up interviews with the recipients. As a last resort, it should be read by family and friends not involved in the campaign to ensure that there are no typing errors, double entendres or other bloopers and that it makes sense. There is certainly evidence that combining direct mail with telephone contact increases the cost effectiveness of campaign-voter contact (Persinos 1994).

Direct Mail Examples

One of the simplest and most effective direct mail efforts in the 2000 US election cycle was from Rick Lazio who was the highly fancied Republican candidate for Senator from New York. Lazio had strong support from popular and effective New York Mayor Rudolf Giuliani, and was opposing a Democratic contender who had never lived in New York, Hilary Clinton. Mrs Clinton was, of course, well connected within her party and America at large and had no trouble raising finances. Lazio realised that if he was to be an effective opponent he would have to raise a lot of money. He decided on a simple appeal to potential conservative backers that said *in toto:*

Dear Stephen (or whoever),
I'm Rick Lazio.
It won't take six pages to convince you to send me an urgently needed contribution for my United States senate campaign in New York.
It will only take six words:

I'm running against Hilary Rodham Clinton.

Sincerely

Rick Lazio

Lazio included a reply paid envelope and a card pitching for contributions from $25 to $1,000. On the card he also compared his small government conservatism with Clinton's radicalism and belief in a "vast right wing conspiracy". The mail out was to a list of known conservative contributors and helped raise more than $13 million. The short, sharp delivery certainly attracted attention and shows the value in honing down the campaign's argument to the very heart of the matter. In the final event, Lazio was narrowly defeated by Clinton but he had successfully established his credentials as an effective candidate.

Despite conventional wisdom on the importance of positive direct mail, in recent years there has been an upsurge of a different style of campaigning often called "attack mail" (Schlackman & Douglas 1995) or "glossy direct mail" (Barnes 1989). Rather than a formal letter, this style of direct mail contains a glossy pamphlet, dense with images and aiming for an emotional impact not unlike a television advertisement while much cheaper than a television ad to produce and distribute. Most effectively, this pamphlet is addressed directly to the voter, but its impact rests not in a personal relationship established by the codes of correspondence but by the visual-tactile experience of television.

A logical extension of attack mail is to post targeted swinging voters a carefully packaged video cassette (Faucheux 1994a). This gives the candidate the opportunity to directly address key issues straight to camera and at length, unmediated by journalists and newsroom agendas. The video can be topped and tailed with television ads that tie the candidate's pitch to the general campaign and add some excitement. Research shows that up to 40% of those who receive such a video will watch it, giving this strategy a higher hit rate than any other campaign activity (Tait 1994). The direct mail of video tapes is a relatively expensive project, but if the campaign has generated a list of undecided swinging voters then it can be a cost-effective way to give the campaign's message to just those people who need to see it.

Telemarketing

The success of direct mail has led consultants in the United States to consider the potential of an even more personal form of communication, the telephone. Commercial and charity organisations were already using the telephone to sell products and raise money when campaigners realised the potential of the medium. Using the telephone to sell a product or raise money in a systematic way, usually aided by a computer, is called telemarketing or phone-banking. Campaigns themselves were using the telephone to randomly poll the citizenry, so it was just a short leap to see the telephone's usefulness in fundraising and persuasion. Proponents of telemarketing point out that the telephone is truly interactive because it supplies what no broadcast medium can: a real time exchange of message and response that is fundamental to effective communication (Johnson 2001: 162–3).

The political possibilities for telemarketing include targeting campaign contributors, recruiting and supervising volunteers, taking polls, canvassing the electorate and, of particular interest here, persuading voters to support the candidate (Boim 1989). Integrated computer-telephone systems, similar to those used in qualitative polling, can improve the efficiency of the telemarketing process by having the next call ringing as the last is finished and screening out fax machines or disconnected or busy phones. These computer programs prompt the caller with scripts, record results and produce instant tabulations. They can also print out direct mail follow-up that reflects the candidate's positions on the voter's interests and preoccupations (Garber 1993).

There is a danger that those called may react adversely to what they perceive as an intrusion. The phone is seen as a somewhat more private medium than the mail. It is important that scripts for the callers are casual and conversationally based so the person called can become involved in the conversation. To be most effective, contact goes over stages, with repetitive contact to build towards the final goal. Asking too much straight up can alienate the targeted citizen (Johnson 2001: 162).

Telemarketing technology can also be used for push-polling, that is pseudo-polling directed at identified swinging voters to highlight opponent's negatives in the period immediately before an election. Most established pollsters reject this practice as unethical because it is based on a lie – while the caller says it's a poll, it is not. The problem is that push-polling is very similar to what pollsters already do when they are seeking to establish the strength of the electorate's negative perceptions of the opponent. This practice may backfire when the person called perceives the call as both intrusive and manipulative. While US pollsters defend the practice as "negative advocacy" (Ceresa 1995: 10) and consider it an expression of free speech where it uses only factual statements, it will continue to be poorly received where it is perceived as manipulative. However, using telemarketing techniques in the few days before the election usually means that complaints about the technique do not receive much press attention and there is not sufficient time for opponents to turn push-polling into an issue. Of course there is also the potential for telemarketing to deliver positive messages to swinging voters though not much has been written on the subject and its viability is untested.

New Technologies

Campaign deployment on the internet is a difficult and developing area. Of course the internet has some useful purposes for the campaign. Web pages are a good repository of policy detail that will be useful to both campaign workers and hardcore supporters. Email is also a good means to keep those groups up to date with latest developments, spread the message for the day and draw people together for meetings, rallies and work. But the main aim of internet work, like all other campaign work, is to convince the targeted audience. It is clear that just setting up a web site is useless: the target audience do not necessarily know it is there and even if they do know, they have very little reason to visit. Even if they visit, how will they be convinced? There is a propensity to build the web pages and wait for the target audience to find it, failing either to draw the target audience in to the campaign or even updating the pages so they have a sense of currency and excitement. As one critic said after the 1996 US elections: "More campaigns wasted more money on home pages than they should have" ("Lessons Learned" 1997).

   To make effective use of the internet requires the campaign to think through how citizens use it generally and how the campaign can draw in the target audience in particular. The campaign has to step beyond the broadcast paradigm to engage in "viral politics" (Painter and Wardle 2001). The campaign is the host which produces messages which are spread around to take on a life of their own but nevertheless infect other people to make them hosts and so the message moves on through networks of connection. This is heresy to traditional campaigns that keep a close control on the message, but to make use of new technologies campaigns have to do something counter-intuitive and harness the energy of strong supporters to convince the targeted audience, "they have to hand the rifle over to the deer." (Lytel 2002: 57) Thus the integration of web pages with email in a strategic fashion is the most effective campaign use of the internet. The aim is to use permission-based email strategies and pay-per-action advertising to spread awareness of the web page that in turn gathers email addresses of targeted citizens "to build lists of unprecedented scale and generate the kind of impact that so far the internet has not achieved." (Lytel 2002: 57)

The use of email to make people aware of the campaign's web page can be a dangerous affair. People generally have a negative attitude to spam, that is unsolicited emails, and any campaign that just purchased a list and started to spam addresses on that list would be taking the very real risk of alienating not only potential supporters but hardcore supporters as well. To generate a permission-based email list, the campaign should spread word of the existence of the web page through a three-part plan: spread the web page address through traditional media, spread it through personal networks and create a humourous email presentation that takes the reader to the web address. One great example of the political use of humour on the web is a spoof of George W. Bush and Dick Cheney as the "new Dukes of Hazard" at http://www.bushcartoon.com/index2.html. Note that Bill Clinton and Al Gore are also spoofed but that after the fun, the message is delivered subtlely. Once people get to the web site, besides having easy access to policies and interactive and humorous activities, they should also be able to leave their email address and some basic information about themselves, including zip or post code, whether they are undecided and what issues are important to them, so that the campaign can target the information sent out.

In 2001 the Blair campaign in the United Kingdom used these methods to send 2.5 million emails in the four-week election period at very little cost (McCarthy and Saxton 2001: 134). In the last days of the campaign period, the aim is to send messages not only to targeted individuals but also to all list members in targeted seats so they can spread the local reasons to support the campaign. The campaign might also consider the use of spin-off sites to appeal directly to young people or those with particular interests. Campaigns can also invite website visitors to send text messages from the site to their friends' phones. Where the receivers respond positively they can then get bulk text messages about key issues and to remind them to vote.

Direct contact offers one antidote to the concern that people are drifting away from an interest in politics. Where campaigns pursue direct contact imaginatively, deploying new technologies in user-friendly ways and responding to the messages citizens send back, then the campaign will keep the relationship between itself and the citizen alive. Direct contact methods keep developing and the campaign that can combine those methods effectively can ride them to success.

9
Organisation and Fundraising – Managing the Machine

Project Management

There is always the temptation among campaign strategists to relegate the organisational infrastructure of the campaign to the "boring detail" side of the campaign to be looked after by people not initiated into the mysteries of media manipulation. But keeping a close watch on the infrastructure is vital to ensure that the infrastructure is delivering resources to targeted demographics, paying the creditors on time and, most significantly, to see the opportunities to shift the resources to greatest effect.

The 2000 US presidential election was won in the state of Florida as we now know and it is most instructive to review what Karl Rove (George W Bush's chief campaign strategist) was saying in the week before the election: "It will be decided in the last precinct with the last ballot in the last hour of the last day. It's going to be a close, exciting election. We're looking great in Florida." (Rove 2000) The reason that Rove was so confident a week before the election was that he knew the details of the logistics that had been deployed in Florida: not only was the advertising and direct mail in place to convince likely supporters, but all possible steps had been taken to disenfranchise certain opponents in the black community. Using legislation that precludes former felons from voting, the Florida Government overseen by George Bush's brother, Jeb, had removed many non-felons from the electoral roll. As the government's own Commission on Civil Rights said: "This disenfranchisement of Florida voters fell most harshly on the shoulders of African Americans. Statewide, based on county-level statistical estimates, African American voters were nearly 10 times more likely than white voters to have their ballots rejected in the November 2000 election." (CCR 2001) Rove knew what all the polling in the world wound not reveal: a lot of Democrat supporters who thought they were going to vote for Al Gore, were going to be denied a ballot. Dubious as these practices may be, they point to the deep levels of planning and logistical management that are required to prevail in a campaign.

To achieve strategic effectiveness, the campaign requires a high degree of project management so there is no duplication of processes or diversion of energy to non-productive exercises. The organisational flow chart is useful in defining roles and setting timelines to ensure a coordinated approach to achieving goals. Computers play an important role in managing and tracking the target audience, personnel, finances and resources. Fundraising is a crucial campaign activity and should be coherent with the campaign message. Compliance reporting requirements now apply to most campaigns and great care must be taken to ensure that returns are accurate, transparent and in the appropriate form.

The effective campaign develops the external communication strategies discussed in previous chapters as the work of the campaign director, pollster, background researcher, media consultant, advertising agent, direct mail consultant and telemarketer. But the campaign also requires internal organisation strategies to implement those external strategies. Turning strategy into action requires organisation. The campaign can be a fast, perilous journey through an obstacle course in a minefield. Mistakes will be made and damage will be done. Some would argue that "campaign organization is a contradiction in terms (because) by their very nature, political campaigns defy traditional organizational rules." (Lebel 1999: 132)

The aim of organisation is to minimise the impact of the problems while maximising the impact of the campaign. To do this requires a high degree of project management: pre-planning, establishing objectives, tactical allocation of resources, delegation of roles and checking to ensure that objectives are being realised on-time and on-budget. Where objectives are not achieved or unforeseen events occur, the campaign has to engage in trouble-shooting to get the plan back on track.

These practices have their origins in Taylorism. Taylor was an American industrial engineer working around 1900. He believed that it was possible to organise industry in a much more rational and efficient way by eliminating movements and activities in the work process that were superfluous to the end result. In his book *Scientific Management*, Taylor worked out the optimum way of shovelling pig iron into furnaces by calculating the maximum amount in each shovel-load against the minimum number of motions a worker required to do the job. Taylor's ideas were first implemented on a large scale in the motor industry. Henry Ford applied Taylor's work to introduce the assembly line where the worker no longer wasted time walking around a static vehicle as he put together its different parts. Rather the worker was restricted to doing the same task over and over again in a fixed position as vehicle after vehicle passed him on the production line. This approach is called Fordism and its dehumanising features that are apparent in the industrial process can be fatal to service activities like campaign work (Murray 1990: 38–53). The antidote to the problems of dehumanisation is to provide participants with the information they need to be empowered in their jobs, which in turn ensures that they are capable of producing the best result for the campaign.

The aim of project management is to ensure that money and energy are expended most effectively and that all sectors of the campaign and all supporters are working cohesively towards the one end. In the hurly-burly of the campaign it is to easy for effort to be expended reinventing the wheel time after time. Two or more sectors of the campaign may be vying to achieve one goal while more important goals are left unattended. Even worse, one part of the campaign may set off in pursuit of particular objectives to the detriment of the rest of the campaign. These internal strategies are essentially the work of project management, which begins with background analysis to define the campaign's organisational strengths, weaknesses, opportunities and threats. The campaign also applies cost/benefits analysis to assess the efficiency of various alternatives and it then prioritises campaign activities to achieve the most beneficial result. The campaign then produces plans, estimates costs and labour (both paid and volunteer) and prepares detailed work schedules outlining commencement and conclusion dates for all tasks.

Useful in this planning process are tools like the flow chart which is a diagram that shows the step by step operation of the campaign. Also useful is the timeline which breaks down tasks and sets them out against the calendar. This is an appropriate opportunity to differentiate between the major campaign that operates across a nation, state or city and the local campaign which operates within limited geographical space. Every campaign is different with different objectives, personnel and resources. But planning the campaign is just half the job: close monitoring, careful tracking, regular reports, intensive audits and sympathetic but prompt management of change increase chances of success. One useful way to organise the campaign is in phases that are scheduled to build towards the goal. Thus the campaign can assess its success as it reaches milestones along its critical path and change the campaign plan where necessary.

To produce a high degree of coordination requires a high degree of discipline and to achieve discipline in a temporary, voluntary environment under close media scrutiny requires that everyone from key financiers to envelope stuffers must understand their role and its contribution to the goal. The campaign is not in the position to insist on discipline through fear. It must achieve discipline by communicating to campaign workers the knowledge they need to keep them committed to the cause and on track. The workers need to be able to ask questions and clarify not only the elements of their tasks but also how they can best do their job to the benefit of the campaign.

The remainder of this chapter discusses roles and techniques that have particular organisational application to campaigns: resource management, fundraising and legal compliance.

Resource Management

All campaigns need both physical and human resources. How those resources are expended will dictate the outcome of the campaign. Physical resources covers the gamut from a bumper sticker to a network of computers and includes office equipment, phones, stationery, placards, posters, signs, public address system, cars and trucks. It is easy to lose things in the rush of the campaign where things can be handed around without much material control. While the campaign should promote productive use of resources, it should also keep an inventory to ensure that significant items are insured and that their whereabouts is tracked at all times. Distribution of campaign materials should always be approached in a methodical fashion to make sure that the material gets to the most beneficial locations and to people who will make the most effective use of it. The production of distribution lists is a useful aid in arranging delivery and phoning to double-check that the materials have arrived promptly at the right spot. Testing the distribution system early maximises chances that it will be working efficiently at the height of the campaign.

Local Campaign Check List

- **Media** Regular releases to local newspapers (with photos). Letters to the Editor by candidate and supporters. Newspaper advertising.
- **Contacts with Local Organisations** Letters and visits to all schools' parent associations. Letters to community groups, clubs and societies.
- **Information Stalls** At shopping centres on Saturday mornings.
- **Visits to Nursing Homes** Contact management. Visits and letters to residents.
- **Coffee Mornings/Afternoons** In supporters' homes.
- **Door-Knocking** Advance work by volunteers, follow-up by candidate.
- **New Enrollees** Letters welcoming all new enrollees and offering assistance.
- **Contact with Unions/Employer Groups** Arrange to address workplaces.
- **VIP Visits** Co-ordinate series of visits by notable supporters to electorate venues and for fundraising activities. Advertise itineraries in local newspaper.
- **Activities with Supportive Locals** Utilise the contacts of previous campaigns.
- **Hotel/Clubs Visit** Friday /Saturday visits to local hotels and clubs to meet locals.
- **Local Businesses** Letters and visits to all businesses introducing candidate, offering assistance and seeking donations.
- **Telephone Canvassing** Supporters ring electors with set questions.
- **Direct Mailing** Mail to groups (teachers etc) and localities with targeted voters.

- **Intro Pamphlet** Prepare intro pamphlet. Delivered by supporters.
- **Posters** Candidate posters for information stalls, functions and yards.
- **How to Vote Card** Prepare and distribute card.
- **Postal Vote/Assisted Vote** Letters to all previous applicants offering assistance. Follow-up with visits to assist in completion.
- **Campaign Office** Establish shopfront as focus to centralise all activities.
- **Issue Pamphlet** Prepared regularly for use at the information stall etc.
- **Politics in the Park.** Monthly event in each area of the electorate. Letterbox homes near park. Provide family activities, clowns, sausage sizzle and speakers.
- **Community Issues Forums** Monthly event on a weeknight about specific issues e.g. education, women, health. Mail invitation to interested community groups.
- **Street Meetings** At strategic locations, from truck with loud speaker.
- **Candidate's Vehicle** Decorate candidate's vehicle to increase visibility.

Source: Phil Reeves and Peter Hogan, Mansfield 1998

In the last 30 years computers have remade political campaigns so they "power most of the political technologies in use... today."(Mills 1986: 200) Their ability to carry out many computations at high speed provides a valuable tool "to canvass, store and retrieve the interests of the electorate" (Bruce 1993: 17) and also to communicate quickly and effectively with individual citizens. The nature of computer mediated communication is truncated when compared to the physical interaction of democratic practice in ancient Greece, but any communication is more effective when it is an exchange and computers offer the opportunity for the campaign and the citizen to engage in a meaningful exchange even though that exchange is systematised and at several removes. Computers cannot replace the "human" elements in campaigning. Humans still need to do the thinking to produce the strategy that sets its direction. It is humans that provide and judge the performance on which credibility is assessed. It is the interaction of human ideas by which the campaign persuades the citizenry and the citizenry (through polling etc) persuades the campaign.

Nevertheless, the computer is a valuable tool to facilitate human interaction in mass society as it is used for many other jobs besides the standard business applications. They can have an impact in small campaigns (McGillicuddy & Robinson 1989: 165–172) and are an essential strategic tool in large campaigns (Jensen 1989: 173–190). Computers are the means to automate fundraising, control campaign finances, phone respondents for opinion polling then analyse the results, ensure the most effective bookings for advertising, organise volunteers, carry out research on opponents and their policies and even provide assistance in phoning key voters (Shannon 1994: 37–39) but "...the core application used during campaigns remains the database coupled with a robust mail-merge facility" (Bruce 1993: 17).

Selected Campaign Software

Campaign Management Software
http://www.electinc.com
Overview: allows you to contact voters, get them to the polls on Election Day. Uses common Windows conventions. Most operations require only a few clicks of the mouse.

Features: Look up Voters, Targeting, Walk/Phone/Worksheets, Mailing Labels, Voter Contact, Volunteer Management, Manage Sign Locations.

GOTV Campaign Optimizer
http://www.americangotv.com
Overview: a campaign management and financial reporting software focused on the management and reporting needs of either the individual candidate or the multi-campaign needs of campaign management firms. Windows compatible.
Features: Fully supports political fundraising, financial, and campaigning activities; prepares necessary Federal (FEC) and State reporting forms and is approved for electronic filing; Campaign Scheduler; generates reports, including Precinct Walk Sheets and Telephone Bank Call Sheets; campaign writing, mail merge and data analysis.

Keep In Touch® Campaign Solution
http://www.gnossos.com/webhelp/index.html
Overview: a comprehensive campaign management solution designed to assist in all areas of campaign activities.
Features: Comprehensive Fundraising Module with Donor Histories, Seamless Thank-you Letter Generation, Bank Account Management and Reconciliation, Receipts Tracking, Volunteer Management, maintains voters, donors, key supporters, volunteers, press contacts and vendors lists, 150 report formats; Disbursements Tracking, FEC and State Reporting.

Human resources covers not only key campaign staff (whose contracts and salaries are typically handled by the Office Manager) but also the party stalwarts and other volunteers attracted by a successful campaign. Some consultants question the cost efficiency of volunteers and argue that the campaign can get more done with paid workers. While there is some truth in these observations, perhaps it is better for the campaign to spend its money communicating the message via advertising and direct mail and employing a competent volunteer coordinator. The volunteer coordinator strives to keep building the volunteer base by organising productive, rewarding jobs that keep volunteers coming back and attract others to put their names forward. Volunteers are useful not only for staffing the office and information booths but also for the work they can do by directly persuading the targeted audience, enrolling them and getting out the vote via door-knocking, letter drops and phone canvassing. Even those documenting the growing professionalisation of political campaigns hope that elections do not become a spectator sport because "there is much that the citizen-volunteer can do to reclaim a voice in the conduct of the campaign" (Johnson 2001: ix).

The volunteer coordinator's job is to make the grassroots work for the campaign. They make a virtue of necessity as they cobble together and train whatever talent comes their way. The political campaign is different from most other forms of organisation: the campaign is temporary plus it is under intense media scrutiny. This is the environment in which the volunteer coordinator must put together a focused and supportive team capable of working together to implement complex projects. To achieve this difficult goal, to make temporary organisations effective, the volunteer coordinator in particular and the campaign generally needs to abide by two interconnected principles: "communication and accountability" (Lebel 1999: 132).

Effective coordination of the volunteer effort requires free flowing vertical and horizontal communication where people receive comprehensive training and then have the opportunity to clarify tasks and negotiate resources up and down the command chain and within groups. A culture of good communication is also the basis for a process of accountability resting on inquiries about progress from the coordinator, reports back about how resources have been expended and confirmation that tasks have been accomplished and independent validation that the task has been achieved. Volunteer coordinators seek to build a level of professionalism into their teams by instigating an environment where people feel comfortable communicating and know they will be held accountable for what they promise to do. The forms of direct contact (at the door, through the letterbox, via the phone, and on the internet) were discussed in chapter 8 but how these forms are turned into productive campaign activities by the volunteer coordinator is investigated below. In particular, enrolment drives and get out the vote (GOTV) exercises in election campaigns and the petition in community and public affairs campaigns are discussed.

Enrolment drives are an early election campaign use of volunteers and a good basis for testing and developing the volunteer apparatus. The aim is to enrol voters who are not on the electoral roll but who will vote for the campaign's candidate. Running an efficient enrolment drive requires strong organisation and disciplined use of time and energy. In marginal seats, this will give the candidate an edge. As with most campaign techniques, targeting is crucial: hold the enrolment drive in the areas where your strongest supporters reside, re-sort the electoral roll by address to see where the gaps are, hone in on new developments. Send out volunteers with a contact list of those on the roll in the area they are covering. Volunteers need training to present a prepared script that will quickly ascertain whether the citizen is a supporter or undecided. A few role plays will prepare volunteers for most eventualities and get them off to a good start. Send out volunteers in pairs to keep them motivated, secure and honest. Send experienced volunteers with the inexperienced. Enrolment work is hard, so show the volunteers how successful they have been by counting completed cards and keeping a chart on the wall to show their achievements. Explain how their efforts set in train follow-up work: letters to the new enrollees on issues significant to them. Keep good records, enter names and addresses onto the database and follow up those who were not at home.

Getting citizens onto the electoral roll is only the first step. In the actual campaign period, there is much work for volunteers in getting the campaign's persuasive messages to targeted citizens through various forms of direct contact. But as the election approaches, the volunteer effort turns to its third phase: getting out the vote. A strong GOTV effort rests on tracking and compiling the results from all voter contact programs so strong supporters are reminded to vote and assisted to polling places where necessary and undecided citizens are provided with persuasive materials and even the personal attention of the candidate. But not all votes are cast on election day. People who will be absent from the electorate on polling day or who are too infirm to get to the polling booth need special attention. The campaign must be ready to offer and support postal voting, the campaign must maintain an active presence at pre-polling stations and the campaign must assist infirm supporters to make use of mobile polling booths. The rules governing application for and collection of the various forms of absentee voting vary from contest to contest and it is crucial that the campaign utilises local knowledge to get the best result. The more people who are assisted by the campaign to exercise their vote, the better the candidate will do in this segment of the electorate that can become crucial in a close finish. A pamphlet drop will turn up people who need the campaign's assistance but lists from previous elections (ensuring that anyone who has died is deleted) and a close relationship with the managers of nursing homes will produce even better results. Timing is everything in this process and the campaign must be ready to mobilise to assist in the application for absentee votes as soon as it is legally possible, so as to beat opponents to them.

Sample Enrolment Door-Knock Script

Introduce yourself: "Good afternoon, Nancy Drew, Democrat candidate for this area has asked me to call to find out if there are any Democrat supporters at home."

If they don't respond positively: "Nancy asked me to offer you this pamphlet on home security. Her contact details are on the back. If she can help you in any way please contact her office." Mark them on the contact list as an opponent and move on.

If they respond positively: Either: "Our records indicate that no-one is enrolled at this address." Or: "I am just calling to make sure all Democrat supporters are on the roll."

Offer to check if they are on the roll and to complete the card for them. Remember this is only for likely Democrat voters. Make sure the card is signed and witnessed. Offer to submit the card for them.

If they can't fill the card in immediately arrange a time for it to be picked up: suggest it be left under the mat or in the letterbox.

Ask if there is anyone else in the house over 17 who is not on the roll and check if anyone needs a postal vote.

If no one is at home, note the address on the contact list for follow-up. Bring the contact list and cards back to the campaign office immediately.

The right to petition the government is one of the basic principles of representative democracy. It is a way the people can send a signal to authorities outside the electoral process. While petitions are often presented to the legislature without fanfare or effect, the petition can also be a powerful organising tool that galvanises support in the community and provides media opportunities to build public opinion in support of a cause. In twenty of the United States and in many other jurisdictions, it is petitions of citizens that initiate issue ballots or referenda. A well organised volunteer effort can gather together the signatures required to turn an idea into a political issue. The petition has become such an important political weapon in California and other western states that professional signature gathering has become another arm of the campaign industry and consultants were responsible for 90% of the successful petitions in the 1990s (Johnson 2001: 210). Nevertheless there are still opportunities for volunteer campaigns to use petitions as part of their strategy to raise issues and expand debate.

Fundraising and Finance

No matter how big or small the campaign, fundraising is a vital part. The fundraising plan should be written into the overall campaign plan at the outset and should be coherent with the campaign message. Concern about the malignant effect of election fundraising on the body politic is a common theme. The concern is that when parties and politicians are required to raise millions of dollars to run campaigns to get re-elected, then the government is effectively on sale. Bribery is institutionalised where businesses and lobby groups contribute to campaigns in order to ensure they have contacts with the successful politicians. Many corporations contribute to all sides in a campaign to ensure that they have access and influence no matter who wins. Attempts to limit the influence of large contributors have by and large failed. Limiting campaign expenditure to minimise the need for fundraising has been ruled as a breach of political rights in Canada (Hiebert 1998: 91) and as an unconstitutional infringement on free speech by the United States Supreme Court in *Buckley v. Valeo* (Johnson 2001: 196). Complex arrangements to limit large donations have merely led to even more complex schemes to skate around the law. The antidote to the influence of large financiers is to have a lot of small scale financiers and raising money from the broad population requires a systematic approach utilising the organisational capacity of the computer.

As we saw in chapter 8, direct mail was originally developed for fundraising purposes rather than persuasion. In the United States in the early 1960s, Richard Viguerie saw the potential of harnessing the power of computers to communicate directly with potential contributors (Mills 1986). Direct mail fundraising is now seen as "a political alchemy by which even obscure candidates can transform lists into gold" (Persinos 1994: 20–25). The mailing list is crucial to the success of this type of campaign and an industry has developed in managing and refining potential contributor lists for a range of issues and geographic locations (Shea 1996: 192–193; O'Shaughnessy 1990: 94–95). Sabato (1989: 92) details five sources of mailing lists in the context of fundraising: in-house list previously developed; outside contributor to a sympathetic organisation; compiled by campaign staff; commercially purchased; and universally available like the phone book. Direct mail provides a very powerful tool for fundraising in the United States where political action committees use it to raise large amounts of money and have broken the nexus between parties and candidates. Direct mail fundraising has become so prevalent that it is sometimes difficult to tell the difference between real special interest groups and "direct-mail mills" that are merely fronts for fundraising, much of which is eaten up by consultants' fees and remuneration for the director of the exercise (Serafini 1995: 1089).

Even with the best lists in the world, the campaign still needs to make a pitch to potential contributors that is in tune with their interests and beliefs in order to win their monetary support. The characteristics of particular lists give some assistance: there is no point in talking about youth issues with senior citizens and vice versa. The key triggers for eliciting financial support are affection, agreement and antipathy (Steen 1999). Some contributors will support a campaign because they have an emotional attachment to the candidate or spokesperson that arises either from the speaker's previous political stances or from their activities before entering politics. For example, Oliver North continues to be a successful fundraiser for himself and many other Republican candidates because of the emotions he inspired when he took responsibility for the Iran-Contragate scandals and diverted further inquiries away from president Ronald Reagan's role. Other supporters will give funds if they agree with the campaign's policies and goals or, and this is an equally powerful reason, if they strongly oppose the campaign's opponents. Deep-felt opposition to Hilary Clinton's personality and politics was the source of Rick Lazio's successful fundraising efforts in the 2000 New York Senate race.

The fundraising plan requires that key personnel be given responsibility for ensuring its timely execution. While the fundraiser manages operations, drawing on volunteers and professional assistance as required, those operations are closely scrutinised by both the treasurer and legal adviser to ensure that they comply with legal and financial reporting requirements. The treasurer might also chair a finance committee that not only plans and oversees the campaign budget but that also gathers together wealthy and well-connected supporters who can act as conduits to further potential contributors. Besides direct approaches to companies, organisations and individuals by mail and phone, the campaign also stages fundraising events where the price of admission becomes a de facto contribution (Feld 1989). Fundraising possibilities are limited only by the imagination and creativity of the fundraiser and can stretch from black-tie celebrity events to wine-tasting or spit roasts. It is important to think laterally when choosing fundraising targets and to look for supporters not only within the target audience but also beyond. Fundraisers are inured to knock-backs but unexpected returns can be very rewarding.

While established party machines have well-organised networks to solicit corporate, union and supporter donations, many also receive electoral funding from taxpayers in proportion to the number of votes each receives. With so much fundraising institutionalised, direct mail appeals, particularly to lists of likely supporters, offer emerging political groups a potential path to connect directly with their supporters.

Fundraising and Finance Plan Check List

Game Plan and Timeline
The Finance Committee
Budget and Cash Flow
The Fundraising Campaign
Within Target Audience
Outside Target Audience
Individual Appeals
Corporate Appeals (business and labour)
Major Fundraising Events
Minor Fundraising Events
The Direct Mail Pitch
Telemarketing
Institutional Support
Political Party Support
Political Action Committee Support
Reconcile Budget
Complete Compliance Reporting
Thanks to Supporters
List Preparation for Future

While fundraising is a vital part of the campaign process, close supervision by the campaign treasurer is required to ensure that funds raised are expended effectively so that the most is made of the money that comes to hand. Often the roles of fundraiser and treasurer are combined and responsibility for both aspects of the campaign is given to the one person. This can be counter-productive as these roles cover very different campaign activities and require different personality types. The fundraiser is ideally gregarious, with strong external networks and deeply committed to the campaign's goals. By contrast the treasurer is pedantic, penny-pinching, closely focused on the mechanics of the campaign and committed to getting value for money. In the rough and tumble rush of the campaign, decisions can be made to spend a lot of money quickly and having an eagle-eyed treasurer who can apply a reality check is a good way to ensure that the campaign's expenditure is actually the best value for money and in accord with the law. There is always a danger in election campaigns that the candidate will be so committed to their campaign that they will go into personal debt. The treasurer is on hand to remind the over-enthusiastic candidate of the problems that personal debt can stir up if they win and most particularly if they lose.

Compliance

Since the 1970s there has been increased scrutiny of not only election campaign funding but also the formal qualifications of the candidate. The legal adviser takes a close interest in the legislation outlining who can run in an election. In particular, the legal adviser checks that the candidate's electoral enrolment and citizenship are in order and that they are not excluded from running because of previous criminal offences. The legal adviser also fills out the nomination form, ensuring that the proposer and seconders are properly qualified and that the form is lodged in time.

Most jurisdictions now have campaign finance laws which require public disclosure of funds raised and spent, and restrictions on contributions and expenditures made to influence federal elections. In some areas, the quid pro quo for these limitations to political activity is the public financing of campaigns. Great care must be taken to ensure that disclosure returns are accurate, transparent, in the appropriate form and in accordance with the law. As was seen above, there are now computer programs available that systematise this process. Typically, legislation has stringent disclosure requirements for candidates, political parties and supporters (particularly political action committees or PACs in the United States). The legislation also sets limits on contributions by individuals, political parties and supporters and may preclude altogether donations from foreigners or government contractors.

Electoral law is usually overseen by an independent agency which is charged with enforcing the law, facilitating disclosure and (in some jurisdictions) administering a public funding program. In the United States, the Federal Election Commission (FEC) is the independent regulatory agency charged with administering and enforcing the federal campaign finance law with jurisdiction over campaigns for the US House, the US Senate, the Presidency and the Vice-Presidency. In Australia, the Australian Electoral Commission fills that role and in the United Kingdom, parties and candidates have had to report to the Electoral Commission only since 2000. All jurisdictions have different requirements and the treasurer and legal adviser have the joint responsibility to ensure close compliance with the legislation.

The legal adviser should also be on hand to ensure that all aspects of the campaign comply with laws, regulations and other rules. Sometimes fundraising events may involve an element of gambling and the legal adviser must be ready to provide effective counter-arguments within the campaign when gambling is not within the letter or spirit of the law or at least to ensure the campaign is distanced from any improper behaviour by enthusiastic supporters. Campaign advertising must comply not only with campaign law but also with laws governing broadcast, fair trade, defamation and contempt of representative institutions and the courts. Advertising must also meet the requirements of the broadcasters who now want to see research proving every claim made in every advertisement. Legal advisers also take a close interest in competing campaigns to ensure that each of them is complying with every law and regulation applicable because if other campaigns are not in full compliance then the campaign has the opportunity to make the public aware (as long as the campaign is in full compliance).

In conclusion, a campaign's strategy is only as good as its organisation. The campaign might be dominating the media battle but unless phones or booths are staffed at the appropriate times, unless the targeted citizens can convert their decisions into actions, then the campaign can fall over in the run to the straight. The energy put into planning is never wasted. If foreseen events come to pass then the campaign is ready. If foreseen events do not come to pass then the campaign is no worse off. If unforeseen events come to pass, as they always do, then they are quickly apparent, because they do not gel with expectations, and plans to hand can be quickly adapted to deal with the situation.

10
THE PERMANENT CAMPAIGN – LAYERS OF GOVERNMENT

Representative Governance

Representative government has now become the site of permanent campaigns, a form of governance designed to win the next election. While critics are concerned that elections change nothing, another reading suggests that elections are the central democratic moment when citizens exercise power to produce unexpected results. Once in government, the permanent campaign goes on using communication managers and press secretaries to work public opinion. The permanent campaign also crosses over into the public education campaigns which governments use to pursue valid policy objectives, though the line of propriety can be blurred when governments use such campaigns for electioneering purposes.

Sidney Blumenthal popularised the notion that the process of representative government has become a permanent campaign for electoral support. He argues that the technocracy of the "permanent campaign" is now not only the decisive determinant of electoral outcomes, but also "the political ideology of our age" (Blumenthal 1980: 7). Like Trotsky's notion of permanent revolution, the permanent campaign is "a process of continuing transformation", but where Trotsky argued that the ends justify the means, for the permanent campaign "the means are the ends" (Blumenthal 1980: 8–9). That is to say the permanent campaign integr... 's image and strategy into one seamless whole that becomes not just the road to government but, as Blumenthal (1980: 7) says: "truly a program of statecraft".

To many critics the rise of the permanent campaign leads inexorably to the dumbing down of democracy, the centrality of image and the ubiquitousness of spin. By and large, election campaign research has been pessimistic about the possibility for campaigns to provide relevant and timely information to the electorate. These critics are all essentially repeating the mantra of Melvyn Bloom (1973: 273–4): the new politics of public relations, technology and professional management removes the electorate from the politician and "runs the risk of alienation, apathy and indifference." The gap between political rhetoric and reality is widening, the argument continues, because the politician and his or her image are manipulated, blurred and different. This critique does point to the abiding problem for representative government – that the image-reliant mass media are an imperfect forum – but any mass democracy will have to accept that by its very nature there will be some distance between participants, and image is a vital tool in traversing that distance.

There is a growing awareness of the hyper-reality of political campaigning, that "the dominance of representation and the explosion of the media (means) it is difficult, if not impossible to distinguish between that which is "real" and that which is represented and mediated" (Parry-Giles & Parry-Giles 2002: 1). One might go further to suggest that in politics the real is always represented and that the represented takes on a reality of its own. As Blumenthal (1980: 5) says: "Image-making, no matter how manipulative, doesn't replace reality; it becomes part of it." The question is how well does the image represent reality? Politics has always been about image and the saving grace of democracy is that it allows debate and discussion about the images the leadership puts forward and whether those images mesh with reality or do not relate to it at all.

Volumes have been written about the problem of representation in art, linguistics and politics because representation is always seeking to do the impossible, to make the absent present. Of course, once the absent is present then it is no longer absent; if all citizens are in attendance then it is direct not representative democracy. Perhaps aesthetics have some solutions when it points out the temporary, unfinished nature of representation. Pitkin (1967: 66) notes that "Even when accurate rendering is the goal (of representation), the very standards of what counts as accurate rendering vary with time and place and school." Accuracy of depiction is not the key to representation in art, detail may obscure the essence of what is represented just as a few well-formed lines may represent deep and universal meaning. Pitkin (1967: 67) concludes that a successful representation allows "no false information" to be derived.

By applying Pitkin's principles to the political field, it can be appreciated that while what counts as effective representation varies over time and place, the decision on whether that representation is "true or false", effective or ineffective, in keeping with the wishes of those represented or not is made at a subsequent election. Of course election campaigns are complex products, mediated and constrained by almost all the forces of power in society. The choices offered to citizens appear to be quite limited. But disregarding, for a moment, the constructions of power overlaid on the electoral process by the media, by tradition and by the citizens' own deference, the formal parameters of the election mean that any citizen with the deposit has a right to stand and all voices have a right to be heard and so, theoretically, any citizen can play a role in the election campaign. Then, in the final moment, in the polling booth, there is a freedom for every citizen to vote according to their own conscience and desires. Together, and admittedly at a formal level, the election provides the opportunity to represent oneself as one wishes. While elections may be unsatisfactory means to determine the exact preferences of the collective citizenry at any particular moment, they nevertheless have a vital role in both theory and practice as the occasion when citizens participate in their own representation.

Australia, lacking both the protections of the US First Amendment and the bustling, brawling press of Fleet Street, has developed a whole of government approach to media management that is fundamentally changing the nexus between politics and the media. Over the past 20 years, governments from both sides of politics have been party to decreasing transparency and increasing involvement in the management of public expectations. The Hawke and Keating governments created the National Media Liaison Service (nicknamed the aNiMaLS) to monitor and interact with the media. Members of parliament had access to sophisticated computer databases to track each constituent. Whole electorates were phone-polled to ascertain voters' individual intentions. More recently, the Howard Government has systematised its relations with the public to circumvent the media where it can and to control the media otherwise.

John Howard likes to portray himself as a politician with an innate feel for the Australian people so that when he speaks his mind he is speaking for all Australians. This is true only because Howard has developed a comprehensive polling capability and immaculate media skills that allow him to play back what people are thinking with his own spin as they are thinking it. Thus he has been successful in "fusing his ideology onto the national psyche", as Bill Hayden puts it.

Howard honed his information-management skills through long years of trial and error. From his failure to grab the economic agenda as Malcolm Fraser's treasurer in the '70s, through the hokey "incentivation" and "white picket fence" campaigns that doomed his 1987 bid to be prime minister and the loss of agenda control that prompted the Peacock coup that retook the Liberal leadership to his long period in the wilderness in the early '90s, Howard learnt a lot about how the media works and how public opinion is formed.

He re-emerged in 1995 with the skilful non-campaign that neutered the Canberra press gallery and toppled Paul Keating. Liberal Party pollster Mark Textor ably assisted Howard by developing soft rhetoric on ideological objectives in industrial relations and the environment, skilfully playing the race card in a circumspect fashion and totally avoiding the tax issue by issuing the blanket "never, ever" formula on the Goods and Service Tax. Howard's successful 1996 election strategy was to give broad and bland headland speeches then avoid controversy and only release his policies in the last weeks of the campaign.

In government, Howard has built a ruthlessly efficient information-management machine. The University of Queensland's Ian Ward has asked: "Is Australia a PR state?" The answer is that it has become much more than that. From the gun-control campaign he ran after the Port Arthur massacre, Howard has closely managed the information flow to avoid difficult areas of the media and gone directly to the public, either through tame talkback hosts or via advertising and direct mail. This process has not been cheap. MPs' budgets for printing and mailouts have been increased. There's an army of ministerial advisers working behind the scenes to spike stories before they are written. Through the Government Communications Unit there is careful coordination of the whole Government's advertising budget that reached $100 million in the lead-up to the 2001 election, while funds are cut to NGOs that do not toe the Government line.

Howard's successes include convincing many Australian republicans to vote against the republic in the 1999 referendum and managing the introduction of the GST in 2000 by making debate irrelevant with a massive advertising spend to the strains of Joe Cocker's *Unchain My Heart*. The failure of image management during the waterfront dispute, allowing news photographers to get pictures of guards in balaclavas with dogs, convinced Howard that he should be even stricter in excluding the media from hot spots.

The 2001 federal election saw Howard at the peak of his information-management powers. The year had not started well: his party was behind in all opinion polls and Labor's Kim Beazley was beginning to outrank him as preferred prime minister. Then the Liberals lost the Western Australia state election and the conservatives were whitewashed in Queensland. Then, in the Ryan byelection, the Liberals lost a heartland seat. But Howard's middle name is Winston and he provided a Churchillian fight back. His first step was to look at the research, which revealed that education, health, unemployment, environment and family issues were the most important concerns of voters and Labor was seen to be the best party to handle each of these issues.

The only issues on which the Government maintained a lead were tax, economics, defence and immigration. Howard sought ways to use his lead on these issues to win back small-business and blue-collar voters. He commissioned a report from the Federal Liberal Party president, Shane Stone, which said that Howard was seen by the voters as "mean and tricky, out of touch and not listening". The report was leaked so that the Prime Minister could respond that he was addressing these issues and would mend his ways. Appealing directly to the male, working-class "battlers", the Prime Minister ordered cuts to taxes on beer and petrol. To lure back small business, he made the GST collection process simpler and less time-consuming.

But most significant were his moves on immigration and defence. In late August, the Government began taking a hard line against refugees, informing the Norwegian ship Tampa of refugees in distress and so obliging it to take them on board and then refusing the Tampa permission to land them on Australian territory. The Government immediately implemented a strict media-management regime as Howard directed relevant departments to refer all press inquiries direct to ministers' offices. These restrictions ensured the flow of information was limited to a handful of press advisers and only the bare details of the operation were made public.

The Government created an exclusion zone around the Tampa, enforced by the military, which prevented journalists talking to the refugees or photographers getting shots that may have humanised the refugees. And while the Tampa stand-off continued, the events of September 11 occurred and Australian troops were committed to the US "War against Terror" in Afghanistan. The "Pacific Solution" to the Tampa problem and the Children Overboard furphy all kept immigration on the front page and made the Labor Party irrelevant to the election.

Most disconcerting in Howard's command-and-control approach to information management is how national security and the military's chain of command are used as excuses to deny transparency. Since the Tampa was declared off limits, Australian journalists have covered US military activity in Iraq while being denied similar access to Australian combatants; Australian journalists were refused access to Howard's barbecue with George Bush for security reasons while US journalists were ushered right in. And draconian laws have been introduced that limit reporting about ASIO.

But over-manipulation of reality does come with costs: Howard's claims that we would "never ever" have a GST, that the children were thrown overboard and that we went to war over weapons of mass destruction are coming back to haunt him. When you promote your pronouncements as "barbecue stoppers" then they need to be so good that people are so busy discussing them that their steaks go cold. It would seem that Howard is now so concerned about his communications with the punters that even when he goes on talkback radio with its friendly hosts, with the options of a screening process for callers and a seven-second delay button, he does not actually take calls from the public but just sits there chatting with Alan Jones or whomever. What we see here is a government that is no longer comfortable talking to its constituents who are all spun out.

This is the danger of too much spin. There comes a time when it is too easy for your opponents to put out the spin that all your pronouncements are spin. There will never be a return to a time without spin because politics is always about spin, but as the public become more media-savvy, the observation of spin and criticism, not only of its techniques but also its contents, will become a media staple as journalists and citizens learn to create democracy from within the information flow.

There is no doubt that the campaign techniques discussed in previous chapters are currently used predominantly by large and powerful political parties or corporations in highly controlled ways that limit the quantity and quality of democratic debate and deliberation, particularly in the electoral process but also throughout the permanent campaign. However the use of these techniques by powerful forces makes them available for cooptation by citizens as they develop their own versions of these rhetorical practices, improve access to the channels of deliberation and increase the transparency of debate. Access to the political debate around election campaigns is, in the first instance, available through a variety of mundane techniques such as personal contact, street stalls, street advertising, pamphlets, community meetings, local newspapers, low-cost direct mail and other "grassroots" communications. In themselves, the communications and exchanges produced by these techniques can quickly disappear into the mass of material from the major parties, but their effectiveness may be maximised where they are interwoven into processes of coalition-building and "grassroots" networking and they are in the language and about the issues relevant to targeted citizens. Thus an awareness of campaign techniques provides all citizens with the opportunity to represent their interests and to insist on them being represented in the permanent campaign.

Elections and Democracy

Much of the critique of the permanent campaign rests on the concern that things are getting worse, that there is greater distance between citizen and politician and a growing sense of alienation. But there never was a golden age where politics was real, debate was rational and citizens were in charge. Politics has always been about image and manipulation and Athenian democracy, the American Revolution and the Paris Commune were all managed by elites. Aristotle was probably the first to point out that elections were predominantly aristocratic rather than democratic: the choice of the "best" candidate presupposes the rule of the elite (Finley 1973: 19). More recently, Pareto and Mosca have applied sociological analysis to argue that democratic elections are only a camouflage for elitist manipulation of power (Hyland 1995: 247–51). Michels (1959: 377–392) generalised these insights to formulate "the iron law of oligarchy" as was discussed in chapter 1.

There is the concern that this may be no more than a minimalist democracy that fails to be representative government because it is, in Schumpeter's (1976: 269) words: "that institutional arrangement for arriving at political decisions in which individuals acquire the power to decide by means of a competitive struggle for the people's vote." Democracy, under this construction, does not seek to represent the citizenry at all and has become "elective despotism" (Macaulay in Hirst 1988: 198). But universal suffrage gives the election a legitimacy as expression of the collective will. To those who would declare "society" or "the people" empty categories, the only effective response is to pose the question: then who is casting all those votes? Barry Hindess (1989: 6) would define society as a "spurious actor" because it has "no identifiable means of reaching and formulating decisions, let alone of acting on them." But where citizenship is available for all those resident in a society for more than one or two years, then elections are precisely such opportunities for society and the people to make and act on decisions.

The difference between democracy and all other forms of elite management is that democracy allows a critique of elites and actively encourages, or at least allows, those outside the elites to strive to produce change even if that only means a circulation of elites. Democratic elections are the moment the elites put their authority and existence on the line and because there is the chance of an upset, chance of a change of government, then the election is a moment when power is in the hands of the citizens and democracy is at work. An election is the one moment when the boot is on the other foot, when people have power over politicians. Politicians dread that moment and the fear of electoral backlash is always at the back of their minds. Some would argue that where the party system is not strong (eg the US Congress) then electoral considerations dominate the political process (Mayhew 1974).

As the moment of mass decision-making, the election provides the opportunity for direct participation and election campaigns have the potential to be open spaces where new and marginal ideas can be introduced and deployed against powerful, entrenched interests. While electoral politics may appear peripheral to the construction of the politics of everyday life, it actually plays a central role. There is a sense in which an election does not change anything – self-obsessed bureaucracies are still overseen by paid politicians. But there is also the sense in which an election changes everything – the ideas and language formations formalised or deflated by the rhetorical interchanges of the election campaign act on individual consciousness to produce a collective outcome expressed in the election results that themselves legitimise the changed realm of discourse. Elections are the glue of democracy. They are an unavoidably real, experiential bond between the people and the government. Despite the formal problems discussed above, the reality is that when people cast a vote they give a (grudging, perhaps) acceptance to the democratic system which, in turn, supplies the government with a working legitimacy.

Where anyone can put themselves forward for election and where there is no coercion in the polling booth, then there is the possibility for the people to exercise their will. Of course the individual's experience of elections is formed by the rules and rituals of citizenship and moulded and manipulated by politicians, parties and governments. The media's often simple reconstruction of complex facts has also been criticised for distancing the citizen from the election but Michael Alvarez (1995) argues that election campaigns are more informative than critics allow because those critics have not studied "the dynamic elements of campaigns" that lead readers and viewers through softer material to substantive coverage. Others criticise the attention-displacement model which holds that public attention on polls cuts back the amount of attention they have available for real issues. Against this model is the "catalytic model" which argues that polls generate the interest in a campaign which leads voters to the important issues. So US research indicates that knowledge about polls in August of an election year had a small but positive impact on knowledge about issues in November when elections are predominantly held (Meyer & Potter 1998). This study has been confirmed in other recent work which claims interest in the horse-race aspect of the election "increases voters' attention to other election messages, including issue information, which in turn leads to a better understanding of public policies" (Bleske & Zhao 1998: 13).

Strategy and Spin

One of the classic examples of spin occurred during the primary elections to choose the Democrat nominee for the 1984 US presidential elections (Matthews 1989). Front-runner Walter Mondale was under attack by a young challenger, Gary Hart, who was expected to do well on Super Tuesday when primary elections were to be held in nine states. Mondale's campaign realised that he would be lucky to win even his strongest state, Georgia. So while the campaign staff directed all their energies to winning Georgia, the campaign manager began ringing journalists to admit that the campaign had a problem and if Mondale lost Georgia, he would be out of the race. Then, while he had their attention because he was being so frank, he made the point that if Mondale won Georgia then he would still be on track for the White House.

There is a logical fallacy at the base of this: if A then B does not imply that if not A then not B or to put it in concrete terms if it is a duck then it flies does not mean that if it is not a duck then it does not fly because the non-duck may be a sparrow or an airline pilot. Luckily, not all journalists are familiar with the details of formal logic so no one pointed out that "if he loses Georgia he is out of the race" does not imply that "if he wins Georgia he is still in the race". So even though Mondale only won two of the nine states, one was Georgia and Mondale and his supporters were seen to be celebrating what they were successfully selling to the media as a comeback. Mondale went on to win the Democrat nomination only to be defeated by Ronald Reagan's superior positioning.

Gary Hart was also a candidate for the 1988 Democrat presidential nomination – he provides a salutary lesson on how not to spin an issue. When faced with allegations of sexual impropriety he shrugged them off by inviting reporters to "put a tail" on him. One reporter took up Hart's invitation and discovered him in a compromising situation on the good ship "Monkey Business". Hart's presidential campaign imploded because he forgot that spin has to have substance to work.

Beyond that, there is always the potential for free elections to produce upset results, particularly while the party system based on the simple left/right divide is in retreat and the number and volatility of swinging voters is increasing. Campaigns thus become more about the creative application of new technology and less about rallying traditional supporters. Democracy is reinvigorated where marginalised groups and aggrieved – or just interested – individuals can use the space afforded by elections to creatively construct their very own representations. To do that requires a capability to enter the meta-narrative of the campaign by deploying the rhetorical techniques and technologies from which it is built. While there are powerful interests constantly seeking to obscure and mystify these techniques and technologies, close examination reveals some trajectories of intervention available even to marginalised groups.

New Media Strategies

The permanent campaign abides in time but it is not permanently fixed to particular methods of organisation or channels of communication. In fact the permanent campaign is constantly seeking out new ways to connect with the citizenry. The rise of new social movements based on participative debate and new technologies that offer peer-to-peer connection is creating the potential where "[c]ommunication comes to be seen as flows among publics rather than as an exchange of discrete commodities" (Keane 1991: 162).

Virtual coalitions are one form of political organisation made possible by new forms of organisation and new forms of communication. Once political coalitions were deeply entrenched configurations where much interpersonal trust and commitment was invested; now virtual coalitions allow people to coalesce around particular issues and then, once the matter is resolved, to move on to new issues and new coalitions without rancour or a legacy of disruption. Virtual coalitions can be gathered by closely analysing the policy positions of key sectional groups and offering aid and comfort to those positions. Sometimes it is necessary for the campaign to do the research to convince those sectional groups that their supporters do in fact support the campaign's policies. Often the members of the campaign's virtual coalition make an interesting list of disparate and often conflicting groups but the members are never in coalition with each other, only with the campaign. This view of society as the sum of social groups contrasts with the alternative view, derived from public choice theory, of a society constituted by rational individuals (Jupp & Sawer 1994).

Celebritisation of politics is an on-going process as the line between serious, broadsheet journalism and tabloid entertainment blurs. In order to connect to the tabloid audience, the campaign must make-over its candidate or spokesperson in a familiar form. As a former actor, Ronald Reagan produced a seamless persona that was both politician and celebrity but it was Bill Clinton who showed the potential for a politician to create celebrity. When he played saxophone on *The Arsenio Hall Show* during his 1992 presidential campaign, he was taking the notion of the permanent campaign to its logical extension. Clinton's campaign sought to permeate the mass media. Here was a politician eschewing the main news channels, and the journalists who are paid to filter and form that information, in order to communicate directly to the citizenry through an entertainment oriented tonight show. Clinton did not even try to talk about policy but played the role of a celebrity and shared with the audience something about himself and his love of music.

Moral panics as a media effect were first isolated by Cohen as he sought to explain the media frenzy that greeted the now-seemingly innocent frolics of the Mods and Rockers at the British sea-side in the 1960s (1973). The media cast the young fashion victims as "folk devils" who were subjected to media outrage for just being there. The small amount of violence that actually occurred was beaten out of proportion by "the moral entrepreneurs" (Cohen 1973: 111–132) as they engaged in the "ideological exploitation of deviance" (Cohen 1973: 166). Forty years after the Mods and Rockers imbroglio, the moral panic has become a staple of the media mix and the potential is there for the campaign to employ the very same methods to pursue moral panics about the devils they judge to be real. There is plenty of scope for campaigns to introduce the topics that lend themselves to indignation by appropriate moral entrepreneurs who can be trusted to produce a moral panic in the campaign's interests.

Government Media Management

Modern governments seek to manage their interactions with the mass media. They strive to strategically communicate key messages to citizens in order to build a consensus of support for the government's policies that will ensure its re-election. Elections come and go but the real day-to-day, hand-to-hand combat in the permanent campaign is done by media managers, press secretaries and political "minders" who are members of a politician's or party's staff and who seek to promote their cause by the application of campaign techniques outside formal campaign timelines. Media managers use their own journalistic skills and their knowledge of media work practices to develop and place news stories for political advantage and electoral success. They are responsible for ensuring that the lines they produce are concocted to maximise their political impact and that those lines are communicated to all interested media. They put a lot of their energy into convincing opinion leaders of the validity of their position. As one "minder" remarked of his own move from journalist to media manager: "...the transition from poacher to gamekeeper was simple: you use the same weapons, you just point them the other way" (Atkins in Electoral and Administrative Review Commission 1992: 17).

The techniques of media management are covered in chapter 6 but a few points need to be made in the context of the media manager's responsibilities. To earn editorial coverage, media managers mould their material to the needs of busy political journalists who have to meet tight deadlines while being pushed by editors to produce more with less resources. Because journalists find themselves reacting to news with little time or support to fully understand it, the media manager seeks to assist journalists to comprehend, write and file stories and with the aim that their position is portrayed in as positive a light as possible. The media manager can make a major contribution to the quality of coverage the position they represent received by providing:

- Media releases that explain issues simply;
- Well-researched background material;
- Strong photo opportunities;
- Spokespeople for community groups with different (though generally supportive) viewpoints; and
- Opportunities to file stories by deadline via phone, broadband, cable, satellite etc.

To summarise the discussion in chapter 6, the media manager must establish a media contact system based on a media list of all relevant journalists, their deadlines, cell and mobile phone numbers, direct work numbers and even their home numbers. This list needs to be constantly updated and programmed into a computer that can quickly send media releases as facsimiles or email (depending on newsroom requirements). But pumping out media releases is pointless without personal contact to develop the close relations with key journalists and media executives that will allow the media manager to contribute to the setting of the media agenda and thus ensure positive coverage of their media events.

The permanent campaign is not without its problems for media managers, particularly where they are also part of the governing apparatus. For example, in the United States there is an increasing preponderance of presidential staff in presidential re-election campaigns. Dickinson and Dunn Tenpas (1997: 51) argue that this crossover effect is contributing to a higher incidence of staff turnover, as presidents juggle their advisers to respond to the diverging tasks of governing and campaigning. From the other direction, there is also a potential for trouble as ebullient and rambunctious campaign staff, who are naturally risk-takers, find themselves constrained by the protocols and etiquette of office as the adventures of Dick Morris (1997) reveal.

Public Education Campaigns

Besides the political media management discussed above, governments also manage the media via departmental public affairs officers, public servants employed by government departments to assist in the dissemination of information on government policy and operations. Departments use publicity techniques to:

- Inform the public about their rights and obligations;
- Acquaint the public with available benefits and services;
- Educate the public about departmental initiatives;
- Pursue departmental goals;
- Clarify and explain the impact of legislation;
- Foster debate; and
- Aid recruitment.

Publicity officers utilise a broad range of techniques to identify and communicate with a diversity of audiences. While their work involves some day-to-day media liaison, the publicity officer also seeks to communicate directly with the public by commissioning advertising, coordinating community events, ensuring a web presence and designing and distributing brochures and other information materials.

One important tool used by departmental publicity officers in pursuit of their departmental work is the public education or information campaign. Governments employ the same techniques used in election campaigning to make people aware of information that assists in attaining policy objectives and, in particular, to persuade people to socially beneficial and less life-threatening behaviour. These campaigns are growing more numerous and sophisticated but whether this is because "citizens have a desire to be informed about the actions of the government" (Klingemann & Rommele 2002: 1) or whether the campaigns are an effective way for governments to manage the population remains a moot point. There is clearly a significant cost benefit for governments in preventing health problems before those problems are out of the work force, on benefits and taking up space in hospital beds.

If You Drink & Drive, You're a Bloody Idiot

With a rising road toll, road safety stakeholders in the Australian state of Victoria (VicRoads, Victorian Police and the Traffic Accident Commission (TAC)) adopted an integrated approach to addressing the road trauma problem. The TAC launched a number of campaigns with drink-driving themes to support Police enforcement, especially random breath testing (RBT) using highly visible "booze buses". The TAC took an aggressive approach in confronting the key causes of the road toll: drink driving, excessive speed, poor concentration, fatigue and not wearing seatbelts (Cameron et al 1996). The advertising campaign used the following slogans to act as the 'brand names' of the campaign.

ISSUES	SLOGANS – brand names
Drink-Driving	If you drink and drive, you're a bloody idiot.
Speed	Don't fool yourself, speed kills.
Fatigue	Take a break, fatigue kills.
Concentration	It's in your hands, concentrate or kill.
Seatbelts	Belt up, or suffer the pain.

The first TAC campaign went to air and placed drink-driving firmly on the public agenda by graphically illustrating a potent deterrent – the fear of drink-drivers finding themselves responsible for the death or serious injury of another human being. The ad, called "Girlfriend", was set in hospital casualty ward where the parents of a maimed girl confront the boyfriend whose drunk-driving is to blame. The naturalistic style and emotional intensity achieved in the ad gave force to the slogan "If you drink, then drive, you're a bloody idiot" which rapidly became part of the national idiom.

The message was reinforced by a string of ads repeating the slogan including:

Joey – Drunk youth insists on driving, the car rolls, and kills his brother.

Country RBT – Driver gets fined; loses licence; will lose his job as a result.

Silent Night – Set to the Christmas carol Silent Night; horrific accidents intercut with scene of a friend trying to talk man out of driving home.

Other ads addressed particular themes:

Speed: Six O'Clock News – Young men set out on fishing trip. Shocked family recognises their mangled car on the television news.

Fatigue: Nightshift – Young couple sets off for the country after working late; the exhausted driver nods off, collides with a truck.

Concentration: Motherless Child – Two giggling young women miss a stop sign, have a collision; kill the mother of a baby heard crying in the back seat.
Seatbelts: What Hurts Most – A young man is blinded in a collision after taking off his seatbelt to reach for the street directory.

The combined effort by the road safety stakeholders has produced a dramatic result in Victoria. Road deaths have more than halved since 1989 dropping from around 17 to eight per 100,000 population – this also saved the Victorian community $2.9 billion (Cameron et al 1996).
Source: TAC web site http://www.tac.vic.gov.au/DOCS/b4.htm

After Lazarsfeld's (et al 1944) work on minimal effects theory of political campaigns there was scepticism about the usefulness of the information campaign. However, by the 1960s and early 1970s there were some successful campaigns against cancer and for energy conservation that led to a growing awareness of the effectiveness of the public education campaign (Mendelson 1973). Since that time, governments have run or sponsored information campaigns that have warned of the dangers of smoking, drinking alcohol, abusing other drugs and that have taught people how to recognise the early symptoms of and avoid skin cancer, breast cancer and venereal disease. Road safety campaigns, combined with prominent enforcement activities, have targeted drink-driving, speeding, seat-belt compliance and driver fatigue (see the case study above). Positive campaigns have encouraged people to stay active and eat a healthy diet.

The Australian AIDS awareness campaign was a great success that used a variety of techniques. On the one hand there was a TV advertising campaign that employed horror movie motifs (The Grim Reaper) to generate public discussion, awareness of safe sex methods and sympathy towards victims. On the other hand there were very specific harm minimisation tactics at the locales and in the sub-cultural media relevant to those who might engage in infectious activities. The breadth and intensity of the AIDS campaign has led to a significant drop in new infections and is regarded as world best practice.

Other government departments have used public information campaigns to send simple messages through a complex array of communication channels to confront sexism in the workplace, address bullying in schools, promote tourism and public transport and advocate compliance with plant and livestock quarantine. It has reached to the stage where every minister needs a public awareness campaign underway so people can see that they are active in their portfolio. There is the danger that departmental publicity activities may become focused on departmental image building and political persuasion rather than providing factual and balanced information. These issues become particularly pertinent as elections approach and they often require the use of bureaucratic skills to ensure that departmental budgets are not used for political purposes.

The campaigns have relied on the careful analysis of problems, the application of practical countermeasures in a integrated, programmatic fashion and the evaluation of those programs has resulted in effective and sound strategies. The first task of the public information campaign is to develop 'product' or 'brand' names that give the campaign message a strong presence in the media marketplace and that encourage targeted citizens to 'buy' that message. Such names need to be memorable, striking and short, summing up a particular theme or issue central to the campaign. In order to monitor public attitude to the themes and how that affects behaviour, market research is conducted regularly to monitor the effectiveness of campaigns. To encourage targeted citizens to change their behaviour, it is vital to adopt an approach that is both attention-grabbing and relevant. Market research indicates that the key to modifying behaviour is to portray its harsh consequences and leave targeted citizens thinking "this could happen to me".

The personal connection is everything in public education campaigns. Providing people with information is only half the work. The campaign has to also show how it relates to the targeted citizen's life. Paul and Redman's (1997) work on the effectiveness of pamphlet-based health campaigns confirms this point. They found that pamphlets were more successful in changing knowledge and attitudes than changing behaviour but they were more effective when used by doctors for patient education rather than distributed freely for general public education. Paul and Redman also found that the effect on targeted behaviour improved when the pamphlet was used along with another form of intervention. Similar findings emerged from evaluation of the TAC program discussed in the box above. Where RBT was conducted systematically by police cars operating alone and without significant publicity, there were less serious crashes. In similar conditions but with a medium level of publicity there was a statistically significant reduction in accidents. However, when both police cars and "booze buses" were deployed and high-level publicity accompanied the enforcement, there was an increase in serious crashes as people taking unfamiliar "back roads" had accidents. This led to police patrolling and making it known that they were patrolling back roads as part of their operations. (Cameron et al 1998)

Public information campaigns have also been successful in countering sudden infant death syndrome (SIDS). The effectiveness of these sorts of campaigns was tested in Tyrol, Austria, after the 1994 national intervention campaign which explained how to reduce risky behaviour (Kiechl-Kohlendorfer et al 2001). Researchers collected data on child care practices four to six weeks after birth for all infants born in Tyrol and evaluated new SIDS cases over a four year period. Risk behaviours such as maternal smoking during pregnancy, putting baby in a prone sleeping position and early cessation of breast feeding all declined. The incidence of SIDS decreased from 1.83 per thousand live births between 1984 and 1994 to 0.4 per thousand live births between 1994 and 1998. Kiechl-Kohlendorfer et al (2001) show the long-term efficacy and relative cost efficiency of health education intervention campaigns. One interesting finding in the research was that the social status of mothers of SIDS infants tended to be lower than that before the campaign. This suggests that health messages need to be explained in simple terms to ensure that it can be understood by people from the full range of socio-economic backgrounds. Messages also need to be in the full range of media consumed by the target audience.

An interesting example of a non-health public information campaign is offered by the program to re-introduce the bearded vulture (gypaetus barbatus) into the European Alps (Robin 2001). The vulture had been eradicated by farmers and shepherds because it was suspected of preying on domestic animals. There had been an earlier attempt to re-introduce the species using captured birds from Afghanistan and Russia but that had not sought public support and was thus unsuccessful. Another attempt at repopulation was then attempted using captive-bred bearded vultures. This attempt was accompanied by a long-term information campaign that sought to raise public awareness of the vulture's benign feeding habits: it is not a predator but rather a scavenger and bone-eater that feeds on animals that are already dead. The program drew on the expertise of researchers, museums and specialised journalists whose explanations were accorded a high degree of credence. As a consequence of the campaign, the bearded vulture is now generally accepted by the people of the Alps as it repopulates its traditional haunts.

There is a danger that what is ostensibly a public information campaign might be used for party political purposes. Particularly in the lead-up to an election, many governments are tempted to extol the virtues of their policies with slickly produced advertisements funded by the taxpayer. This kind of electioneering is often seen as an improper extension of the permanent campaign but it is a difficult activity to legislate against, even if governments were inclined to so legislate, because there is a danger that such legislation would outlaw campaigns that could save the lives of humans and vultures. Perhaps the strongest deterrent to such campaigning is a well-informed citizenry who can appreciate the electioneering aspects of these activities and an active opposition that can quickly turn such excesses to their advantage.

11
PUBLIC AFFAIRS –
LOBBYING AND ACTIVISM

Public Affairs

The term public affairs covers the pursuit of political goals without the primary objective being electoral success. Public affairs activity aims to achieve governance without becoming the government. Those engaged in public affairs proceed by lobbying (with direct appeals to politicians and government officials) or activism (which seeks to affect public opinion so that government is forced to respond) and often a combination of both. Interest groups from local environmental organisations to large corporations seek to influence the outcome of government decisions by engaging in public affairs so that the systematic development of sustained public affairs campaigns has now become a standard part of the control of governments. The growth in public affairs activities is altering the nature of representative government, making government less responsible to the citizenry as a whole and within its constituencies, and more beholden to the special interests who use strategic campaign donations, background research and media management to affect government policy.

Sociologist Anthony Giddens (1994) is concerned, like many others, with the declining effectiveness of representative government and thinks that to remake democracy it is necessary to move beyond the duopoly of left and right that has transfixed politics for two centuries now. At face value, present systems of representative democracy offer most citizens little more than the formal minimum for participation: every two to five years, the citizen gets one vote among millions. In a mass society, voting in the formal democratic

213

process can appear futile. The size of the citizenry dilutes the power of each vote. The complexity produced by so many opinions can barely be approached by the simple dichotomies offered by the two-party system. A protest vote might occasionally be used to strategic effect but generally one or other of the major parties mould themselves to appeal to the middle ground whose support they require to form a government. Thus the two big blocs in most democratic systems are constantly moving closer together, converging on policy and presentation to appeal to that middle ground but manufacturing shrill differences to produce the Tweedledum/Tweedledee effect, satirised by Lewis Carroll in *Through the Looking Glass*. There is a danger that this effect will in turn produce a cynical citizenry, alienated from political debate and convinced that they are unable to make a difference even if they do get involved.

While there is cynicism about the efficacy of representative politics, the remarkable thing is that people are not fleeing the political field altogether. Giddens (1994: 249) argues that in the "double dissolution of tradition and nature" as the old parties lose their relevance, there is the potential for a "utopian realism" which provides a creative way to deal with social change. He points out that when citizens gather together as interest groups and engage in public affairs without seeking election then they are producing "dialogic democratization" and creating new forms of social interchange that contribute to reconstructing the social connectedness at risk from a growing cynicism about politics (Giddens 1994: 111–112). For Giddens, democracy is not a gauge of the "general will", but rather a process of debate and deliberation where greater transparency of the operations of representative government creates greater effectiveness because "democratization combats power, seeking to turn it into negotiated relationships" (Giddens 1994: 132). He argues that his practical dialogic democracy is already evident in "the pure relationship" of personal life, self-help groups and social movements (Giddens 1994: 117–124).

These interest groups forming outside the traditional political parties are using strategic organisation and media management to realise their potential to intervene in the governmental process: "voter discontent is opening an opportunity for a new political force" (Persinos 1995: 20). These groups, described variously as interest groups, pressure groups, lobby groups or social movements use most of the campaign techniques discussed in previous chapters to engage in public affairs. These groups may be corporate or community-based, they may concentrate on a range of issues or a specific topic, they may seek to affect government by subtle means or by rowdy demonstration, but they all seek to intervene in the political process, without standing for election, to mould public opinion to force governments to act in particular ways. As interest groups become better organised, they are using the segmentation and differentiation in society to create "the changing market for representation and participation where the decline in the market share of parties may be as much a sign of vitality as depoliticisation" (Richardson 1995: 61).

The public affairs of interest groups have always been a part of politics – farmers, professions, churches and unions (or guilds) played a role in the political process even before democracy developed but they have become more politically influential in recent years as fewer citizens choose to involve themselves in the traditional political parties and instead work through groups with the specific goal of safeguarding the citizen's particular interests. The anti-Vietnam War moratoriums and student movements of the 1960s are often singled out as the beginning of this heightened form of interest group activity on the left. On the right, counter-movements emerged from conservative Christians, gun owners and proponents of liberal economic policies. As parties concentrate on the centre, old allegiances are breaking down and blue-collar conservatives and white-collar radicals are emerging who do not find a place in the traditional parties and express their opinions through interest groups. At the same time governments are expanding their influence and intervening in more aspects of life, so citizens have more about which they can complain. Interest groups are relatively easy to organise and through the media they can have an impact on government that would otherwise require years of involvement in the often boring and mundane logistics of political parties.

The term "public affairs" covers a range of activities. An effectively organised interest group can intervene in the political process to promote policy and produce effects not originally in the world views of the major parties. Other groups have much more diffuse goals and merely seek to extend the field of debate. Some interest groups are radical and use direct activities to seek to achieve their aims by protest and the circulation of their ideas through the mass media. Others might lobby politicians and bureaucrats or intervene in election campaigns by rating parties and politicians on their attitudes to the matters of interest to the group. They might even provide election campaign assistance. Yet other interest groups seek influence by indirect activities – encouraging people to write to or phone their MPs or by drawing up petitions that are presented to the government. They might also build alliances with like-minded groups to maximise their impact in the media and with the public. Most groups use a mixture of the approaches above. To win elections some parties seek to build a coalition of interest groups whose members will support a party because of its position on a matter of particular interest to that group. Democracy is reinvigorated where interest groups use the space afforded by the operations of representative institutions to construct their own representations and introduce these into the broad debate. The remainder of this chapter discusses the two main forms of public affairs: lobbying and activism.

Lobbying

As society becomes more complex, so does the work of government. Federal, state and local governments are constantly making decisions that affect peoples' lives so individuals and interest groups (from local environmental organisations to large corporations) seek to influence the outcome of government decisions by lobbying politicians and public servants. Only in the last decade of the twentieth century was there a growing academic interest in the work of the lobbyist in the United States (Mack 1997) and the United Kingdom (Jordan 1991, Moloney 1996). The term "lobbying" comes from the lobby just outside legislative chambers where citizens traditionally meet politicians. The systematic development of sustained lobbying campaigns utilised not only personal and institutional contacts but also media management techniques and coalition-building among supporters to now become a standard part of the democratic control of governments. The process of making law, from the development of policy to the final vote on the floor, is a competition among interest groups. As in most competitions, the legislative process has its winners and losers. Those with the best communication skills and techniques, those employing the most thoughtful strategy and tactics will have the most impact.

The traditional lobbyist was typically a retired "minder" or journalist, politician or public servant who could tap the "old boys' network" to have a word in the client's interest to the right person in the right place at the right time. The changing nature of government and the intensity of media scrutiny means that lobbyists now have to organise complex campaigns to advance their client's position. Today, lobbyists are more likely to be communications graduates who can utilise new information technologies to research and deliver decisive arguments in the appropriate forums at the right moment. This work requires a high degree of flexibility. A typical day might see the lobbyist selling stories to breakfast radio, appearing with a client before a government inquiry, commissioning research, lunching with prospective clients or contacts, drawing diverse materials into a submission to government, writing and coordinating a direct mail push and making introductions between clients and contacts over dinner.

While international firms like Hill & Knowlton and Burson Marsteller dominate the lobbying industry, there is still plenty of opportunity for small operations or individual practitioners to develop expertise and contacts in particular areas that give them a competitive advantage over the large organisations. Industries that depend on government financial support and regulation have become particularly adept at lobbying. The pharmaceutical industry is a good example: it requires government approval to introduce new drugs and also receives government financial support through subsidies that make their products generally affordable. Thus the pharmaceutical industry, and particular pharmaceutical corporations, can be observed lobbying vigourously to expedite the often lengthy approval processes for drugs with a ready market (such as Viagra) or to seek the inclusion of particular drugs on the list of government-subsidised pharmaceuticals.

Lobbying requires a constantly updated contact system that lists politicians, journalists and public servants relevant to client interests. The lobbyist must be able to monitor current events continually with particular attention to shifts in political factions and bureaucratic alignments that may impact on their clients' interests. They must also remain informed on the minutiae of government decision-making processes and the progress of policy initiatives, legislation and regulation through parties, governments, cabinet and parliament. Access to a comprehensive database of relevant historical material is also useful, as is the technology to turn all this raw data into useful and timely intelligence for the client.

Lobbyists begin by assessing the political position of the client and developing the strategy and infrastructure to achieve the client's goals. The lobbyist must have a clear understanding of the client's needs and objectives and be frank about what can be achieved. The goals of the lobbying effort are identified and agreed upon by lobbyist and client. To maximise the lobbying effort, each action builds on the last. Making contact with politicians and bureaucrats in the right order and context allows the lobbyist to refine the arguments put forward, integrating the reigning language and concepts to maximise comprehension and chances of success. The careful lobbyist never snubs a junior or middle-ranking bureaucrat because they most likely will be promoted and may be a help in the future. Choosing who to talk to – and when – requires close attention and switching attention from bureaucrats to politicians or vice versa can generate internal friction that is not helpful to the lobbyist's cause. An integrated approach is often best. Governments are never interested in hearing about problems unless there are politically saleable solutions attached. The lobbyist becomes adept at looking at the issue from the politician's or bureaucrat's point of view and prepares for all eventualities. Identify the problem and lay out all the solutions, even those opposed by the client. Chart the effects each solution has on clients and all other interests and prepare arguments against all unacceptable options and for the client's objectives while simultaneously explaining why it is in the government's interest to pursue the proposed course of action. The lobbyist is constantly searching for the win/win solution because that is much more palatable to all concerned than any alternative. While having primary goals and a number of ways to achieve them is important, it is also vital to have one or more fall-back positions.

Generally, the client wants to motivate the members of cabinet or legislators to introduce or amend legislation or exercise their regulatory or decision-making powers in some way. Access to members of the cabinet requires briefing papers, presentations and close liaison with the cabinet member's personal and departmental staff. Departmental staff often wield great power behind the scenes and the lobbyist develops a strong working relationship with them. The client's interests may be affected by minute drafting decisions in the legislative process. The placement of a comma might put them out of business. The lobbyist has the contacts among departmental staff to keep aware of developments and nudge the decision-making process, avoiding the traps of legislative procedure, towards the client's best interests.

On the legislative front, the lobbyist keeps in touch with committee and legislative staff who steer legislation through. Whether the client is supporting or opposing pending legislation or arranging for new legislation, the lobbyist will have to win the support of the committee with responsibility for the issue. Committee staff may help the lobbyist become familiar with committee members and their staffs, explain where committee members stand on the bill, give hints as to what actions would be helpful from grassroots supporters and what language will strengthen the client's chances. The lobbyist will make sure that a strong, clear message is getting through to supporters and waverers alike to maximise committee and chamber votes. It is crucial to know which committee and sub-committee members hold the power to influence the direction of the client's legislation. These legislators have a responsibility for this legislation and from among this group will come the supporters and potential sponsors of the legislation and, given the conduct of humans in small groups and their propensity to factionalise, the most implacable opponents of the legislation. Legislators not only accept being lobbied on an issue, they even welcome it because listening to the various sides of the argument from competing lobbyists assists them in clarifying the issue and saves much research which would otherwise be required to understand the issue.

The lobbying campaign requires the reverse of the strategy and tactics discussed previously in this book. Instead of a campaign based on a few people contacting a lot, to effectively lobby a lot of people must get their message through to a few. The lobbyist might arrange for each member of the sub-committee and full committee to be contacted by a number of constituents who support or oppose particular legislation. Letters and visits from constituents are the most effective forms of communications in attracting the legislators' attention and drawing their minds to the issue. To generate the volume of contacts needed to convince politicians that the issue is important to their own welfare often requires a coalition of a number of groups working together.

Ten Reasons to Lobby for Your Cause

1. You can make a difference. It takes one person to initiate change. Gerry Jensen was a single mother struggling without the help of a workable child support system. She put an ad in a local newspaper and brought together other moms who built the Association for Child Support Enforcement which has changed child support laws across the USA.

2. People working together can make a difference. Mothers Against Drunk-Driving convinced dozens of states to tighten their drunk-driving laws and the road toll dropped.

3. People can change laws. Women didn't even have the power of the vote when they started their struggle for suffrage. Our history is full of stories of people who changed the law and the way we live. Their successes include: child labour laws, public schools, clean air and water laws, social security.

4. Lobbying is a democratic tradition. The act of telling policymakers how to change our laws is at the very heart of our democratic system. It is the only alternative to tyranny or revolution. Lobbying keeps democracy evolving.

5. Lobbying helps find real solutions. Family service organisations working to place abused children into safe homes needed changes in the judicial system so kids did not have to wait for years for a secure place to grow up. Advocacy of innovative solutions can overcome the root-cause of a problem.

6. Lobbying is easy. Many of us think lobbying is some mysterious rite that takes years to master. It isn't. You can learn how to lobby— whom to call, when, what to say— in minutes. Lobbying is easier when many committed people work together.

7. Policymakers need your expertise. People see problems first-hand. They see what works and what doesn't. They can make problems real to policymakers. Personal stories are powerful tools for change. Policymakers can learn from your story.

8. Lobbying helps people. Everything that goes into a lobbying campaign—the research, the strategy planning, the phone calls and visits—will help fulfill your goal. You may not personally provide a direct service, but through your advocacy work, you enable many others to do so. Even failure can inspire others to take up the cause.

9. The views of locals are important. More decisions are being made at the local level than in the past. This change gives locals even more responsibility to tell local policymakers what is needed and what will work. As more decisions are being made locally, your lobbying can have an immediate, concrete impact on people in need.

10. Lobbying advances your cause and builds public trust. Lobbying gains public trust by increasing your organisation's visibility. You advance your cause if you show that you have the public interest at heart.

Charity Lobbying in the Public Interest, http://www.clpi.org/

While a single, large organisation may have the contacts, usually it needs a coalition to produce enough varied and influential contacts to achieve a major success on an issue. Though coalitions have the ability to gather legislative support, they nevertheless remain fragile. Coalition members will not agree about every issue and it is often difficult to keep the members focused on what they have in common. Then there is always the danger that some members of the coalition will seek to take it over despite the majority view. The lobbyist needs the people skills to steer everyone back to the main game in order to achieve what is achievable.

While an awareness of policy initiatives and the capability to intervene in the policy making process will remain key work for lobbyists, more and more lobbying campaigns have an activist aspect and are also about developing and utilising public opinion. Lobbyists may use media management including background briefings, media releases, media conferences, information kits, letters to the editor and less publicised activities such as sponsored third-parties and unsourced tip-offs to get their message across. Some lobbyists have been tripped up through their involvement in underhand activities that, besides being wrong, take the focus off the campaign's positive messages. If the message is not getting through in the editorial or free media then advertising, direct mail, petitions, brochures, posters, strategic use of the internet and physical demonstrations help develop targeted support for the client's position. The lobbyist seeks to turn public opinion into a political force by using grassroots networking to encourage supporters to communicate key messages directly to politicians and public servants in order that government appreciates the strength of public sentiment (Bonner et al 1999: 22–26). Lobbying is more an art than a science and the lobbyist develops a gut feeling for issues and an intuitive appreciation of the right moment to display aggression or steely resolve and the right moment to do a deal. Lobbyists are always assessing the alternatives in developing situations and are ready to be flexible in pursuit of the client's goals.

Areas of specialisation for lobbyists include trade, defence and environment. Their work entails not only presenting a client's views and promoting them in the media but also serving as a source of information for governments and keeping the client informed of often subtle developments that impact on their interests. Lobbyists have become the conduits between government and a diverse range of interests in society.

Activism

While lobbying concentrates on persuading politicians to a course of action, activism is much more concerned to draw citizens to its cause. While activists may lobby politicians and seek legislative change, they appreciate that politicians will not be pushed to make changes until there is a groundswell of popular support for that change. Activism concentrates on gathering and motivating citizens so that they gather and motivate others to produce the groundswell that makes any alternative to change look unfeasible. It is difficult to theorise activism because every activist has their own theory but suffice to say that activism, like lobbying, seeks to produce a political effect without becoming the government but, unlike lobbying, it is not concerned only with legislative and regulatory regimes but also with the social and particularly with producing thorough-going social change.

Saul Alinsky is an abiding role model for activists. For Alinsky, ideology was secondary to the strategy required to produce the desired outcome. His brand of community organising developed in the rough and tumble of Chicago street politics during the Great Depression. He was confronted with party political corruption and a strong Mafia organisation feeding off the poverty and powerlessness of citizens living around the stockyards. Alinsky drew together ideological and ethnic opponents, socialists and Catholics, Serbs and Croats etc, but most importantly the people themselves, to confront the need for social improvement in impoverished, run-down, inner-city slums. *Reveille for Radicals* (Alinsky 1969), argues that the poor could reclaim democracy through a program of realistic organisation that exercised their strength of numbers at the ballot box and through strikes, boycotts, demonstrations and talking to the media. He summed up his political philosophy: "I tell people the hell with charity, the only thing you'll get is what you're strong enough to get." *Rules for Radicals* (Alinsky 1971) explains the strategies that he developed over years of practice: if you've got plenty of support then flaunt it, if you haven't got much support then make a lot of noise so opponents think you have plenty of support and if you have no support then cause a stink and the support will find you.

Alinsky's Strategy and Tactics

1. Power is not only what you have but what the enemy thinks you have.

2. Never go outside the experience of your people. When an action is outside the experience of the people, the result is confusion, fear, and retreat.

3. Wherever possible go outside of the experience of the enemy. Here you want to cause confusion, fear, and retreat.

4. Make the enemy live up to their own book of rules. You can kill them with this, for they can no more obey their own rules than the Christian church can live up to Christianity.

5. Ridicule is man's most potent weapon. It is almost impossible to counterattack ridicule. Also it infuriates the opposition, who then react to your advantage.

6. A good tactic is one that your people enjoy. If your people are not having a ball doing it, there is something very wrong with the tactic.

7. A tactic that drags on too long becomes a drag. People can sustain militant interest in any issue for only a limited time, after which it becomes a ritualistic commitment...

8. Keep the pressure on, with different tactics and actions, and utilise all events of the period for your purpose.

9. The threat is usually more terrifying than the thing itself.

10. The major premise for tactics is the development of operations that will maintain a constant pressure upon the opposition.

11. If you push a negative hard and deep enough it will break through into its counterside; this is based on the principle that every positive has its negative.

12. The price of a successful attack is a constructive alternative. You cannot risk being trapped by the enemy in his sudden agreement with your demand and saying "You're right – we don't know what to do about this issue. Now you tell us."

13. Pick the target, freeze it, personalize it, and polarize it. Blame someone at the top of the organisation under attack and refuse to accept that anyone else is to blame. Soon others to blame will come to the frozen target's support.

Source: *Rules for Radicals* (Alinsky 1971, 126–140)

Emerging from the Vietnam moratorium in the 1960s were a raft of new social movements with a left-wing orientation. Many of these movements were based on newly defined identities dependent on gender, ethnicity, age, disability or community. Other groups gravitated around new issues that mainstream parties had trouble comprehending such as environment, animal welfare or urban development. The strategic use of the media by those groups has been instructive to activists from all parts of the political spectrum.

At the core of the social movements' media strategy is what Sean Scalmer identifies as the gimmick. The central role of the political gimmick in no way trivialises the work of these social movements. Rather, Scalmer (2002: 176) argues, gimmicks are "at the root of democratic advance, social movement mobilisation and theoretic renewal." The gimmick is any action, legal or illegal, that is so scandalous, outrageous, shocking, new or different that it draws the attention of the media. In the sixties, the gimmick could be as simple as a white person sitting in a seat reserved for a black person or visa versa. The gimmick could involve one person burning their draft card or ten thousand people holding hands around the Pentagon with the stated aim of levitating it off the ground. The point is, and this is where its theoretical significance lies, the gimmick seeks not only to draw the media's attention but also to create new perspectives for the audience. The aim of the activists is not to get on the evening news for their own gratification but to jolt the audience's world view so they come to new understandings. The social movements' interventions aimed to produce "an exhilarating chase across social space, as radical actors joyously opened up new issues" (Scalmer 2002: 80). Once the gimmick breaks into the public arena it sets new parameters against which moderates judge themselves, forcing them to shift their position towards that of the activists in order that they remain moderate.

While money is useful in achieving desired results, the innovative use of volunteers, technologies and most particularly media events can disrupt entrenched positions as the work of activists like Greenpeace and the anti-smoking lobby show. Green activists have been particularly successful using campaign techniques to pursue debates both within and far beyond the electoral context. Greens have long appreciated the importance of making their case clearly and succinctly in the media at local, national and international levels, both to build a grassroots organisation and to pursue their arguments among the citizenry generally. Typical of their systematic approach to contemporary campaign techniques is the practice common among Green groups around the world to themselves provide broadcast standard video and magazine standard photos of protests to mainstream media outlets who may not have assigned staff to cover the event. As Guy Barnett (1994: 9), a strident critic of the Greens, points out: they argue "with pictures and images rather than words and figures. They appeal to the hearts and to the emotion. Their determination, imagination and ruthlessness have enabled them to tap concerns held by a substantial number." This critique glosses over the rational argument at the heart of the environmentalist cause, it nevertheless captures the pro-active manner in which the Greens have utilised media opportunities to pursue a broad-ranging process of debate.

Media activism is not just a tool for radicals. The tobacco industry has long run an activist campaign against government plans to restrict the sale and advertising of cigarettes. They have used third party fronts to promote arguments in favour of free choice and supported genuine grassroots groups who have raised questions about the economic future of tobacco-growing regions (which is of particular political relevance where those regions are in marginal electorates). Those concerned with the health effects of cigarette smoking have effectively countered the work of the tobacco industry. Of particular interest here is the counter-activism organised by BUGAUP (Billboard Utilising Graffitists Against Unhealthy Promotions) which pursued a campaign of defacing outdoor cigarette advertising to turn it into anti-cigarette advertising. The continuing efforts of tobacco industry lobbyists is evident in the increased consumption of cigarettes among young people.

Since the 1960s, activists have been aware of the leverage they can extract from an issue in the media and this has led to a form of media activism that seeks not only to highlight an issue in the media but also to insist on the media as a public resource for the pursuit of democratic debate. Thus media activists not only use the media for advocacy but also monitor it for accuracy and fairness, promote media literacy, lobby for public access to the media and co-opt it for culture-jamming. Media activists play the difficult game of working with the media, arranging media conferences, running media events and engineering appearances on talk shows while at the same time challenging media power. Media activists are building on a general and widespread dissatisfaction with the mainstream media which is a corporate-controlled oligopoly that buys acquiescence from politicians, avoids serious concerns, gets things wrong and is arrogant in its lack of concern for the power it has. Activists create an alternative to mainstream media when they make their own media via public access TV or radio, on the internet and on the street. Any attempt to communicate will gather an audience and the persistent activist who is willing to learn will build that audience.

12
CAMPAIGNS AND THE GLOBAL–
BIRTH OF THE CITIZEN HACKER

Democracy and Global Society

What will democracy look like a hundred years from now? Will it still exist? Will it make sense? Will it be a religious incantation that barely disguises the fact that it is no longer real? Or will it be a vibrant idea, carried out in practice, in ways that ensure that government is for the people. If we start by looking back a hundred years, we can see that democracy has come a long way – women are involved now in ways they barely were a century ago, and you no longer need to be a rich guy to be involved, but it still does help.

Democracy has slowly seeped into other aspects of life and not just because we get a vote on who to eliminate from Big Brother. Student councils at schools, representation for consumers and customers on boards and tribunals and groups lobbying governments and companies with the expectation that their opinions will at least be taken seriously... all point to a growing demand for, and comfort with democracy among the people. People are communicating more one-on-one via the internet and text-messaging, lending their support to particular organizations on particular issues.

This is perhaps an indicator of the direction democracy could go. As nation-states become less relevant, new forums and new institutions will arise and where they allow for discussion and debate among people then they may point to a new path for democracy, which is also a very old path: people make the democracy, and one of the main jobs for democracy is to constantly remake itself to keep itself relevant to the world around it.

A hundred years from now, democracy will either be remade on a global scale or it will be dead. It will use the technology that we now use to communicate around the world for debate and discussion around the world or it will be irrelevant to the concentrations of power that are emerging and so to the actual lives of the people. Only we, in our own individual ways, can save democracy from itself by creating it anew.

As politics becomes globalised, there is an urgent need and a great opportunity for democracy to do what it has always had to do to survive – to change and develop in light of emerging practicalities. As national representative institutions decline in power and authority, it is crucial that global citizens take the debate to the centres of global power and to do that citizens must harness the campaign strategies and new technologies on which this phase of globalisation depends. Political campaigns have always been early and enthusiastic adopters of new technology. Future US presidents have a particular propensity to ride the technology wave. Abraham Lincoln used the newly built rail system to good effect in his first Senate race during the 1850s, William McKinley used the recently developed channels of mass advertising in the 1890s and Lyndon Baines Johnson used the helicopter in his first campaign for Congress in the 1940s. Early adoption of new technology has long been recognised as giving military campaigns an edge over their opponents and this is a lesson that political campaigns have learnt well (Pitney 2000: 128).

New technologies have already changed the nature of campaigning. Computers have been used since the 1960s for database management that allows candidates and groups to appeal directly to their supporters. Direct mail, telemarketing and the precise placement of advertising to reach the target audience are all made possible by the power of the computer. But the internet brings a whole new paradigm. It is the first major technological advance since the telephone that allows real reciprocity in a two-way flow of information. Jon Katz argues that with its multiplicity of "speakers" and "listeners" and its equality of viewpoint, the internet would appear to offer the opportunity for the increasingly freer flow of information and decidedly deeper levels of deliberation (1995: 154ff). Many point to the democratic possibilities inherent in the internet's ability to invite discussion and tabulate views which could become the means of achieving large scale participatory democracy (Abramson 1990; Jones 1995; Leslie 1993; Negroponte 1995; Williams & Pavlik 1994). Mark Taylor and Esa Saarinen (1994: T7) argue that the emerging information economy will so blur the flow of power that while the government presently communicates to a diffuse audience, technical adaptation will allow that same audience to define itself in great detail as it communicates with governments so "the 'leader' becomes the recording surface for the will of the people".

In the early years of the internet, some were cautious about overstating the likely influence it would have on politics, pointing to its use for "downward information dissemination" (Gibson & Ward 1998: 14) and that it was "more likely to reinforce the existing structure of American politics than to change it" (Margolis, Resnick & Tu 1997: 59). While many extol new media technology for its potential to improve the quality of democracy, its coercive potential is patent. Secrecy and surveillance, command and control, manipulation and instrumentalism are deeply inscribed in the hardware, software and integrated systems of contemporary information technology. This is reflected not only in the origins of the computer and the internet in the purposes of the military but also in the potential for close surveillance over the use of these and other emerging technologies. If the internet is on, people can see every key-stroke you make. If your cell or mobile phone is on, people can know where you are.

Then there are a number of difficult practical problems preventing the internet from being the open system required by a truly democratic global forum. First there is the question of the access to equipment required by the population of the globe and then there is the question of the literacy required to effectively participate via this equipment. But beyond the problems of the digital divide, there is the concern that the rapid commercialisation and regulation of the space means that it can never be a forum for rigourously free speech. Further, the potential for automated replies and surveillance raises the possibility that the internet may quickly become open to even more coercive and invasive manipulation than older forms of media. Interactivity between real people in real time offers some democratic possibilities, as can be seen on organising chat sites and in active email groups. However when interactivity is systematised, as it is on many web sites, then the user is forced down predetermined paths to results determined by the writer and any debate is perfunctory (Meikle 2002).

Further, new technologies provide corporations with the opportunity to restructure human experience of time and space, affecting both the extent of the public sphere available for democratic deliberation, and the formation and exercise of the human freedom required for effective operation in that sphere. The role of corporate interests in producing citizens cannot be underestimated. The commodification of the processes of personal development have been described by Jurgen Habermas (1987) as the colonisation of the life-world while others point out that people's most intimate conceptions of themselves "have been subject to skilled manipulation and construction in the interests of corporate efficiency and profit" (Carey 1995: 11). The flexibility required to operate in the post-industrial information economy seems to preclude traditional notions of ethics and freedom.

Perhaps critics are right to disavow the utopian promises of cyber-democracy which contends that the internet will become our democracy. However it is important to consider at the same time, the utopian cast of the globalising process and the new political formations that this process could call into being. Nevertheless, we should not underestimate the impact that the internet can have on existing democratic formations. As we saw in previous chapters, the emergence of viral campaigning begins to reveal the potential for the internet, not to replace real world politics but to augment it in ways that open up discussion and debate (Painter & Wardle 2001). The internet has not yet been decisive in an election the way television was in the 1960 US presidential election between John Kennedy and Richard Nixon.

Does democracy have a future in the global information economy? How do you do democracy in the global media flow? There is a danger that political campaigns might be used to close political debate if the "industrial" form of politics discussed in previous chapters obscures and limits citizens' deliberations. Global culture is not necessarily an unmitigated universal hegemonic force. When the increase in transnational information flows is combined with the declining role of the nation-state then the space is cleared for the emergence of the "world citizen... encouraged by normative influences to regard particularistic institutions as secondary" (Spybey 1996: 61–66). In order to be reproduced globally, media must interact with local cultures and in doing so "there is no guarantee that it will remain under the control of its originator nor that it will be reproduced exactly as created" (Spybey 1996: 114).

With the advent of the global information economy, it is incumbent on democratic theory to adapt and grow to serve the society so produced. While national representative institutions will continue to function into the foreseeable future and national campaigns will continue to be an important part of political life, their irrelevance will continue to grow as first economic control and then political power is ceded to global bodies. Now is the time for democratic theory to consider what kind of democracy might develop in a global society, what kind of democracy can counter the coercive effects of the global information economy. Some critics do not see much chance of improvement: "What electronic democracy offers is more of the same: more instantaneously mushrooming pressure groups, more fragmented politics, more corrupt public life" (Sardar 2000: 745). But recent work in media theory offers the opportunity to break from the model of the national citizen defined by the institutions of representative democracy and move to consideration of the cosmopolitan citizen of the media defined by participation in the dispersed networks of militant intervention through political campaigns.

A number of recent theorists have pointed out the need for new forms of citizenship. Ian Marsh goes even further, suggesting the "two-party" regime is incapable of dealing with the integration of complex interests as the political agenda is increasingly dominated by the pursuit of international economic competitiveness. This complexity, he argues "can be reconciled at a new substantive level only in a new participatory context." (Marsh 1995: 40) Peter Dahlgren (1991) points out the centrality of the media and its methods in moulding new forms of participation. He discerns four elements in the contemporary social configuration disrupting the representative model: crisis of the state, the new movements, audience segmentation and the available communication technologies. Doing politics under these constraints elicits "the contours of historically new conditions for the public sphere, a new nexus to set in contrast to the dominant one of the corporate state and its major media" (Dahlgren 1991: 14). McKenzie Wark (1992: 145) goes so far as to argue that emergent media forms invite subversion because "the speed of new communications vectors themselves produce feedback loops in the global information environment which can become so rapid and unpredictable that they breach the hegemonic forms of policy response and media management."

Citizens as Hackers

The concept of "citizens of the media" (Hartley 1996: 57–76) has its roots in Walter Benjamin's observation that mass media techniques of reproduction have a liberating potential because they permit "the reproduction to meet the beholder or listener in his own particular situation" (1992: 215). This insight presages a crucial shift from the "ritual" around issues of production and ownership to the "politics" of audience reception. Stuart Hall (1980) pointed to the power of the audience in the communication process when he analysed the differences between *encoding* and *decoding* media texts. He argued that the message intended by the producers may be read in a variety of ways by the audience: they might accept the preferred reading; negotiate their own reading by contesting the preferred message; or produce an oppositional reading by rejecting the preferred strategy.

Citizens appropriate media output for their own purposes, they subvert it and "read between the lines" to produce their own interpretations. This provides great opportunities for emerging political groups to piggyback on existing campaigns to legitimate and coordinate citizens' alternative readings. This is precisely what is happening when anti-World Trade Organisation groups cyber-squat at wto.org (not an official site) to direct visitors to arguments against the WTO. While for Marshall (1964) citizenship was the product of national history, the tendency towards a global information economy suggests the opportunity for a new account of citizenship as the product of global history. In this context, the globalising effects of the mass media give rise to the possibility of citizens of the global media, giving their own subversive readings to Hollywood and CNN and developing new forms of political campaigns around global events. While Hartley returns immense political power to the audience as "citizens of the media", it is not clear how they might exercise that power beyond changing the channel. He concludes

Popular Reality with the advice that "now the outcome is up to you" (Hartley 1996: 43).

The challenge that remains is to theorise the means to create greater deliberative participation in democracy generally and emerging global structures in particular. Citizens must have the potential to make their voice heard or it is not a democracy. There is potential for democratic use of the existing mass media: through the gaps provided by their commercial, competitive nature; by building public spheres for debate free from direct government or corporate intervention; and by playing to the audience's abilities to decode their own, subversive interpretation. Already the traditional media gatekeepers, the journalists, are engaged in jurisdictional demarcation disputes for control of political communication that is slipping not only to TV talk show and radio talkback hosts but also to citizens themselves via electronic town meetings and email campaigns (Dooley & Grosswiler 1997). Nevertheless, the questions that remain are: exactly how might "citizens of the media" create greater deliberative participation in existing representative institutions and emerging global environments and, given the development as the pre-eminent form of political organisation, how can citizens gain the necessary skills to mount strategic campaigns in the media in order to realise their democratic voice?

Answering these questions requires a return to classical accounts of citizenship to appreciate the significance of what Minson (1998: 20–21) describes as "certain mundane ethical abilities of a *disciplinary* and *rhetorical* character which are required of a responsible participant." In considering the nature of participatory abilities expected of a citizen, it is useful to recall Perry Anderson's (1974: 33) observation: "The precondition of later Greek 'democracy'... was a self-armed citizen infantry." Thus before democracy was a theoretical construct, it was an assertion of practical power by the hoplite citizenry. The political reforms that institutionalised the power of the *demos* into democracy flowed directly from the practical power of citizens to organise collectively and fight in their own interests, at first physically and then in participatory politics. In classical Athens there was the expectation that citizens would actively participate in the democracy. As Pericles puts it: "we do not say that a man who takes no interest in politics is a man who minds his own business; we say he has no business here at all" (Thucydides 1972: 147). Access to political forums was not granted to citizens; rather they created it. The challenge for global citizens is to create the global campaigns that will carry their voices into the global media forum.

In surveying the contemporary public sphere we find some of these classical characteristics of the citizen, to participate and speak, in the emerging notion of hacking. While often derided as a criminal activity, and some hackers do cross that line, the core ideas informing hacking are essentially militant media practice. Hackers were originally computer programmers with a desire to understand the intricacies of computing systems so that they could move freely through the machines and their networks to find obscure and hidden information. Hackers regard computer systems not as corporate property but as part of the common wealth and find nothing wrong in exploring systems to understand where power lies and to liberate information that should be common knowledge. They get so close to the machines that they have thought through them and surfed around their coercive contours to reveal their secret substance. In his seminal 1985 work *Hacker's Handbook,* Hugo Cornwall notes two other uses of 'hacker' besides computer criminal: "those involved in the recreational and educational sport of unauthorised entry into computers" and, more generally, the enthusiasts "who love working with the beasties for their own sake, as opposed to operating them in order to enrich a company (because this is) where the fun is... developing an understanding of a system and finally producing the skills and tools to defeat it"(Cornwall 1985: vii).

The word "hacking" has a number of meanings that reunite in the work of the hacker: it suggests both cutting through thick foliage and managing or coping with a difficult situation, often with an appropriate application of ingenuity or a creative practical joke. Hackers are descendants of phone phreakers who used anomalies in the phone system to make free calls. "It all started in the early '60s" on university and research computers where people created unofficial areas of memory to share information and play games. (Cornwall 1985: 2). Since the 1960s, hackers have adhered to The Hacker Ethic... a code that championed the free sharing of information and demanded that hackers never harm the data they found. Rather, hackers say, they are searching for the most elegant and concise programming solution, using simplicity and serendipity to cut through the complexity, a regard for the rules would only be a hindrance. They are anti-authoritarian, anti-bureaucratic, anti-centralisation and really believe that information wants to be free.

They are both opposed to and utilise both anonymity and security weaknesses in computers. They exist because of the perennial software crisis – that gap between expectation about and actual performance of any given computer program. We are all hackers when we seek ways around bugs, through back doors, using tricks and guesses and not quite understanding what we are doing until the program works the way we want it to work. Every time we get a bit of troublesome software to work we are taking risks, making magic, conjuring up memory and power and tinkering with inter-relations to subtly change the world. Hacking, says Sterling (1993: 53), "can signify the free-wheeling intellectual exploration of the highest and deepest potential of computer systems. Hacking can describe the determination to make access to computers as free and open as possible..." There is an attitude among hackers that "beauty can be found in computers... (and) the fine aesthetic in a perfect program can liberate the mind and spirit..." (Sterling 1993: 53). Hacking also came to mean anything either particularly clever or particularly whacky, with or without a computer, as long as the tweaking of a complex system was involved: "To members of the computer underground *hacking* still refers, in the first instance, to the imaginative and unorthodox use of any artefact."(Taylor 1999: xii)

Hackers are at work on the free speech frontier, "opposing the re-establishment of traditional (property) rights in the newly emerging information society… they oppose the commodification of information…" (Taylor 1999: 61) and spend a lot of time crunching program protection codes. Unlike the anti-technology aspects of the counter-culture, hackers don't demonise artefacts, they prefer to use them to their fullest advantage. The demonisation of hackers as is a form of fear of technology and our inability to control our own curiosity: Prometheus, Icarus, Frankenstein, Neuromancer, Bladerunner, Terminator (Taylor 1999: xiii). In refusing to be bound by the constraints of the expanding command and control communication channel and the rule of corporations, hackers created the space for a free exchange of ideas down to the level of data. In ways we barely understand yet, this is the zone from which a new wave of political campaigns will emerge.

Hacking takes a militant attitude to working in the media flow. It has developed beyond its "geek" origins to incorporate any approach to any media that seeks to use hidden potentialities and anomalies in that media to open interpretation and debate. Thus the work of "culture-jammers" in adapting billboards to carry anti-corporate messages is a kind of hack, just as is doing similar adaptation to a corporate web site. We may distinguish culture-jammers who work entirely in the media flow subverting and re-purposing software from "hactivists" who keep strong links to traditional street activism as well as working with both hardware and software as well.

The ethos of hacking is opening up to become a tool to create democracy within the realities of the information economy. Hacking sustains and extends the means of civic engagement within existing political structures and beyond. Hackers are imbued with the cynicism of the machine, refusing to accept the "official" story at face value, always digging and exploring to find their own truth beyond the standard explanation. Thinking like war machines, stepping around the surveillance, living behind the screen, the hackers find the space to ride decoded machine languages to free the information. In this, they share the passion, humour, temerity and self-sufficiency of the hoplites and they have thus created the ethos on which a new stage of democracy might be built. Himanen (2001) summarises hacker values: passionate and free work; the belief that individual imaginations can create great things together; and a commitment to existing ethical ideals, such as privacy and equality. Wark (2001) captures the sense of possibility hackers bring: "...in any process of knowledge where data can be gathered, where information can be extracted from it, and where in that information new possibilities for the world produced, there are hackers hacking the new out of the old."

Hacking New Campaigns

Within the globalising environment, the campaign is showing a high degree of resilience. The complex meta-narrative of the campaign is eminently adaptable to the many channels of communication offered by the globalisation process. Further, campaign workers already have many of the attributes and attitudes of hackers. They find themselves hacking through thick foliage of logistical detail and media frenzy and applying ingenuity as appropriate. More significantly, campaign workers have to develop a self-sufficiency to work collectively in an often distributed system. Campaign workers too have to think through the system, and indeed they spend a lot of time hacking computers to get them working and communicating, but campaign workers are also immersed in the political system which is usually a lot more complex and unpredictable than a computer.

Just as the "hacker" ethos that has developed from its geek confines to encompass any militant and creative intervention in the media flow, the realm of the campaign worker is expanding from the professional consultant to every citizen who participates in or actively responds to a political campaign. Thus arises the possibility of citizen-hackers utilising technology to create new deliberative forums and new techniques of grassroots political campaigning on any scale from local to global. When they get up off the couch and plug in, then "citizens of the media" transform their role beyond the passive reading of the public sphere to hack greater deliberative participation in democracy by increasing the democratic use of the mass media as a locus of debate. Just as citizenship in the classical model depended on a militant citizenry with the rhetorical skills and ethical attributes to make an impact in deliberative forums, the global citizen must acquire the campaign skills to intervene in, and hack, the "media game".

New technologies give hackers, campaign workers and citizens the tools to produce alternative spaces for discussion within cyberspace and thus open up its democratic potentialities. While new communications technologies are no panacea for the creation of universal democratic deliberation, they are already playing a part in extending the opportunities for democratic deliberation by 1) providing access to debates for a multitude of voices that could never be heard through existing mainstream broadcast media, 2) creating a greater quantity of available information that increases the level of transparency over political debate generally, and above all 3) allowing people the opportunity to fiddle, improvise or "kludge" their own communication solutions. In short, the internet blurs the distinction between hacker, campaigner and citizen and allows them all to create their own political spaces for campaigns.

Further, given the commodification of personal development addressed above, citizen-hackers also need to acquire the ethical attributes required to make responsible and effective use of campaign skills in order to transform currently existing representative institutions and to create new global associations by producing new deliberative and participatory practices. Once again classical sources offer useful insights. Aristotle's (1953) *Rhetoric* concerns the practical reason which binds ethics and politics together. For Aristotle, rhetoric concerns not only technical skills but also an ethical imperative to produce compelling arguments for virtue. Athenian citizenship and its mode of life have passed, but the impetus to integrate ethics and politics remains a significant force in contemporary moral and political philosophy. Recurring questions include: "how values can and ought to be embodied institutionally" and how theorists might "shift attention... from values to mechanisms for implementing them" (Goodin 1993: 158, 176).

As the national institutions of representative democracy wane in relevance, it is time for democratic theory to escape the tyranny of the institutions and to return to the people at the heart of the democratic project. Democracy is not a set of ideals informing a set of institutions, but rather a method by which people who make up institutions argue about ideals. Democratic institutions are only useful to the extent they are used by citizens, and to put democracy to use, global citizens require the ethical discipline to utilise their technical expertise to campaign and otherwise produce collective action through participation. Citizens surmount their passivity as citizen-audience by projecting themselves into the media as citizen-hackers. Just as a crucial part of citizenship in ancient Greece was to summon the courage to overcome "stage-fright" in order to speak in the Assembly, contemporary citizen-hackers need to draw on moral energy and discipline to hack their arguments into the media flow. The ethical responsibilities of the citizen of the media extend to intervening in the media not only to respond to the news but also to create and promote the campaign images required to make an impact.

While the Athenian citizen had the confidence and commitment to stand in the assembly to communicate a message to all interested parties, citizen-hackers define themselves with the same confidence and commitment to hack through all available gaps that come and go in the media monolith, creating their own niches in the public sphere and producing campaigns that put their arguments to a variety of audiences, through a variety of media, in a variety of genres and that develop and respond to counter-arguments, all over an extended time period. The power of the new forms of campaigning is perhaps best seen as it confronts the globalisation process itself.

Greens around the world have honed the art of the citizen-hack into a set of successful and ongoing campaigns. Greens have long appreciated the importance of coopting the media machine to make their case clearly and succinctly in order to build a grassroots organisation and to take their arguments to the wider community. Greenpeace has led in using media manipulation techniques against corporations (see http://cybercentre.greenpeace.org). Greens have built a number of campaigns on environmental issues and pursued them in a variety of media at local, national and international levels. Typical of their systematic approach to contemporary rhetorical technique is their practice of providing broadcast standard video of protests in remote locations to broadcast television outlets. In recent years Greens have made creative use of computer mediated communication technology "to publicise their campaigns, mobilise participation, co-ordinate actions and as a tactical tool in itself" (Pickerill 2001: 69).

Another useful example of citizen-hack that subverted corporations, the law and the media is the case of the "McLibel Two" discussed in chapter 6. There is also the use of the internet to distribute anti-publicity that calls corporations to account (http://www.flamingfords.info/). Similarly, while the considerable resources of the international community have been used to campaign for support of the General Agreement on Tariffs and Trade (GATT), opponents use the internet to coordinate the case against GATT (see, e.g., http://www.rtmark.com/ gatt.html). Opposition to the Bush administration's response to the terrorist attacks on September 11 2001 is finding the internet to be a useful tool for organising dissent in an environment where any attack on the government is portrayed as unpatriotic. People opposed to the war use free, disposable email addresses and do not identify themselves as they explore alternative viewpoints and debate relevant issues (Harmon 2001).

The Mexican Zapatista movement is another powerful citizen-hack that has ridden the media cycle, feeding it simple but eloquent images and coopting it to spin a local dissatisfaction into a global story played not only in the mainstream media but also with a life of its own on the internet (http://www.ezln.org/). Consider also Belgrade Radio Station B92 which used the internet in 1999 to thwart Milosovic's censorship (http://www.wired.com/news/culture/0,1284,19705,00.html) and the success of net-savvy artists at etoy.com in fending off a bid to take their domain name by heavy-duty online retailer, etoys.com.

The rise and rise of the cell-based Independent Media Center (IMC at http://www.indymedia.org) provides a particularly cogent example of the global potential for solutions that pit the technology of the global information economy against itself. The first stirrings of Indymedia occurred around the opposition to the World Trade Summit held in Seattle in 1999. Using an available open source, free-ware program that was a fore-runner of the now popular web-log, activists established a web site that allowed people to instantly upload stories and images. This produced a dynamic information exchange, with debate and discussion among the many disparate interests who used the Seattle meeting as an opportunity to highlight deficiencies of the emerging global economy. The site also spread that debate to many interested parties who were not in Seattle: "The IMC was an end run around the information gatekeepers, made possible by the technology of the Internet...During its coverage of the weeklong "Battle of Seattle", Indymedia.org received 1.5 million hits, and its audio and video clips were rebroadcast on community radio stations and cable public access channels." (Tarleton 2000: 55)

Since 1999, more than 100 local IMC Collectives have been created in more than 40 countries, utilising the inherent properties of the global information economy to create a durable and self-supporting network systematically linking local issues to a global perspective: "In addition to the local pages there is a 'Global' page which features news from other local web sites, displays of original material for the site, and links articles from the other local sites into a common feature story... All the pages, including Global, stand alone and link to each other." (Pike 2000)

While it is difficult to aggregate quantitative information about the large number of Indymedia sites, examination of the Internet server traffic reports of eight North American Indymedia websites from January to May 2003 by Opel and Templin (2005) reveals a significant increase in traffic at all of these websites from March 2003, the month when open hostilities broke out in Iraq, which suggests a connection between Indymedia and the mobilization against the war.

What the emerging global information infrastructure does offer is the chance for citizens to campaign in a myriad of ways, not just to affect traditional representative races but also to intervene as the continuing process of change in commerce, government and media occurs. Thus global citizens can harness the breaks and irregularities in power that such change produces and use new forms of media to foster democratic deliberation, at least until control is established over those new forms. The deliberative potential of the global media rests in the willingness and ability of people to claim global citizenship in order to pursue new debates designed to civilise national governments, international corporations and other forms of power that are not yet apparent.

The Persistence of Strategy

Only the wealthiest of citizens has the financial resources to intervene in democratic politics at the level of the entrenched parties. Money remains a key determinant of the impact of the campaign, but good organisation, innovative use of new technologies and skilful management of volunteers and other resources can cause upsets. It is important for all campaign workers to appreciate the potential to continually adapt campaign technologies and techniques for strategic use. Because, in the end, it is the strategic use of money and technology that decides outcomes and while the elements of strategy remain constant, they take new forms in the emerging global system. Campaigns require a creative approach to extend into this arena and as they manage their intervention in new channels of communication and the new ways they are used.

Compared to the rational choice offered by the measured campaign speech of yesteryear, democratic deliberation has become a diffuse and second-order exercise which typically occurs in a multitude of moments: watching TV in the living room, listening to the radio in the car, in the five seconds between opening a piece of direct mail and throwing it in the bin, in rushed conversations at the canteen and cafe and text messages on the way to the polling booth. This is the context for political campaign strategy today. The aim remains the same: to use these many channels to send the same message, variegated as necessary to appeal to particular audiences, developing as external events impact and the campaign rolls out, but nevertheless the same message.

The campaigner continues to look for strategic breaks. As the major parties strive to mould themselves to appeal to the middle ground whose support they require to form a government, they are increasingly ignoring their traditional supporters and moving closer together, converging on policy while remaining adversarial, mostly at the level of personality. One result is an alienated and cynical electorate who see themselves too far from political debate to make a difference, even if they were involved. Another, and converse, result is that "voter discontent is opening an opportunity for a new political force" (Persinos 1995: 20). A growing potential exists for campaigners to look to building alliances with traditional foes or, outside the mainstream, putting together coalitions strong on just one issue. Jeremy Richardson (1995: 61) points to "the changing market for representation and participation" and suggests that "the decline in the market share of parties may be as much a sign of vitality as depoliticisation."

Another strategic break is offered by the growing distance between citizens and their representatives. The distance between the professionalisation that typifies two-party, machine politics and the everyday life of the citizens is creating opportunities for the entry of different political viewpoints into representative politics. These opportunities may be pursued to maximum democratic effect by the creative utilisation of the media, both established and emerging, to expand existing occasions for debate and to establish new ones. Political campaigns can also feed off the cynism produced by the growing distance between citizen and representative by integrating their media interventions with effective grass roots organisation so that the campaign can take its arguments into the community and the everyday lives of citizens. The aim, as Bob Hodge and Gunther Kress (1988: 160–161) note in their analysis of Ken Livingstone's campaigns for Greater London Council, is "to deploy a variety of alternative modes of communication to create a strong alternative, oppositional community."

Campaign finance is another area that offers strategic purchase for campaigns. While all parties and most interest groups are seen as beholden to financial interests, campaigns that disavow big donations have an advantage but they have to work at a very grassroots level to make sure everyone knows about it. In fact, given the failure of previous campaign finance reforms to staunch the flow of big money into campaigns, it would appear that the only way to combat the influence of a few wealthy contributors is to foster the entrance of low-budget campaigns. To these ends, the citizen-hacker or campaign worker who uses the strategies and technologies of the campaign to open debate or makes those strategies and technologies available for more general use by the citizenry are subverting the big money campaigns and saving democracy from itself.

Democracy can never be an end in itself. At its best it is the means to a better, fairer and more humane life for the whole society. But society is not a constant and by the time discussion and debate has achieved even the smallest democratic reform, new problems have arisen and new challenges present themselves. To confront this task which will never be completed, there is only the meta-narrative, conceptualised as strategy, communicated through language and image and felt as emotion. To promote the arguments necessary for democracy in a mass society requires not only a systematic approach to reach fellow citizens, but also the creativity to continually produce the open forums where the arguments can be placed. To create greater deliberative participation in existing representative institutions and to recreate democracy by extending the possibilities for deliberative participation beyond representative institutions and onto the global stage, citizen-hackers seek to remake political campaign strategy as both a technical and ethical exercise based in subverting it to broader democratic purposes.

BIBLIOGRAPHY

Abramson, Jeffrey B., et al 1990, *The Electronic Commonwealth*, Basic, New York

Adams, Chris 1993, 'Good researchers are observers, not oracles', *Sydney Morning Herald*, 10 June, p. 36

Adams, Robert 1994, 'The Origin of Cities', *Scientific American*, Special Issue 5.1, pp. 12–16

Alexander, Jeanette 1994, 'Presentation makes all the difference', *Campaigns & Elections*, June, p. 54

Alinsky, Saul 1969, *Reveille for Radicals*, Vintage Books, New York
____ 1971, *Rules for Radicals: a practical primer for realistic radicals*, Vintage Books, New York

Alvarez, R. Michael 1995, 'The Dynamics of Issue Emphasis', Political Methodology Working Papers, <http://wizard.ucr.edu/polmeth/working_papers95/alvar95a.htm l> [27 November 2002]

Anderson, Perry 1974, *Passages from Antiquity to Feudalism*, New Left Books, London

Ansolabehere, S. and Iyengar, S. 1995, *Going Negative*, Free Press, New York

Arblaster, Anthony 1987, *Democracy*, Open University Press, Milton Keynes

Arieff, Irwin B. 1979, 'Computers and direct mail are being married on the hill to keep incumbents in office', *Congressional Quarterly Weekly Report*, vol. 37, pp. 1445–8

Aristotle 1940, *Art of Poetry*, Oxford University Press, London
____ 1946, *Politics*, Oxford University Press, London
____ 1953, *Ethics*, Penguin, Harmondsworth
____ 1991, *The Art of Rhetoric*, Penguin, Harmondsworth

Arnhart, Larry 1981, *Aristotle on Political Reasoning*, Northern Illinois University Press, De Kalb

Barbalet, J. M. 1988, *Citizenship: Rights, Struggle and Class Inequality*, Open University Press, Milton Keynes

Barber, Benjamin 1984, *Strong Democracy*, University of California Press, Berkeley

Barnes, James A. 1989, 'Campaign letter bombs', *National Journal*, vol. 21, pp. 2881

Barnett, Guy 1994, 'The Green Lobby's Strategy and Tactics: a Tasmanian Case Study', *Environmental Backgrounder*, no. 14

Barrett, Harold 1987, *The Sophists*, Chandler & Sharp, Novato

Bartels, Larry M. 1993, 'Messages received: the political impact of media exposure', *American Political Science Review*, June, pp. 267–285

Bayley, Edwin 1981, *Joe McCarthy and the Press*, Pantheon Books, New York

Beiler, David 1989, 'White Knights, Dark Horses: The Kentucky Governor's Race of 1987', in *Campaigns and Elections: A Reader*, ed. Larry Sabato, Scott Foresman, Glenview

Bell, Allan 1991, *The Language of News Media*, Blackwell, Oxford

Benjamin, Walter 1992, *Illuminations*, Fontana, London

Berelson, Bernard 1952–3, 'Democratic theory and public opinion', *Public Opinion Quarterly*, Spring/Winter, no. 16, p. 313

Berger, Peter 1973, *The Social Reality of Religion*, Penguin, Harmondsworth

Bergmann, K. and Wickert, W. 1999, 'Select aspects of communication in German election campaigns', in *Handbook of Political Marketing*, ed. Bruce Newman, Sage, Thousand Oaks

Bernstein, Carl 1992, 'Journalism and the growth of the idiot culture', *Guardian Weekly*, 14 June, p. 21

Bianchi, E., Righi, N. and Terzaghi, M. 1997, *The Doge's Palace in Venice*, Electa, Milan

Bindman, D., Ekserdjian, D., Palin, W. 2001, *Hogarth's Election Entertainment*, Sir John Soane's Museum, London

Birch, Anthony 1993, *The Concepts and Theories of Modern Democracy*, Routledge, London

Bleske, Glen L. and Xinshu Zhao 1998, 'Horse-Race Polls and Audience Issue Learning', *The Harvard International Journal of Press/Politics*, vol. 3, issue 4, Fall, pp. 13–34

Bloom, Melvyn 1973, *Public Relations and Presidential Campaigns*, Thomas Y. Crowell Company, New York

Blumenthal, Sidney 1980, *The Permanent Campaign*, Beacon Press, Boston

_____ 1992, 'The secret war for the White House' *Vanity Fair*, June, pp. 32–43

Bobbio, Norberto 1987, *The Future of Democracy*, Polity Press, Cambridge

Boim, David 1989, 'The telemarketing centre', in *Campaigns and Elections: A Reader*, ed. Larry Sabato, Scott, Foresman Glenview

Bolce, L., De Maio, G. and Muzzio, D. 1996, 'Dial in Democracy', *Political Science Quarterly*, Fall, No. 3, pp. 457–82

Bonner, J. et al 1999, 'Trends in grassroots lobbying', *Campaigns & Elections*, February, pp. 22–25

Boorstin, Daniel 1962, *The Image*, Atheneum, New York

Bourdieu, Pierre 1978, 'Public Opinion Does Not Exist', in *Communication and Class Struggle*, eds A. Mattelart and S. Siegelaub, IG/IMMRC, New York

Bowra, C. M. 1962, *Primitive Song*, Weidenfield and Nicholson, London

Bremmer, Jan 1993, 'Walking, standing and sitting in ancient Greek culture', in A Cultural History of Gesture, eds Jan Bremmer and Herman Roodenburg, Polity Press, Cambridge

Bremmer, Jan and Herman Roodenburg (eds) 1993, *A Cultural History of Gesture*, Polity Press, Cambridge

Brown, Lillian 1994, 'Looking good', *Campaigns & Elections*, June, pp. 40–42

Bruce, Linda 1993, 'PC (politically correct) vote gathering', *The Australian*, 9 February, p. 17

Burnet, John 1968, *Greek Philosophy*, MacMillan, London

Butler, David and Ranney, Austin (eds) 1992, *Electioneering – A Comparative Study of Continuity and Change*, Clarendon, Oxford

Calder, D. G. (ed.) 1983, *Sources and Analogues of Old English Poetry II*, DS Brewer, Cambridge

Cameron, M. et al 1996, 'Mass media publicity supporting police enforcement and its economic value', *Public Health Association of Australia Annual Conference*, <http://www.general.monash.edu.au/muarc/media/media.htm> [27 November 2002]

Cameron, M. et al 1998, 'Evaluation of the country random breath testing and publicity program in Victoria, 1993–1994', *Monash University Accident Research Centre*, Report no. 126

Campbell, Joseph 1991, *The power of myth*, Anchor Books, New York

Cappella, J. N. and Jamieson, K. H. 1997, *Spiral of cynicism: the press and the public good*, Oxford University Press, New York

Carey, Alex 1995, *Taking the Risk Out of Democracy*, University of New South Wales Press, Sydney

Castro, Fidel 1969, 'The duty of the revolutionary is to make revolution' in *Fidel Castro Speaks*, (eds) Martin Henner and James Petras, Grove Press, New York

Ceresa, Maria 1995, 'US pollster defends "negative advocacy"', *The Australian*, 9 May, p. 10

Chapman, R. J. K. and Wood, Michael 1984 *Australian Local Government – The Federal Dimension*, Allen & Unwin, Sydney

Clausewitz, Carl von 1968, *On War*, Routledge, London

Cohen, J. 1989 'Deliberation and democratic legitimacy' in *The Good Polity*, eds A. Hamlin and P. Pettit, Blackwell, Oxford

Cohen, Stanley 1973, *Folk Devils and Moral Panics*, Paladin, St Albans

Commission on Civil Rights 2001, *Voting Irregularities in Florida During the 2000 Presidential Election* at http://www.usccr.gov/pubs/vote2000/report/ch9.htm

Commune di Firenze 2000, *Cosimo's Court* Museo dei Raggazi, Firenze

Conrad, Roger 1994, 'Winning votes on the information superhighway', *Campaigns & Elections*, July, pp. 22ff

Corcoran, Paul E. 1979, *Political Language and Rhetoric*, University of Texas Press, Austin

Cornwall, H. 1985, *The hacker's handbook*, Century Communications, London

Crichton, Michael 1993, 'The mediasaurus: today's mass media is tomorrow's fossil fuel' *Wired*, September/October, pp. 56–59, <http://www.wired.com/wired/archive/1.04/mediasaurus_pr.htm l> [27 November 2002]

Crouse, Tim 1972, *The Boys on the Bus*, Random House, New York

Curry, Bill 1994, '1993 Election', *Australian and New Zealand Communication Association Conference*, University of Technology, Sydney, 13 July

Curtis, G. L. 1983, *Election Campaigning Japanese Style*, Kodansha, Tokyo

Curtis, Michael 1965, *The Great Political Theories, Volume 1*, Avon, New York

Dahl, R. A. 1984, *Modern Political Analysis,* 4th edition, Prentice-Hall, Englewood Cliffs

Dahlgren, Peter 1991, 'Introduction' in *Communication and Citizenship*, eds Peter Dahlgren and C. Sparks, Routledge, London

De Kerckhove, Derrick 1983, 'Classical rhetoric and communication theory', *Communication*, vol. 7, pp. 181–200'

Diamond, Edwin & Bates, Stephen 1984, *The Spot: The Rise of Political Advertising on TV*, The MIT Press, Cambridge

Diamond, Jared 1992, *The Rise and Fall of the Third Chimpanzee*, Vintage, London

Dickinson, Matthew J. and Dunn Tenpas, Kathryn 1997, 'Governing, Campaigning and Organizing the Presidency: An Electoral Connection, *Political Science Quarterly*, vol. 112 no. 1, Spring, pp. 51–67

Dilenschneider, Robert L. 1998, 'Spin Doctors Practice Public Relations Quackery', *Wall Street Journal*, 1 June, p. 18

Dinken, Robert J. 1989, *Campaigning in America – A History of Election Practices*, Greenwood Press, Connecticut

Diogenes Laertius 1972, *Lives of Eminent Philosophers*, Harvard University Press, Cambridge Mass

Doob, L. W. 1954, 'Goebbels' Principles of Propaganda' in *Public Opinion and Propaganda*, eds D. Katz et al, Holt, Reinhart & Winston, New York

Dooley, P. L. and Grosswiler, P. 1997, 'Turf Wars: Journalists, New Media and the Struggle for Control of Political News', *Harvard International Journal of Press/Politics*, no. 2, issue 3, Summer, pp. 31–51

Downs, Anthony 1957, *An Economic Theory of Democracy*, Harper, New York

Dryzek, John S. 1990, *Discursive Democracy*, Cambridge University Press, Cambridge

Duquin, Lorene Hanley 1989, 'Door-to-door campaigning', in *Campaigns and Elections: A Reader*, ed. Larry Sabato, Scott, Foresman Glenview

Electoral and Administrative Review Commission 1992 *Proceedings: Public Seminar on Review of Government Media and Information Services* EARC Brisbane 16 June

——— 1993, *Review of Government Media and Information Services*, EARC, Brisbane, 16 April

Eliot, T. S. 1957, *On Poetry and Poets*, Faber, London

Emery, Merrelyn 1987, 'The Dynamics of TV Marketing of Products and Concepts', *Media Information Australia*, November, no. 46, pp. 35–49

Evans, Fred 1987, *Managing the Media: proactive strategy for better business press relations*, Quorum, New York

Farrell, D. and Schmitt-Beck, R. 2002, *Do political campaigns matter?: campaign effects in elections and referendums*, Routledge, London

Faucheux, Ron 1993, 'Great Slogans', *Campaigns & Elections*, June, pp. 26ff

_____ 1994a, 'Versatile videos', *Campaigns & Elections*, August, pp. 34–36

_____ 1994b, 'Candidate Debate Checklist', *Campaigns & Elections*, September, pp. 42–44

_____ 1994c, 'Paper drive', *Campaigns & Elections*, October, pp. 48–49

Feld, Karen 1989, 'Special event fundraisers', in *Campaigns and Elections: A Reader*, ed. Larry Sabato, Scott, Foresman Glenview

Ferguson, John 1972, *Aristotle*, Twayne, New York

Fenwick, Ian et al 1985, 'Dealing with indecision – should we … or not', in *Political Marketing*, eds Bruce Newman and Jagdish Sheth, American Marketing Association, Chicago

Field, Mervin D. 'Political opinion polling in the United States of America', in *Political Opinion Polling*, ed. Robert M. Worcester, MacMillan, London

Finley, M. I. 1973, *Democracy Ancient and Modern*, Rutgers University Press, New Brunswick

Franzen, John 1994, 'Lights, camera, action!: Creating effective commercials for low budget campaigns', *Campaigns & Elections*, August, pp. 30–31

Freeman, Mara 1995, 'Word of Skill', *Parabola*, Spring, <http://www.celticspirit.org/wordofskill.htm> [27 November 2001]

Fukuyama, Francis 1992, *The End of History and the Last Man*, Avon, New York

Garber, Robert 1993, 'Computer-telephone integration', *Campaigns & Elections*, October/November, p. 58

Gawenda, M. 2005, 'Bill and (mostly) Hillary's excellent new adventures', *Sydney Morning Herald*, 11 June, p. 21

Gerbner, G., and Gross, L. 1976, 'Living with television: the violence profile', *Journal of Communications*, vol. 26, no. 2, pp. 173–199

Gibson, Rachel K. and Ward, Stephen J. 1998, 'U.K. Political Parties and the Internet: "Politics as Usual" in the New Media?', *The Harvard International Journal of Press/Politics*, vol. 3, issue 3, Summer, pp. 14–38

Giddens, Anthony 1994, *Beyond Left and Right*, Polity Press, Cambridge

Glover, Richard 1993, 'Blink and you'll miss it', *Sydney Morning Herald*, 7 August, p. 40

Goodin, Robert E. 1993, 'The Contribution of Political Science', in *A Companion to Contemporary Political Philosophy*, eds Robert E. Goodin and Philip Pettit, Blackwell, Oxford, pp. 158–183

Godwin, R. Kenneth and Mitchell, Robert Cameron 1984, 'The Implications of Direct Mail for Political Organizations', *Social Science Quarterly*, vol. 65, no. 3, pp. 829–839

Gosling, Adam 1996, 'Marketing Messages to the Masses', *IT Review*, February, pp. 20–29

Graf, Fritz 1993, 'Gestures and conventions: the gestures of Roman actors and orators' in *A Cultural History of Gesture*, in eds Jan Bremmer and Herman Roodenburg, Polity Press, Cambridge

Green, J. R. 1994, *Theatre in Ancient Greek Society*, Routledge, London

'Greer's New Ad: Plagiarism or clever campaign tactic?', 1991, *Campaigns & Elections,* September, pp. 4–6

Guber, Susan 1997, *How to Win Your First Election,* St Lucie Press, Boca Raton

Guevara Che 1969, 'Guerilla Warfare: a method' in *Venceremos,* ed. John Gerassi, Panther, London, pp. 384–388

Habermas, Jurgen 1987, *The Theory of Communicative Action II: Lifeworld and System,* Beacon, Boston

_____ 1989, *The Structural Transformation of the Public Sphere,* Polity Press, Cambridge

Hall, Stuart et al 1978, *Policing the Crisis,* MacMillan, London

Hall, Stuart 1980, 'Encoding and Decoding', in *Culture, Media, Language,* Hutchinson, London

Harmon, Amy 2001, 'Protestors Find Web to be a Powerful Tool', *New York Times,* 21 November <http://www.nytimes.com/2001/11/21/technology/21ANTI.html> [27 November 2002]

Harrison, Tubby 1980, 'Impact Polling: Feedback for a winning strategy', *Campaigns & Elections,* Spring, no. 1, p. 8

Hartley, John 1996, *Popular Reality,* Arnold, London

Held, David 1987, *Models of Democracy,* Stanford University Press, Stanford

Herbert, Christopher J. 1994, 'Listen up: a guide for the focus group observer', *Campaigns & Elections,* July, p. 42

Herm, Gerhard 1976, *The Celts,* Weidenfeld and Nicolson, London

Herman, Edward and Chomsky, Noam 1988, *Manufacturing Consent,* Pantheon, New York

Hess, J. M. 1968, 'Group Interviewing' in *New Science of Planning,* ed. R. L. King, American Marketing Association, Chicago

Hiebert, Janet L. 1998, 'Money and Elections: Can Citizens Participate on Fair Terms amidst Unrestricted Spending', *Canadian Journal of Political Science,* vol. 31, pp. 91–111

Higgins, Ean 1997, 'Big Mac Pays High Price for Win over Small Fries', *Weekend Australian,* 21 June, p. 17

Himanen, Pekka 2001, *The Hacker Ethic*, Random, New York
Hindess, Barry 1989, *Political Choice and Social Structure*, Edward
    Elgar, Aldershot
Hirst, Paul 1988, 'Representative democracy and its limits', *The
    Political Quarterly*, vol. 59, no. 2, pp. 190–205
____ 1994, *Associative Democracy*, Polity Press, Cambridge
Hodge, R. and Kress, G. 1988, *Social Semiotics*, Polity Press,
    Cambridge
Holbrook, Thomas 1996, *Do Campaigns Matter?*, Sage Publications,
    Thousand Oaks
Hoskin, Ned R. 1989, 'Treasure Maps', *Capital*, August
Hughes, K. 1977, *The Early Celtic Idea of History and the Modern
    Historian*, Cambridge University Press, Cambridge
Hyland, J. L. 1995, *Democratic Theory: The Philosophical
    Foundations*, Manchester University Press, Manchester
Jackson, K. H. (ed.) 1971, *A Celtic Miscellany*, Penguin, London
Jamieson, Kathleen Hall 1996, *Packaging the Presidency*, Third
    edition, Oxford University Press, New York
Jaynes, Julian 1977, *The Origin of Consciousness in the Breakdown of
    the Bicameral Mind*, Houghton Mifflin, Boston
Jensen, Dennis 1989, 'Computers, control and communication' in
    Campaigns and Elections: A Reader, ed. Larry Sabato, Scott,
    Foresman Glenview
Johnson, Dennis W. 2001, *No Place for Amateurs*, Routledge, New
    York
Johnson-Cartee, K. S. and Copeland, G. A. 1991, *Negative Political
    Advertising: coming of age*, N. J. L. Erlbaum Associates, Hillsdale
Jones, Stephen (ed.) 1995, *Cybersociety*, Sage Publications,
    Thousand Oaks
Jordan, G. (ed.) 1991, *The Commercial Lobbyists*, Aberdeen
    University Press, Aberdeen
Jupp, James and Sawer, Marian 1994, 'Building coalitions: The
    Australian Labor Party and the 1993 General Election',

Australian Journal of Political Science, vol. 29, Special Issue, pp. 10–27

Juan, Stephen 1992, 'The TV Brain', *Sydney Morning Herald*, 26 November, p. 14

Katz, Jon 1995, 'The Age of Paine', *Wired* 3.05, May, <http://www.wired.com./wired/archive/3.05/paine.html> [27 November 2002]

Kavanagh, Dennis 1995, *Election Campaigning: the New Marketing of Politics*, Blackwell, Oxford

____ 1996, 'New Campaign Communications: Consequences for British Political Parties', *The Harvard International Journal of Press/Politics*, vol. 1, issue 3, Summer, pp. 60–76

Keane, John 1991, *The Media and Democracy*, Polity Press, Cambridge

Kellems, Kevin Shaw 1994, 'Handling the press: 20 rules never to break', *Campaigns & Elections*, August, p. 34

Kenny, Christopher and McBurnett, Michael 1997, 'Up Close and Personal: Campaign Contact and Candidate Spending in U.S. House Elections', *Political Research Quarterly*, vol. 50, no. 1, March pp. 75–97

Kerbel, Matthew R. 1994, *Edited for Television: CNN, ABC and the 1992 Presidential Election*, Westview Press, Boulder

Kiechl-Kohlendorfer, U. et al 2001, 'Epidemiology of sudden infant death syndrome in the Tyrol before and after an intervention campaign', *Wiener Klinische Wochenschrift*, vol. 113 (1/2), pp. 27–32

Klingemann, H. and Rommele, A. 2002, *Public Information Campaigns and Opinion Research*, Sage Publications, London

Knight, Michael 1988, *Winning Against the Odds*, ALP, New South Wales

Kraus, S. 1999, 'Televised debates: marketing presidential campaigns', in *Handbook of Political Marketing*, ed. Bruce Newman, Sage, Thousand Oaks

Labiola, Michael 1993, 'Campaigning on cable', *Campaigns & Elections*, August, pp. 34–35

Lasswell, Harold 1927, *Propaganda Technique in the World War*, Kegan Paul, London

Lawson, Valerie 1993, "The Spin Doctors" *Financial Review-Weekend Magazine* 12 February, p. 1

Lazarsfeld, P., Berelson, B., and Gaudet, H. 1944, *The People's Choice*, Columbia University Press, New York

Lazarsfeld, P. and Merton, R. 1948, 'Communication, Taste and Social Action', in *The Communication of Ideas*, ed. L. Byron, Cooper Square, New York

Lebel, G. G. 1999, 'Managing Volunteers' in *Handbook of Political Marketing*, ed. Bruce Newman, Sage Publications, Thousand Oaks

Lees-Marshment, Jennifer 2001, *Political Marketing and British Political Parties*, Manchester University Press, Manchester

Leitch, Shirley 1992, 'The mass media election?' in *Communication Australia*, ed. G.W. Ticehurst, Griffin, Sydney

Leslie, Jaques 1993, 'The Cursor Cowboy', *Wired* 1.2, May/June, <http://www.wired.com/wired/archive/1.02/cursorcowboy.html> [27 November 2002]

'Lessons Learned', 1997, *Campaigns & Elections*, February, p. 17

Lippmann, Walter 1932, *Public Opinion*, Allen & Unwin, London

Locke, John 1966, *The Second Treatise on Government*, Basil Blackwell, Oxford

Lucaites, J. L. and Charland, M. 1989 'The legacy of Liberty: rhetoric, ideology and aesthetics in the postmodern condition', *Canadian Journal of Political and Social Theory*, vol. 13, no. 3, pp. 31–48

Luntz, Frank I. 1988, *Candidates, Consultants and Campaigns – The Style and Substance of American Electioneering*, Basil Blackwell, Oxford

Lynch, James 1992, *Education for Citizenship in a Multi-cultural Society,* Cassell, London

Lytel, D. 2002, 'The Wire next time; Rethinking the internet's place in politics', *Campaigns & Elections,* June, pp. 56–57

Maarek, Philippe J. 1995, *Political marketing and communication,* John Libbey, London

Machiavelli 1961, *The Prince,* Penguin, Harmondsworth

MacIntyre, Alasdair 1985, *After Virtue,* Duckworth, London

Mack, C. S. 1997, *Business, Politics and the Practice of Government Relations,* Quorum Books, Westport

Mackay, Hugh 1993 *Reinventing Australia,* Angus & Robertson, Sydney

MacNeil, Robert 1970, *The People Machine,* Eyre and Spottiswoode, London

Maddock, Kenneth 1974, *The Australian Aborigines,* Penguin, Ringwood

Maltese, John A. 1994, *Spin Control,* University of North Carolina Press, Chapel Hill

Margolis, Michael, Resnick, David and Chin-chang Tu 1997, 'Campaigning on the Internet', *The Harvard International Journal of Press/Politics,* vol. 2, issue 1, Winter, pp. 59–78

Marsh, Ian 1995, *Beyond the Two Party System,* Cambridge University Press, Melbourne

Marshall, T. H. 1964, *Class, Citizenship and Social Development,* University of Chicago Press, Chicago

Matthews, Christopher 1989, *Hardball,* Perennial Harper & Row, New York

Mauser, Gary A. 1983, *Political marketing: an approach to campaign strategy,* Praeger, New York

—— 1985, 'Positioning political candidates', in *Political Marketing,* eds Bruce Newman and Jagdish Sheth, American Marketing Association, Chicago

Mayer, William G. 1996, 'In Defence of Negative Campaigning', *Political Science Quarterly*, Fall, No. 3, pp. 437–55

Mayhew, D. 1974, *Congress: The Electoral Connection*, Yale University Press, New Haven

McAllister, Ian 1992, *Political Behaviour*, Longman, Melbourne
___ 2002, 'Calculating or capricious? The new politics of late deciding voters', in *Do political campaigns matter?*, eds D. Farrell and R. Schmitt-Beck, Routledge, London

McCarthy, K. and Saxton, A. 2001, 'Labour: the e-campaign is born', in *Viral Politics*, eds A. Painter and B. Wardle, Politicos, London

McCombs, M. and Shaw, D. 1972, 'The agenda setting function of the press', *Public Opinion Quarterly*, vol. 36, pp. 176–187

McGillicuddy, Allyn and Robinson, Vernon L. 1989, 'Running for mayor with a micro' in *Campaigns and Elections: A Reader*, ed. Larry Sabato, Scott, Foresman Glenview

McGinniss, Joe 1970, *Selling the President*, Andre Deutsch, London

McQuail, D. 1981, 'The influence and effects of mass media', in *Reader in Public Opinion and Mass Communication*, eds M. Janowitz and P. Hirsh, Free Press, London

Meadow, Robert G. and von Szeliski, Heidi 1993, '10 myths about political polling', *Campaigns & Elections*, August, p. 49

Media, Entertainment and Arts Alliance 1993, 'Journalist Code of Ethics', *Ethics Review Committee Issues Paper*, December

Meikle, G. 2002, *Future Active – Media Activism and the Internet Pluto*, Pluto Press, Sydney

Melder, Keith 1989, 'Creating Candidate Imagery', in *Campaigns & Elections: A Reader*, ed. Larry Sabato, Scott, Foresman Glenview

Mendelson, H. 1973, 'Some reasons why information campaigns can succeed', *Public Opinion Quarterly*, vol. 37, pp. 50–61

Merton, R. K., Fiske, M. and Kendall, P. L. 1990, *The Focussed Interview*, Free Press, New York

Meyer, Kuno 1970, 'Introduction to the Ancient Irish Poet' in *The Celts*, Chadwick, Nora, Penguin, Harmondsworth

Meyer, P. and Potter, D. 1998, 'Preelection Polls and Issue Knowledge in the 1996 U.S. Presidential Election', *The Harvard International Journal of Press/Politics*, vol. 3, issue 4, Fall, pp. 35–43

Michels, Robert 1959, *Political Parties*, Dover, New York

Mill, John Stuart 1991, *On Liberty and Other Essays*, Oxford University Press, Oxford

Miller, David 1993, 'Deliberative Democracy and Social Choice' in *Prospects for Democracy*, David Held, Polity Press, Cambridge

Mills, Stephen 1986, *The New Machine Men*, Penguin, Ringwood

Minson, Jeffrey 1998, 'Ascetics and the Demands Of Participation', *Political Theory Newsletter 9.1*, pp. 20–33

Mithen, Steven 1999, *The Prehistory of the Mind: The Cognitive Origins of Art, Religion and Science*, Thames & Hudson, London

Moloney, K. 1996, *Lobbyist for Hire*, Aldershot, Dartmouth

Montgomery, B. 1968, *A History of Warfare*, Collins, London

Moore, D. W. 1992, *The Super Pollsters*, Four Walls Eight Windows, New York

Morris, Dick 1997, *Behind the Oval Office: winning the presidency in the nineties*, Random House, New York

Muir, Edward 1999, 'The sources of civil society in Italy, *The Journal of Interdisciplinary History*, vol. 29, issue 3, Winter, pp. 379–380

Mouffe, Chantal (ed.) 1992, *Dimensions of Radical Democracy*, Verso, London

Murray, Robin 1990, 'Fordism and Post-Fordism' in *New Times*, eds S. Hall and M. Jaques, Lawrence & Wishart, London

Napolitan, Joe et al 1994, 'The political campaign industry', *Campaigns & Elections*, December/January, pp. 45–50

Negrine, Ralph and Papathanassopoulos, Stylianos 1996, 'The "Americanization" of Political Communication: A Critique', *The*

Harvard International Journal of Press/Politics, vol. 1, issue 2, Spring, pp. 45–62

Negroponte, Nicholas 1995, *Being Digital*, Knopf, New York

Newman, Bruce 1994 *The Marketing of the President: Political Marketing as Campaign Strategy*, Sage Publications, Thousand Oaks:

Newman, Bruce 1999, *Handbook of Political Marketing*, Sage Publications, Thousand Oaks

Newman, Bruce & Sheth, Jagdish 1985, 'A Model of Primary Voter Behaviour' in *Political Marketing*, eds Bruce Newman and Jagdish Sheth, American Marketing Association, Chicago

Nimmo, D. 1985, 'Image and voter's decision-making processes' in *Political Marketing*, eds Bruce Newman and Jagdish Sheth, American Marketing Association, Chicago

Nimmo, D. 1999, 'The Permanent Campaign' in *Handbook of Political Marketing*, ed. Bruce Newman, Sage, Thousand Oaks

Noelle-Neumann, E. 1974, 'Spiral of silence: a theory of public opinion', *Journal of Communication*, vol. 24, no. 2, pp. 43–51

Norris, Pippa 1999, *On message: communicating the campaign*, Sage Publications, London

_____ 2000, *A virtuous circle: political communications in postindustrial societies*, Cambridge University Press, Cambridge

Omura, Glenn S. and Talarzyk, Wayne 1985, 'Shaping public opinion', in *Political Marketing*, eds Bruce Newman and Jagdish Sheth, American Marketing Association, Chicago

Opel, A. and Templin , R. 2005, 'Is Anybody Reading This? Indymedia and Internet Traffic Reports', *Transformations*, http://transformations.cqu.edu.au/journal/ issue_10/article_08.shtml [7 August 2005]

Orwell, George 1970a, 'Propaganda and Demotic Speech' in *Collected Essays, Journalism and Letters*, vol. 3, Penguin, Harmondsworth

Orwell, George 1970b, 'Politics and the English Language' in *Collected Essays, Journalism and Letters*, vol. 4, Penguin, Harmondsworth

O'Shaughnessy, N. J. 1990, *The phenomenon of political marketing*, MacMillan, Houndmills

Paglia, Camille 1992, *Sex, Art and American Culture*, Vintage, New York

Painter, A. and Wardle, B. 2001, *Viral Politics*, Politicos, London

Parry-Giles, S. J. and Parry-Giles, T. 2002, *Constructing Clinton: Hyperreality and Presidential Image Making in Postmodern Politics*, Peter Lang, New York

Pateman, Carol 1970, *Participation and Democratic Theory*, Cambridge University Press, London

_____ 1985, *The Problem of Political Obligation*, Polity Press, Cambridge

Paul, C. L. and Redman, S. 1997, 'A review of the effectiveness of print material in changing health-related knowledge, attitudes and behaviour', *Health Promotion Journal of Australia*, vol. 7, pp. 91–99

Pepper, Simon and Adams, Nicholas 1986, *Firearms and Fortifications*, University of Chicago Press, Chicago

Perloff, R. M. 1999, 'Elite, Popular and Merchandised Politics' in *Handbook of Political Marketing*, ed. Bruce Newman, Sage, Thousand Oaks

Persinos, John, F. 1994, 'Pushing the envelope', *Campaigns & Elections*, June, p. 22

_____ 1995, 'Gotcha!', *Campaigns & Elections*, August, pp. 20–23

Pickerill, Jenny 2001, 'Strengthening Cohesion, Networking Cells: Environmental Activists On-Line', *Fibreculture Reader*, pp. 69–78

Pike, J.R. 2005, 'A Gang of Leftists with a Website', *Transformations*. 10.

http://transformations.cqu.edu.au/journal/issue_10/article_02.sh
tml [21 March 2005]

Pitkin, H. F. 1967, *The Concept of Representation*, University of
Chicago Press, Berkeley

Pitney, J. 2000, *The Art of Political Warfare*, University of
Oklahoma Press, Norman

Plato 1956, *Phaedrus*, Bobbs-Merrill, New York

_____ 1971, Gorgias, Penguin, Harmondsworth

_____ 1987, *Theaetetus*, Harvard University Press, Cambridge Mass

Plutarch 1965, *Makers of Rome,* Penguin, London

Popkin, S. 1991, *The Reasoning Voter: communication and persuasion
in presidential campaigns*, University of Chicago Press, Chicago

Powell, Di 1993, 'The Language of Television News', *ABC TV
News and Current Affairs*, Sydney

Pratkanis, A. R. and Aronson, E. 1992, *Age of propaganda: the
everyday use and abuse of persuasion*, W. H. Freeman, New York

Richards, Paul 2001, *How to Win an Election*, Politicos, London

Robin, Klaus 2001, 'The re-introduction of the bearded vulture in
the Alps: A success story', *Forest Snow and Landscape Research*,
vol. 76 (1–2), pp. 41–51

Root, Robert L. 1987, *The Rhetorics of Popular Culture – Advertising,
Advocacy and Entertainment*, Greenwood Press, New York

Rosenbaum, Martin 1997, *From Soapbox to Sundbite: Party Political
Campaigning in Britain since 1945*, MacMillan, London

Rove, Karl 2000, *CNN Late Edition*, 29 October

Rust, R. T., Bajaj, M. and Haley, G. 1985, 'Efficient and inefficient
media for political campaign advertising', in *Political Marketing*,
eds Bruce Newman and Jagdish Sheth, American Marketing
Association, Chicago

Sabato, Larry J. 1981 *The Rise of Political Consultants,* Basic Books,
New York

_____ 1989, *Campaigns and Elections: A Reader*, Scott, Foresman
Glenview

Sachs, Christopher 1993, 'Campaigns and Computers', *Campaigns & Elections*, September, p. 59

Sardar, Ziauddin 2000, 'Alt.civilizations.faq', in *The Cybercultures Reader*, eds D. Bell and B. Kennedy, Routledge, London

Sawyer, David 1984, quoted in *The Spot: The Rise of Political Advertising on TV*, eds Edwin Diamond and Stephen Bates, The MIT Press, Cambridge

Scalmer, S. 2002, *Dissent Events: Protest, The Media and the Political Climate in Australia*, University of New South Wales Press, Sydney

Scammell, M. 1995, *Designer Politics: How Elections are Won*, MacMillan, London

Schlackman, R. and Douglas, J. 1995, 'Attack Mail: The Silent Killer', *Campaigns & Elections*, July, p. 25

Schmidt, David D. 1989, 'How they whipped "whoops" in Washington State', in *Campaigns and Elections: A Reader*, ed. Larry Sabato, Scott, Foresman Glenview

Schnur, D. 1999, 'Greater than the sum of its parts: Coordinating the paid and earned media message' in *Handbook of Political Marketing*, ed. Bruce Newman, Sage Publications, Thousand Oaks

chrage, Michael et al 1994, 'Is advertising finally dead?', *Wired*, February, p. 73

Schumpeter, Joseph 1976, *Capitalism, Socialism and Democracy*, Allen & Unwin, London

Seccombe, Mike 1992, 'Poll vaulting', *Sydney Morning Herald*, 21 November, p. 41

Serafini, Marilyn Werber 1995, 'Senior Schism', *National Journal*, no. 27, 6 May, pp. 1089–1093

Shama, Avraham 1985, 'Political Marketing: A study of voter decision-making and candidate marketing strategy', in *Political Marketing*, eds Bruce Newman and Jagdish Sheth, American Marketing Association, Chicago

Shannon, Michael R. 1994, 'Campaign and computers', *Campaigns & Elections*, December/January, pp. 37–39

Shapiro, Robert D. 1993, 'Have camera, will travel', *Wired*, July/August, pp. 74–77

Shaw, C. 2001, 'Counsel and Consent in Fifteenth-Century Genoa', *The English Historical Review*, vol. 116, issue 468, August, pp. 834–62

Shea, Daniel M. 1996, *Campaign Craft – The Strategies, Tactics and Art of Political Campaign Management*, Praeger, Westport

Sirius, R. U. 1994, "The medium is the message and the message is voyeurism', *Wired*, February, p. 48

Solmsen, F. 1975, *Intellectual Experiments of the Greek Enlightenment*, Princeton University Press, Princeton

Spero, R. 1980, *The duping of the American voter: dishonesty and deception in presidential television advertising*, Lippincott and Crowell, New York

Spybey, Tony 1996, *Globalization and World Society*, Polity Press, Cambridge

Steen, J. A. 1999, 'Money Doesn't Grow on Trees: Fundraising in American political campaigns', in *Handbook of Political Marketing*, ed. Bruce Newman, Sage Publications, Thousand Oaks

Sterling, B. 1993, *The hacker crackdown: law and disorder on the electronic frontier*, Viking, London

Stevenson, Nick 1995, *Understanding Media Culture*, Sage, London

Stewart, Morgan 1993, 'Pump up the volume', Campaigns & Elections, October/November, pp. 22–26

_____ 1994, 'Damage control', *Campaigns & Elections*, March, pp. 24–29

Stone, I. F. 1988, *The Trial of Socrates*, Little Brown & Co., Boston

Street, John 1996, 'In Praise of Packaging?', *The Harvard International Journal of Press/Politics*, vol. 1, issue 2, Spring, pp. 126–133

Strunksy, Rose 1914, *Abraham Lincoln*, Methuen, London

Stockwell, S 2000, "From Bard to Spin Doctor: Continuities in Strategy and Style" *Text* vol 5, no. 2 October

Stuart, Ewen 1996, *PR! : A social history of spin*, Basic Books, New York

Sturluson, Snorri 1966, *King Harald's Saga*, Penguin, Harmondsworth

Sun Tzu, 1983, *The Art of War*, Delta, New York

Tacitus 1970, *The Agricola and the Germania*, Penguin, Harmondsworth

Taylor, Mark C. and Saarinen, Esa 1994, *Imagologies*, Routledge, London

Taylor, P. A. 1999, *Hackers: crime in the digital sublime*, Routledge, London

Tait, Paula 1994, 'Eight myths of video cassette campaigning', *Campaigns & Elections*, December/January, pp. 54–55

Tarleton, J.2000 'Protestors develop their own global Internet news service', *Nieman Reports.* 54(4): 53–5

Thomas, Julian and Meredyth, Denise 1996, 'Pluralising Civics', *Culture and Policy,* vol. 7, no. 2, pp. 5–16

Thompson, Hunter S. 1973, *Fear and Loathing on the Campaign Trail*, Popular Library, New York

Thucydides, 1972, *The Peloponnesian War*, Penguin, Harmondsworth

Thurber, J. and Nelson, C. J. 1995, *Campaigns and Elections American Style*, Westview Press, Boulder

Tiffen, Rodney 1989, *News and Power*, Allen & Unwin, Sydney

Tobe, Frank 1989, 'New techniques in computerised voter contact', in *Campaigns and Elections: A Reader*, ed. Larry Sabato, Scott, Foresman Glenview

Totaro, Paola 1995, 'Seven days that made the difference', *Sydney Morning Herald*, 27 March, p. 2

Tuchman, Barbara 1978, *Making News*, Free Press, New York

Verwey, Norma Ellen 1990, *Radio Call-ins and Covert Politics*, Avebury, Aldershot

Ward, Ian 1991, 'Making Television News – Journalists and politicians at work', *Media Information Australia*, August, no. 61, pp. 54–62

_____ 1992, 'Colour-conscious ALP won mailbox battle: researcher', *University (of Queensland) News*, 28 October, p. 4

_____ 1995, *Politics of the Media*, MacMillan, South Melbourne

Ward, Ian and Cook, Ian 1992, 'Televised Political Advertising, Media Freedom and Democracy', *Social Alternatives*, vol. 11, no. 1, pp. 21–22

Wark, McKenzie 1992, 'To the Vector the Spoils', in *Continental Shift*, ed. Elizabeth Jacka, Local Consumption Press, Sydney, pp. 142–160

_____ 1993, 'Selling the President', *21C*, Autumn, p. 40

_____ 2001, 'Hacker Manifesto 2.0.', <http://www.feelergauge.net/projects/hackermanifesto/version_2.0 [21 September 2001]

Watson, Don 1995, 'In defence of the noble art of rhetoric', *Sydney Morning Herald*, 23 November, p. 15

Wertheimer, F. 1997, 'TV Ad Wars: How to Cut Advertising Costs in Political Campaigns', *The Harvard International Journal of Press/Politics*, vol. 2, issue 3, Summer, pp. 93–101

West, D. M. 1994, 'Television Advertising in Election Campaigns', *Political Science Quarterly*, vol. 109, no. 5, Winter

West , D. 2001, *Checkbook Democracy*, Northeastern University Press, Boston

White, Joe Slade 1993, 'Wavelength winners', *Campaigns & Elections*, June/July, pp. 4–5

White, T. H. 1961, *The making of the President 1960*, Atheneum, New York

_____ 1966, *The making of the President 1964*, The New American Library, New York

_____ 1969, *The making of the President 1968*, Atheneum, New York

_____ 1974, *The making of the President 1972*, Jonathan Cape, London

Williams, Fred and Pavlik, J. P. (eds) 1994, *The People's Right to Know – Media, Democracy and the Information Highway*, LEA, Hillsdale

Williams, J. D. 1966, *The Compleat Strategyst* (revised edition), McGraw-Hill, New York

Witherspoon, John 1989, 'Campaign Commercials and the Media Blitz', in *Campaigns and Elections: A Reader*, ed. Larry Sabato, Scott, Foresman Glenview

Wolin, Sheldon 1960, *Politics and Vision,* Little Brown, Boston

Worcester, Robert M. (ed.) 1983, *Political Opinion Polling*, MacMillan, London

Wright, Tony 1995, 'What people think', *Sydney Morning Herald*, 24 August, p. 4

Wring, D. 1999, 'The Marketing Colonization of Political Campaigning' in *Handbook of Political Marketing*, ed. Bruce Newman, Sage Publications, Thousand Oaks

INDEX